18th November 2003

To Stephen,

Take it slow

with ! _____ om

Geo.

II9I3600M3

Naive Metaphysics

A theory of subjective and objective worlds

GEOFFREY V. KLEMPNER
Workers' Educational Association
Rotherham College of Arts and Technology
University of Sheffield

Avebury

Aldershot · Brookfield USA · Hong Kong · Singapore · Sydney

© G. V. Klempner 1994

All rights reserved. No part of this publication may be reproduced, stored in a retrieval system, or transmitted in any form or by any means, electronic, mechanical, photocopying, recording or otherwise without the prior permission of the publisher.

Published by
Avebury
Ashgate Publishing Ltd
Gower House
Croft Road
Aldershot
Hants. GU11 3HR
England

Ashgate Publishing Company
Old Post Road
Brookfield
Vermont 05036
USA

British Library Cataloguing in Publication Data

Klempner, Geoffrey V.
  Naive Metaphysics: Theory of Subjective
  and Objective Worlds. - (Avebury Series
  in Philosophy)
  I. Title   II. Series
  110

ISBN 1 85628 962 1

Library of Congress Cataloging-in-Publication Data

Klempner, Geoffrey V., 1951–
  Naive Metaphysics : a theory of subjective and objective worlds /
Geoffrey V. Klempner.
      p. cm.   -- (Avebury series in philosophy)
  Includes bibliographical references.
  ISBN 1-85628-962-1
  1. Metaphysics. 2. Subjectivity. 3. Objectivity. I. Title
II. Series.
BD161.K554 1994   94-34576
110--dc20   CIP

Printed and bound by Athenæum Press Ltd.,
Gateshead, Tyne & Wear.

Contents

Dedication

For June-Allison:

No personal relationship is so secure that it has not, on some occasion, been unexpectedly thrown into question by a word or gesture. The sense of certainty, of which we were perhaps not even conscious, gives way to intimations of something unknown and dangerous; an unexplored region, a depth that has never been plumbed, an order threatened by chaos. Before the threat has time to materialize, the moment passes and certainty returns. And so it is with our relation to the world itself. Unconsciously taken for granted as the backdrop to all our experience and action, the world suddenly becomes visible as a subject towards which one stands in a precarious relation. At such a moment, the very attitude of certainty seems a distortion of reality; the world is and will always remain something absolutely other than I, it is not mine to take for granted. But then, as before, the moment passes and is forgotten.

Preface

OVER the last two weeks of 1988 and the Winter and Spring of 1989, a group of six would-be philosophy students made their way on Thursday evenings to a flat next to Dore Railway Station, on the outskirts of Sheffield. The group comprised of a retired headmistress, a business man, a young woman who worked as an administrator in an EFL school, a retired fireman turned spiritualist healer, an elderly woman who had studied eastern religions and Theosophy before joining the Quakers, and a young man from the local radio station who nursed the ambition to do a degree in philosophy. (He subsequently gained his BA at Warwick University.) Despite wide differences in their day-to-day lives and academic attainments, the members of the group soon learned that they shared a common belief in the power of pure reason to uncover fundamental truths about reality; although their attitudes towards this discovery ranged from naive optimism to bemused scepticism. They had come as the willing guinea pigs in a philosophical experiment. For their pains (and the payment of a modest entrance fee of £2) they sipped their tea and coffee and hot chocolate while a would-be author, unused to speaking before an audience of strangers, discussed chapters from a work of metaphysics that he was in the process of writing.

The idea behind this curious set up was simple. As an unemployed philosopher, I had much time to think, but little inspiration for putting pen to paper. Scattered amongst various notebooks was the outline of a metaphysic – the theory of subjective and objective worlds – whose detailed structure seemed somehow to elude me. I knew if I was to make any progress, I had to begin for once from the very beginning; to develop my theory from first principles. What better discipline could there be for my project than to seek to make the arguments intelligible to an audience of complete beginners?

Or perhaps not so simple. Of all the branches of philosophy, metaphysics, at least in its modern guise, holds a particular distrust of all starting points and assumptions. Our most basic beliefs are but raw material for philosophical dissection, the pathology of the intellect. In the light of this critical, analytic stance – the legacy of Hume's fork – my search for first principles, whether conducted alone or in the company of persons who did not know any better, appeared indeed naive. Even if I did succeed in gaining my students' acceptance of my ideas, what would that prove? Only, at best, that my audience shared my own pre-reflective prejudices.

On the other side, it must be said that a suspicion of all starting points is no small task to state even in theory, let alone put into practice. Philosophical reason is hard put to question its own rationality: even the most skilful surgeons are disinclined to operate on themselves. The theoretical problem is compounded by the psychological fact that groups of individuals who share expertise in a field of inquiry are only too ready to mistake their agreed assumptions for the perception of self-evident truth. Philosophy is no exception to this rule. A new theory thus faces one or other of two possible fates. Either it fits established preconceptions, in which case its novel features are made the object of intense industry, until all sharp corners are chipped away and roughnesses smoothed over; or it fails to follow the familiar pattern, whereby it is summarily deemed beyond the pale of serious academic discussion.

Professional philosophers, to their credit, are not unaware of the problem. From time to time, fortunately not too often, one finds oneself afflicted by a disconcerting form of cartesian doubt concerning the validity of the philosophical enterprise itself. How can anyone tell when a survey of underlying assumptions is complete? How can we be sure that our critique will not fall to a yet more radical critique? In my defence, I could point out that all I aimed to do was make a contribution to that process of healthy self-appraisal.

I already knew the general tenor of the informed objections, by no means unjustified, that would be raised against the theory I was seeking to develop. For the time being, it did not matter that my listeners lacked the equipment to criticize my views that a philosophically trained audience would have possessed. I was looking for a different kind of criticism, in a way more challenging yet also more constructive; an audience who would pester their teacher with questions that those who knew better were more likely to pass over in complacent silence.

viii

Our legal system enshrines the principle that the guilt or innocence of an accused be capable of being decided by a jury comprising of ordinary persons with no special legal training, using nothing but their common sense and native intelligence to assess the force of arguments for and against. So it is, I told my group, with metaphysics: the conflicting theories arising out of the debates of the philosophical schools ought to be able to be made intelligible to men and women whose only training is the school of life.

Privately, my only residual concern was that as counsel for the prosecution, and at the same time judge directing the jury, it would be all-too easy for me to sway the outcome of the trial in my favour. As things turned out, I need not have worried. Week after week, after listening politely while I read out my latest chapter, my audience would subject me to a barrage of questions and objections. At times, I am ashamed to admit, I found myself reacting with ill-disguised impatience when one of the group members raised an objection that seemed obviously mistaken or irrelevant, only to realize long after everyone had gone home that my critic had been right and I had been wrong. At other times, after I had tied myself up in knots trying to get across a difficult point, someone would say, 'Do you mean...?' and then proceed to explain the point in a few pregnant words. Whether I succeeded in winning over any of my students to my theory I do not know. As we said our good-byes at the end of the last meeting, several assured me that they had been converted to the cause of metaphysics. I considered that success.

Starting in the Summer of 1989, new versions of the chapters I had written became the basis for a year-long course of philosophy evening classes organized by the Workers' Educational Association at Abbeydale Hall, the local adult education centre. Our meetings followed the same format as before. The classes were lively and enjoyable. Yet it soon became clear to me that my views were hardening. Having originally set off with only the sketchiest idea of the form my work would take, allowing the direction of the argument to be influenced and guided to a large extent by the response of my audience, I was now working within a structured programme whose main features I naturally had great interest in conserving. Whether I liked it or not, the book was beginning to assume its final shape.

By the end of 1989, with my 'introduction to metaphysics' two thirds of the way through its test run, I decided to approach a publisher. The process of appraisal seemed to be going smoothly, if a little slowly, when at the very last hurdle an obstacle appeared that I should have seen coming. I was well prepared for criticism of my book on the part of academic philosophers. My arguments had been elaborated and honed to the point where I felt sure that they made a strong case, whether or not one agreed with their conclusion. This belief was borne out by two very favourable reader's reports. What I had not foreseen was that the publishers would take exception to the way I had vigorously argued my case to an audience of beginners, rather than presenting the reader with the conventional laconic survey of different views, together with a balanced appraisal of their pros and cons. As one of the reports had colourfully put the point, there was a danger that some students 'would find their critical faculties sufficiently impaired by the glare of the work's metaphysical vision for them to become acolytes of it'. A third reader was appointed. When the manuscript arrived one bright July morning like a slab of meat on the doorstep, the accompanying letter from the philosophy editor said simply that it had been judged 'too idiosyncratic to function as a good introductory book'.

It has taken me a long time to reach the point of finally presenting my views to the community of academic philosophers. In response to criticisms, both real and imagined, the manuscript grew to over one and a half times its original size, then, after a brief circulation, remained on the shelf. The longer it rested there, the greater its faults seemed magnified in my eyes. In the end, however, I came to recognize that time would never remedy those faults. Even if one had the dexterity and wit to fill in every new gap as soon as it appeared, there are limits to the amount of fortification a position will hold before sinking under its own weight. Let others now have their say. What ought to recommend the theory put forward in the following pages is ultimately not words which could be spun out ad nauseam, but simply the perception of its truth.

Acknowledgements

IN view of the difficulty in keeping up with the state of our increasingly complex art, it is no small task to find philosophers prepared to set aside their own research in order to trawl through a heavy manuscript for points worthy of comment, or to highlight errors or omissions. I therefore consider myself fortunate that five individuals have given their time to review or discuss different stages of the production of the present work. Jonathan Barnes, Dorothy Edgington, David Hamlyn, Christopher Janaway and Charles Whiteley have each contributed, through their valuable criticisms, to making this a less flawed, and more readable book. They are not to blame if the author has sometimes remained deaf to their advice, or if some of the errors have appeared such as to leave even a sympathetic reader speechless.

To David Hamlyn I owe a unique debt, for providing the original impetus to my investigations – in a pointed remark many years ago about Wittgenstein's 'two godheads' – and also for encouraging me to persist, despite the setbacks, in seeing my project to fruition.

By far the most sustained influence on my ideas, however, has come from the generations of evening-class students with whom I have at different times argued most of the points written down in these pages. Of all those who have stimulated and challenged me, Robert Kerrigan deserves special mention. I should also like to record for posterity the names of the members of my first metaphysics group: Joan Page, Clifford Corton, June Graham, Derek Waters, Ruth Molloy and John Wrigglesworth.

I owe warm thanks to Ian Horsfield, Head of Abbeydale Hall, who gave me my first opportunity to teach philosophy in a formal setting, and to the redoubtable June Fisher, Secretary of the Sheffield Central

Branch of the Workers' Educational Association – who is always reminding me to 'keep it simple'. I am also grateful to the student philosophy societies at Sheffield and Warwick Universities for inviting me, each on two separate occasions, to talk about issues related to the work, and for their stimulating and at times boisterous discussions.

At Sheffield, I have benefited from conversations with Frank McDermott, Robert Stern and David Bell, as well as from the atmosphere of good-natured tolerance that prevails there. A paper, 'The "I"-Illusion', which I read to a staff seminar back in 1986 provoked some pertinent questions. The members of the department will be pleased to see my work in print, as will John McDowell, supervisor of my graduate studies at Oxford between 1976 and 1982, from whom I learned that a proper regard for the limits to philosophical theorizing imposed by our situation as human subjects by no means requires modesty in one's philosophic ambitions, and who accordingly gave me the freedom to pursue my 'grandiose schemes'.

My parents, Paul and Edith, and my two sisters Julia and Elizabeth have followed my meandering progress with hope, and long-suffering patience. Sadly, my mother did not live to see the outcome. Julia's husband, Adam Saltiel, has closely watched the development of the work from its early, barely coherent beginnings, calling my attention on numerous occasions to psychoanalytic aspects arising from the problems that engaged me. Discussions with my sister Rabbi Elizabeth Sarah have shown the way to my taking a less arrogant view of questions relating to theology than might otherwise have been the case.

Finally, I wish to dedicate this book to my wife, who has taught me that the only work worth doing is the work of love.

Part one

'What, you wretch, so you want to avoid talking nonsense?
Talk some nonsense, it makes no difference!'

1 Subjective and objective

1. LOGICALLY, the world ought not to exist. – Brute fact is an affront to human reason, which always seeks the sufficient ground for every contingent given. Yet neither can reason be persuaded to accept (pace Spinoza, Leibniz) that it is necessary that our little planet Earth should have come into being. Or that I should be writing this. Or that the Holocaust happened. Fortunately, as finite beings, we are never brought to the point of having to make that impossible choice. The chain from consequences to grounds is (as Kant observed) never-ending. However, a contradiction that will never have to be faced is still a contradiction. Between logical contingency and logical necessity there is no third modality: either our world is or is not the only logically possible world. If it cannot be either, then it cannot be.

Taking our stand, then, in an ultimately illogical universe, we shall not ask why our world exists, or indeed why there is any world. Still, if there is no explaining contingent existence, nor even accounting for its inexplicability, there remains the modest but important task of definition. What is a world? What is it to be the world? or this world? or our world? (Whence the definite description? Whence the indexicals?) What is it, of which we were once prompted, so foolishly, to ask the question, Why? whose existing in the face of all the alternatives – including the awesome possibility of nothing – has led human beings to wonder, to worship, to speculate, even at the certain risk of talking nonsense?

One might call the state of mind which questions the existence of the world naive metaphysics. It is an attitude anyone can fall into or stumble upon, even if one has never heard of a discipline called philosophy – let alone a philosopher called Aristotle. It could be argued that human beings are by nature naive metaphysicians. (Kant thought that the impulse to transcend its proper boundaries was built in to human reason.) We should not make so strong a claim. Perhaps the impulse indicates merely a serious defect that will one day be eradicated from human consciousness; or, failing that, from the minds of those creatures destined to succeed humankind in the course of evolution. In that case, this book speaks to those who do not wish to be cured (or saved) but who do wish to understand the nature, and consequences, of their affliction.

There is more, however, to naive metaphysics than just a state of mind. Naive metaphysics embodies an implicit theory; a theory which up until now philosophy has, for logically impeccable reasons, either ignored or distorted out of all recognition. In this chapter, we shall identify that theory; the rest of the book is concerned with its defence and application. (In the last chapter, the theory will be extended in response to dilemma put forward in paragraph 1.) For the claim of identification, the author will not cite empirical evidence, but rely upon intuitive generalization from his own case. In saying how things are with oneself, one's aim is always to speak for others. How wide that class of others is meant to be, however, depends upon our view concerning the historical, psychological or even biological roots of the metaphysical attitude.

There is always a risk that, as a trained philosopher, one's intuitions concerning the thoughts or visions of other persons not trained in philosophy may be wide of the mark. However, we intend to make naive metaphysics a partner in the dialectic, to bring it in easy stages to recognize the strange vision to which it is in fact committed. The final, simple test of success or failure is whether the shoe fits; a matter which, ultimately, only the reader can decide. By contrast, the defence of the theory so attributed, rightly or wrongly, is a matter of logical necessity. This might be termed the strictly philosophical component, but the word is only a conventional label. No conclusion of any philosophical interest was ever proved by means of pure logic alone. In both cases the author is aiming to describe something that he sees, and expects the reader to see also.

2. Consulting one's intuitions, it seems that when naive metaphysics asks the question, Why is there anything? it is asking two questions, not one. The first question is why there is a world; the second question is why there is such a thing as I, or my world. (Throughout this book we shall be reserving the first person singular for the cartesian voice.) Consider the familiar expression of perplexity, Why am I here? One may ask why God chose to make a world, and in particular a world like

4

ours containing someone like me. Yet one may also ask why God chose to make me, and there is a compelling sense that there is something extra in this second question that is not in the first. The question, Why am I here? is not intended as an instance of the schema, Why is....here? If it were not about me then it would not be the kind of question that it is. For it is not as if another person could put the question on my behalf, simply by substituting the third- for the first-person pronoun. In so doing, she would merely be repeating the question why the world contains a person with my particular attributes, a person like me.

As it stands, however, this intuition is shot through with ambiguity. In order to delineate the second question sharply from the first, it seems one would have to consider a number of obscure counterfactual suppositions such as, Could God have chosen to make me Napoleon? or Mother Theresa? Could God have chosen to make a person situated at this place and time, with a history identical to mine, indistinguishable in bodily substance (and soul substance if I have a soul) – who was not me? In asking these questions, we have left naive metaphysics far behind. Nor would it serve any purpose to press the point. Philosophical thinking is a search for consistency, and under pressure from such questioning the inchoate vision that we are seeking with its fundamental inconsistency is just as likely to be destroyed as brought into the open. The picture of the world as one thing, and of me or my world as something else not included in the world, something extra on top which might or might not have been there leaving the world as such untouched is, as we shall soon discover, sheer paradox. It owes its long survival only to the fact that naive metaphysics is not equipped, or at any rate does not have the energy to examine it.

How then can philosophy hope to describe this curious vision of two worlds without destroying the very thing it seeks to uncover? Logic is hard pressed to speak consistently of what is by its very nature inconsistent. One is reminded of parallels in psychology and physics: the neurosis which disappears in the course of its being brought to light, the particle which moves when we try physically to observe its position. Yet still, neuroses are uncovered, the positions of particles are observed. In each case, the relation between knower and known reveals an internal complexity, a special dynamic which each form of knowledge works through in its own way. The illusion to be got rid of is that this is somehow second best, the thought that ideally what one would like to have before one's mind is the object itself, rather than the mere knowledge of that object. There is an important moral to be learned here. The knowledge we seek as philosophers is whatever waits to be revealed in the course of the dialectic. Whatever emerges, if

5

one succeeds in avoiding the pitfalls, is no more or less that what was there to be known.

3. It seems that no sooner have we encountered the worrying question mark raised against the world as a whole, than there appear one or other of two standpoints from which we can think about our relation to everything that exists, two ways of making the world as such the object of our thought. It is these two standpoints which give rise to two distinct meanings for the question, Why is there anything? Yet neither standpoint is aware of its opposite, nor is there any logical route from one to the other. For each sees the question, Why is there anything? as having no ambiguity, sees only one question to answer.

Thus it is that on occasion, perhaps during moments of intense perceptual experience, when the self seems to lose itself in a world of sights and sounds, or, by complete contrast, during periods of complete self-absorption, it becomes apparent that the question, Why there is anything? is none other than the question, Why is there anything for me? Why do I exist? The existence of something rather than nothing is simply the existence of a world for me. Take *this* away from the world and there is nothing left. Make *this* and you have made the world. By thinking in such a way, I am adopting the standpoint of my own existence as subject of experience. Whenever I try, in this frame of mind, to imagine or think about anything happening in the world, I find myself representing the events in relation to what is happening to me here and now, or impinging on my senses; even when I picture events on other planets or galaxies, or in the distant past or future.

There are, no doubt, many things which I cannot think about because I lack the requisite concepts, and, moreover, many concepts I shall never have the wit to grasp. Yet my apparent inability, in this mood, to conceive of things happening independently of my I is of a different order. Let my power of thought may be extended ever so far, it seems it will always remain tied down to the same egocentric starting point. It follows that the world is in every respect and in total my world; the sun, moon and stars are all mine just as surely as the objects attached to my arms are my hands. Everything that exists, exists for me; and without me there would be nothing. – We shall call this the subjective standpoint.

4. The frame of mind in which one finds oneself thinking about things from the subjective standpoint appears to most of us only as a passing mood; it is not a point of view which we maintain for very long. Indeed, it soon comes into conflict with our most basic beliefs. For example, if the subjective standpoint were the only point of view from which I

thought about my relation to the world, then I could attach no determinate sense to the thought of my own death. The destruction of a body or a brain – or a soul if there are souls – is something that happens within the world. Yet at the moment of my death there is no world for the event to happen in (as the Wittgenstein of the *Tractatus* observed). Clearly, however, there is no such barrier to my conceiving of the deaths of other persons. Why, then, should I be a special case?

Recognizing that I am just like any other person, and in no way a special case, instantly transports us to the second point of view from which we may grasp our relation to the world as a whole. This second standpoint appears simply that of the world by itself, a world in which I happen to exist but equally well might not have existed. I am merely one amongst the multitude of self-conscious beings who happen to inhabit the world. (In terms of the sheer probability of my having existed, it must be noted, given the state of the world at some arbitrary point in the distant past, it seems that things are, on the contrary, far from equal. Lucky I!)

Now, if I have special characteristics that no-one else has, that is equally true of everyone else. As conscious subjects, we are all the same, for all the uniqueness of each person's physical and mental attributes. Only on the basis of such identity, it seems, could there be such a thing as communication between persons. If the world were only my world, then by seeming to converse with another person, I should in reality be merely altering the state of one of the objects in my world; in effect, I should be talking to myself. For in the world of my subjective standpoint, the sole function of other persons consists in their being there for me, in their playing a part in the story of I. By contrast, from the standpoint of the world itself, what I call the world is simply the one world we are all in, a world which is no more my world than it is my neighbour's. – We shall call this the objective standpoint.

5. The problem with sticking exclusively to the objective standpoint is that it leaves me with no way to express the special, incommunicable meaning that my own existence has for me; the indescribable something I seem to see when I grasp my relation to the world from my subjective standpoint. For once I ascend to the objective standpoint, I have to think of myself as just another person in the world, a subject who exists for other persons to encounter or observe, in just the same way as they exist as subjects for me. The substance, the actuality of all that I experience, all that appears immediately to my consciousness, is translated into a neutral subject matter we can all talk about. The one thing that cannot be talked about, however, is the thing that seems the

7

most important of all: the *this*, which, whether I look into myself or out onto the world, presents itself exclusively to me, but which as soon as I talk about it ceases to be *this* and becomes instead a tickle or a pain, a tree, a house, the sky.

Objectively, what it is to be me is not there being *this*, but simply there being some individual with my unique physical and mental attributes. One of these attributes, let us say, is that I am now perceiving a chair. I, the subject, am seated at my desk in the computer room, having just noticed a broken swivel chair turned over on its side in the corner. In my brain, scattered amongst its intricate workings, there is now taking place the complex information processing, the flickering pattern of physico-chemical reactions, which science tells me constitutes the process of discerning a visible object, such as a chair. Meanwhile, in my consciousness, there occurs a certain experience (therein I differ from my computer) which I describe as my seeing the chair, and which others may attribute to me on the basis of where I am and what I say. Yet the thisness of the chair is nowhere to be found.

6. We have been seeking a way in which each of us can grasp our relation to the world as a whole; and we have discovered that neither the subjective nor the objective standpoint alone is adequate. Each standpoint misses out something that only the other can supply. Now the first, most natural response to this difficulty is to try to locate the common ground, to work out a compromise between the two standpoints. This might seem easy. If I wish to tell the whole truth about my relation to the world, then why not simply combine together the two standpoints, in the way that a novelist might tell a story, first from the point of view of the main protagonist, and then from the imaginary point of view of an all-seeing observer? Surely, once that is done, there is no further story to tell?

On closer examination, however, this analogy appears fatally flawed. In the novel, the full story is the one which would result if the novelist granted the all-seeing observer access to each character's thoughts and feelings. The objective standpoint from which no-one is picked out for special treatment does indeed give the whole truth. The crucial difference between the novel and the account of my relation to the world is that in my case one of the characters in the story is myself. And we have already seen that the objective standpoint cannot accommodate what appears to me as the special, incommunicable meaning of my existence for myself, the thisness of my experience.

One can anticipate an obvious objection to this argument. In a novel, it is not always made explicit how the all-seeing observer is supposed to have acquired its knowledge of the various characters' thoughts and feelings. One way of acquiring this knowledge, the way we normally use, is simply to talk to the persons concerned and encourage them to confide in us. Indeed, one can imagine it written into the novel that the person telling the story has shared the full confidence of all the protagonists. On the other hand, the novelist is free, without having to offer any further explanation, to place the observer in the position in which we imagine God to be, reading each person's thoughts and feelings directly by looking into her mind. Now, if in reality there did exist such a deity, who could see not only the objective chair, not only the process in my brain which constituted my seeing the chair, but also my own subjective experience of seeing the chair, then surely nothing would have been left out of account. For then God would see me, not merely with the limited access of a interlocutor, nor even a scientist of the future probing the hidden recesses of my brain, but would directly intuit my conscious experience as I myself experienced it.

In short – so runs the objection – from God's super-objective standpoint, the view that takes in every side of every existing object, as well as experiencing the world through the eye and senses of every living subject, nothing is left out of the account of my relation to the world. In that case, far from seeking a compromise between the subjective and objective standpoints, we ought instead to reject as superfluous a subjective standpoint which defines itself in opposition to the objective, since it adds nothing to what is given to the standpoint of an all-seeing deity.

This objection is invalid. The reason why it is invalid, however, is highly instructive, for it brings the paradox of the opposition between the subjective and objective standpoints into sharpest possible relief. (It is of course no defence against the objection to insist that the existence of a God first be proved; we are considering a hypothetical deity, to whom we may attribute any cognitive powers that are not logically self-contradictory.) The problem is, to put it succinctly, that God knows too much. Just because he knows everything, there is one thing that God cannot know. While God knows what it is like to be me, just as he knows what it is like to be each one of his creatures, he still does not share in the awareness I have of simply being me. Obviously, he cannot have the sense of being me, since he is not me. The indescribable thisness of my experience, that which marks it as being essentially mine, remains invisible to God; for as far as he is concerned, every person's experience is equally 'this'. (In a similar way, we shall argue in a later chapter, for a God who knows all times, past, present and future, there is no such time as now.)

9

7. We are left, therefore, exactly where we started. The subjective and objective standpoints each present a different account of my relation to the world as a whole. These accounts stand opposed: from the subjective standpoint, I find myself unable to conceive of the possibility of my own death; yet from the objective standpoint, where my death becomes just another event that occurs, I cannot find myself at all. Our natural reaction, when we first encounter this opposition, is to seek a compromise between the two standpoints, a middle ground that somehow encompasses both. Only that cannot be done. Any attempt to compromise with the objective standpoint or incorporate the subjective standpoint into a wider view renders the subjective standpoint invisible. My subjective standpoint stubbornly refuses any kind of absorption into the objective.

In describing the opposition between the subjective and objective standpoints, we have not yet explicitly spelt out the fundamental inconsistency, the paradox implicit in the vision of naive metaphysics; but we are very close to it. Each standpoint has proved defective: by itself it appears incapable of comprehending the whole truth about my relation to the world. It is a fact that I am going to die; but my subjective standpoint cannot see it. Equally, it is a fact that I exist; but the objective standpoint cannot see that. In effect, each cannot see the other, for each denies the very existence of the point of view, the logical space, which the other claims to occupy. From my subjective standpoint, the objective standpoint is inconceivable. From the objective standpoint, there is nothing to which the words 'my unique subjective standpoint' could possibly refer. The contradiction arises because neither will own up to this logical blindness as any kind of defect. Neither standpoint can be eliminated; each appears absolutely necessary. Yet each proclaims that the other is impossible.

In our everyday lives, we pass back and forth between the subjective and objective standpoints without ever thinking what we are doing. All language and communication presupposes the objective standpoint; the objective account of our relation to the world may never once come up for discussion, but it lies permanently in the background, as the logical condition for the very possibility of language. Similarly, the sense that each of us has of being an existing self-conscious individual presupposes the subjective standpoint as its logical condition; even if we never once explicitly think about it as such. We are not aware of any contradiction between the two standpoints because for practical purposes the endless to and fro works perfectly well. Even when we stand back and allow ourselves to indulge in naive speculation about the existence of the world or of our own selves, there is no sense of any strain or inconsistency.

Sooner or later, however, there comes an unnerving experience which calls this easy-going compromise into question. In trying to comprehend the mystery of love, when subjectivity contemplates, in serenity or despair, the enigmatic countenance of the other; or human suffering, where the distance between self and other seems unsurpassable; or the inevitability of our death, we find intimations of a duality impenetrable and absolute. We begin to realize, however obscurely, that no stable compromise between the subjective and objective standpoints could ever be achieved. Each of us stands alone at the centre of our own unique world; we all share one and the same world. Both propositions are true, and at the very same time both propositions are also false. To comprehend that contradiction is the fundamental task of metaphysics.

2 Egocentrism and Nonegocentrism

1. TO say that the discipline of metaphysics takes as its primary point of reference the existence of naive metaphysics at first sounds like a repetition of Plato's remark in *Theaetetus* 155D (echoed by Aristotle in Book I, chapter 2 of the *Metaphysics*) that philosophy begins with wonder. The activity of producing philosophical theories can only arise amongst those who have, for whatever material or spiritual reasons, become sensitive to the force of those questions and perplexities to which theory-making is the appropriate response. It is not enough that the problems are there in some abstract sense, nor even that they have been given a name; one must first feel the real need to solve them. That is all true. As we have seen, however, naive metaphysics, the attitude of wondering about the very existence of the world, does not lead anywhere. It is stuck with a question it does not know what to do with. Metaphysics proper begins only when we question the wonder and reveal the contradiction implicit in its vision of what it takes to make a world.

It turns out – and this could not have been predicted, for it is no part of the notion of a theory as such – that the problems of metaphysics ultimately refer to our actual existence as human beings, to the perennial concerns of human life. For it is here that the unstable equilibrium between the subjective and objective standpoints breaks down. The sense of the wholeness of our life, the unthinking trust with which we gave ourselves to the world and to our projects, which naive metaphysics hardly disturbs, is shattered by the discovery of the contradiction between the subjective and the objective; as when we contemplate the unbridgeable gulf that separates us from others, or from their joy or suffering, or when we fact the unimaginable prospect of our own death. For most persons most of the time, the one effective recourse in the fact of the contradiction is to forget the doubts and carry on as before. Yet we can no longer be satisfied with such a course of action. For we have lost our innocence. Having become aware of the problem, one cannot just wipe the slate clean and start again. If the sense of wholeness is ever to be regained, it can only be by an extended process of abstract thought; in other words, by the construction of a metaphysic.

2. In the light of what has just been said, one will hardly expect the philosopher to recite a few spells, wave a magic wand and so make the contradiction between the subjective and objective disappear. In the first chapter, we argued that the contradiction is not apparent but real. However, this was meant in a different sense from that in which one statement is said to contradict another statement. For example, the statement that I am now sitting at my desk in the computer room contradicts the statement that I am now taking a walk in the park. It is conceivable that I could come to hold both beliefs (under the influence of drugs, or through extreme fatigue). No doubt that would pose a serious problem for me, but it would not be a philosophical one. If it is true that I am in the computer room, then it is false that I am in the park; and, conversely, if it is true that I am in the park then it is false that I am in the computer room.

In the absence of any convincing reasons for giving up one or other metaphysical view we cannot, however, ignoring their prima facie claims, decree on any arbitrary basis of preference one of the two standpoints to be the true way of conceiving of our relation to the world and abandon the other as false. Admittedly, even in philosophy, it happens that one may simply decide to close one's eyes, or one's heart, to one of the sides in a conflict. One can choose not to listen to the arguments. Yet seeking truth about reality can never be the same as throwing in one's lot for a cause.

Nor indeed is there any hope of avoiding conflict by re-describing the two standpoints, so that each may be seen as valid in a different respect, in the way one might say, metaphorically, that it was both true and false that I was in the computer room if I had stopped work and was day-dreaming about where I ought to be on a lovely spring morning such as this; or, more literally, that it was both true and false that I was in the computer room if I was standing in the doorway. Nor again, as we saw in the last chapter, can one say that the subjective and objective standpoints each describe a different aspect of one and the same reality, like the different viewpoints of the protagonist and narrator in a novel. Restoring the sense of wholeness to our life, by constructing an account of our relation to the world which does not fragment into two irreconcilable halves, is not simply a matter of finding the right words or inventing an instant glue to cement the subjective and objective standpoints together. Results in metaphysics are not won so easily.

3. Still, before setting out on such a long journey it would seem only prudent to satisfy ourselves that there are no short cuts to be found. Why go to all the effort of trying to save the vision of naive metaphysics if it is in fact beyond redemption? Logic dictates that there are just three short cuts to consider. The first is the egocentric theory, which takes its stand on the exclusive reality of the subjective standpoint: there is only one world, and that world is mine. Clearly, if one could get the objective standpoint out of the way, then the contradiction between the two standpoints would no longer be a problem. The same is true of the second short cut, the nonegocentric theory, which, as its name suggests, takes the opposite position, rejecting my sense of the uniqueness of my existence, the exclusive thisness of my experience as merely a symptom of philosophic illusion. There is nothing in the world or my relation to the world, says the nonegocentrist, that cannot be fully accounted for from the objective standpoint. The third short cut is quicker than either of the other two. This is the anti-metaphysical view which simply refuses to see any real problem at all. According to this view, our mistake lies in thinking that there is anything to hold a metaphysical position about. For the conflict we seem to perceive between the subjective and objective standpoints, or between egocentrism and nonegocentrism, is only the result of philosophic confusion.

In actual fact, the idea that we have to clear these dissenting claims out of the way before we can get on with the real work would show a complete misunderstanding of the task ahead. For it is not as if we should get to our destination more speedily if we ignored all suspect short cuts and refused to look to the right or the left. Overcoming these other views is part of the problem, part of what is involved in dealing with the contradiction between the subjective and objective standpoints. Both egocentrism and nonegocentrism will crop up again and again as we pursue the problem of the subjective and objective through a range of philosophical issues. As for the anti-metaphysical view, the possibility that we may be deluding ourselves is a challenge which we face constantly. There is no general criterion we can apply that would tell us when we have gone too far and strayed over the borderline between sense and nonsense. The only answer will come from attending closely to the matter in hand, to what we can see of the problem before us, and not losing our way amongst thickets of words. No proof in metaphysics works by magic; nor is there a magical test for deciding when a proof does work.

It should be clear by now that no sharp distinction can be drawn between the positive, constructive work of producing a theory that is able to reconcile the contradiction between the subjective and objective standpoints, and the negative, destructive work of rejecting the mistaken or illusory beliefs of the egocentrist, the nonegocentrist or the anti-metaphysician. For the project of restoring the sense of wholeness to our life necessarily involves fighting against such mistaken philosophical views as preach that we should give up the struggle; either because the theoretical standpoint of a metaphysical construct can never be fully applied to our actual existence but must remain an object of pure contemplation, like the perfect lines and circles of geometry which are never to be found in the real world; or because those questions which seem to call up a conflict between standpoints, and make us search for an adequate theory, do so only because our thinking is muddled.

4. To make the discussion a little less abstract, we shall be taking a preliminary forage into some of the philosophical issues involved in investigating the subjective and objective standpoints. First, however, we need to deal with a point of elementary logic which seems to go against the assertion that the contradiction between the two standpoints is, in the problematic sense indicated, not apparent but real.

The point is this. According to formal logic, the discipline that investigates the relations of logical implication between statements in general regardless of subject matter, it is a law that contradictions cannot be true. If one of a pair of contradictory statements is true, then the other must be false. In ordinary life, of course, there are many cases which have the surface appearance of contradiction, where each of the apparently contradictory statements is in a sense true. We gave examples above involving vagueness and metaphor. That is not the case here. The subjective and objective standpoints are absolute contradictories: either way of comprehending one's relation to the world totally precludes the other.

A simple-minded response might be to say that our apparent insight into the dual nature of reality is the one unique exception to the logical rule, the one contradiction that escapes the law of non-contradiction. The universality of the law of non-contradiction is, after all, just one more belief, which stands to be corrected in the light of new knowledge, just as intuitionist mathematicians question the law of

15

excluded middle or quantum theorists deny that the connective 'and' always distributes over 'or'. Unfortunately, we cannot escape so easily. For another, equally correct way of expressing the law of non-contradiction is to say that if a contradiction is put down as strictly true, and not merely in a sense true, then anything is true. If one has been led so far as to attempt the impossible action of simultaneously asserting and denying the very same statement in the very same sense – and not merely asserting it in one sense and denying it in another – then any statement may be validly asserted; for example, 'I have three heads.' (Once you allow one impossible thing, then every other impossible thing becomes possible.) Thus, if by saying that the contradiction between the subjective and objective standpoints was real one meant that both standpoints are true and yet still contradict one another, then one would have to admit that one did indeed have three heads; something most persons would be inclined to doubt. Philosophers have believed many nonsensical things; on occasion it can take as elementary a point as this to make the nonsense manifest.

The argument can be blocked by pointing to a crucial difference in logical status between the subjective and objective standpoints. All communication presupposes the objective standpoint, the point of view from which I appear as merely one subject amongst other subjects. The only way words can be used to say anything is, after all, if by having the same meanings for different people. It is admittedly sometimes very difficult to know what another person means by a certain word, sometimes we may doubt whether we are really communicating at all; but that doubt or difficulty arises against a background of agreement which we should never think of questioning. The subjective standpoint is something else entirely. For it relates to something given to me alone: the inexpressible *this* which uniquely characterizes my experience as mine. If I try to say anything else about *this* then I find I am using words that another person can be in as good a position to understand as I. For example, if *this* is my experience of looking at the sky, then *this* is blue. If *this* is the sensation of the sun on my face, then *this* is warm. Were I, on the other hand, to try to invent words for describing *this* as I and no-one else can grasp it, words with a private meaning that only I could understand, then, by an argument we owe to the later Wittgenstein, I myself would not know what I meant by them. (In chapter 4, an argument not unrelated to Wittgenstein's critique of private rule-following will be used to refute the egocentrist.)

Now, there is no harm in talking of the truth of the subjective standpoint, as we did at the end of chapter 1, provided that one realizes that the word 'true' is being used in an extended sense. For as far as logic is concerned, the notion of truth applies strictly to the

16

objective domain, to propositions that can be expressed in communicable statements. Indicating my inexpressible *this*, on the other hand, or attempting to refer to my unique subjective world is not meaningful in terms of our public language; for what I intend has a significance only for myself. The statement, 'There is *this*,' is thus strictly neither true nor false. Nevertheless, we shall argue, it indicates something real. The contradiction between the subjective and objective standpoints does not, therefore, hold between conflicting truths but rather between conflicting realities. The contradiction is, in short, metaphysical, not logical.

5. To orient ourselves for the task ahead, we shall take a preliminary look at four issues arising from the dialectic of subjective and objective standpoints. The metaphysical contradiction hits us hardest, we have suggested, just when one is brought to realize the absolute separation of our subjectivity from the subjectivity of others. (One says 'our' but one means 'my': the distance I measure between two others can never be compared with the metaphysical divide that appears to separate myself from others.) It is, for example, a distorted awareness of this problem that has led some thinkers to the pessimistic conclusion that the only mind whose reality I can be assured of, or whose contents I can ever really know anything about is my own. Whatever there may or may not be for others, it seems, is locked away so deep inside that anything I say about it is pure conjecture. The distortion, as we shall discover, lies in failing the appreciate that the separation between self and other amounts to an absolute difference between the two real terms.

From a wider perspective, however, the problem of self and other not only illustrates the equivocal nature of the relation between myself and the world, in the way one runs back and forth between the subjective and objective standpoints without ever finding a resting point; it also provides a compelling metaphor for the attempt to regain the sense of the wholeness of our life. Even though there can be no return to the state of philosophic innocence, we may still hope overcome the loss of the unthinking trust with which we originally gave ourself to the world of others, despite recognition of a distance which can never be overcome.

6. An issue closely connected with the problem of self and other is freedom of the will. According to a well-know dilemma, it appears that no human action can really be called free when viewed from the objective standpoint. Objectively, the body of a human agent is just a complex system of movements, of chemical and electrical changes

17

which take place according to physical laws. Science tells us that what we call our mental states, such as thoughts, intentions and feelings, all ultimately depend on these movements and changes. This might be taken to mean that, given the total physical state of a person's body at any one time, its states resulting from subsequent variations in its external conditions are in every case fully determined. If that is so, then my sense that in performing an action I could have chosen to do otherwise is sheer illusion. For in choosing that action, I was merely following the laws which govern my bodily movements and changes, from which I have no freedom to depart. If, on the other hand, my bodily movements are not fully determined by prior conditions, then my sense of my decision's being up to me or to my will at the moment of choosing is illusory for a different reason; whatever freedom I have is only the freedom of randomness or indifference. Those who seek freedom of the will in the rejection of determinism can still only give us less than we feel we have a right to ask for.

Either way, then, if I wish to hold on to my sense of freedom – the feeling that changes in the world genuinely come from myself, from my will or my I – it seems the only remaining alternative is to refuse to view myself and my actions purely objectively. There is, in me, or in my actions, something more than could ever be comprehended from the objective standpoint. That something more is what is inexpressibly given to my subjective standpoint. Yet a parallel argument will not work when I contemplate the actions of others. I may readily admit that they must take the same attitude to their actions as I take to mine; like me, they must refuse to view their actions purely objectively. However, that does not prevent me from viewing their actions from the objective standpoint, or from interpreting their refusal as just another objective event in the world. It would seem to follow that I am alone in the universe in being the only person who is really free: an intolerable result.

7. The third problem we shall anticipate concerns the nature of time. Just as my incommunicable sense of the uniqueness of my existence might be called my sense of the I-ness of I, so our awareness that the present moment, amongst all possible times, past, present and future is this time and no other, might be called our sense of the nowness of now. We are all immediately aware that this time is uniquely special, even though nothing special may be happening now, simply because it is now. If one wanted an example of something absolutely real, it seems one could do no better than pick the nowness of now.

However, from the point of view of language, that is to say from the objective standpoint, the only reality is the relative order of events.

18

One of these events is the event of the author writing, a few moments ago, 'this time is uniquely special.' That event can be completely accounted for in relation to other events which occur before and after. It will be the same event tomorrow, and the same the day after that, whether I remember it correctly or not; everything that makes the event the event that it is goes with it into the past. Moreover, it was the same event yesterday, and the day before, waiting for its turn to happen. Yet the actual happening of an event, its reality in being now, is not in the past or the future; it is not part of the description of what that event was or will be. Its reality or nowness is something over and above its place in the objective order of events; a feature which remains completely invisible from the objective standpoint.

Another way of putting that point is to say that the statement, 'now is now' is no more able to communicate a meaningful truth than the statement, 'I am I.' Both are meaningless repetitions. I can see or grasp the reality of now and the reality of I, but I cannot say it. One important difference, however, between 'now is now' and 'I am I' is that the same now is uniquely real for all of us, whereas I am uniquely real only for myself. So one cannot say that now has a purely subjective reality, for if it did each of us would be living in a different now. What, therefore, can now be if it is neither purely objective nor purely subjective?

8. The last problem we shall mention relates to the question, Why is there anything? One of the ways in which naive metaphysics seeks satisfaction is in the religious attitude. There are those for whom the sense of awe at the existence of a world or one's own self renders human efforts to puzzle out the nature of existence futile. Others are happy to combine a religious attitude with an interest in metaphysics. Yet there are also persons who fall into neither category, for whom religion, specifically theism, assumes the garb of a primitive metaphysical theory.

Now there are two lines of inquiry which follow from our recognition of the reality of the contradiction between the subjective and objective standpoints. The first is this. We described earlier the theory of nonegocentrism, which believes in the exclusive reality of the objective standpoint, and also egocentrism, which holds to the exclusive reality of the subjective standpoint. When either theory considers the problem of the existence of the world, it has just one question to answer: the nonegocentrist asks why there is an objective world, while the egocentrist asks why there is my subjective world. However, if both the objective and subjective standpoints are real, then we have two questions to answer, not one. If God is the creator in the literal sense, an omnipotent power that forged the world out of nothing, then he had to create both the objective world and my subjective world; or, to put the matter another way, having created the world we all know, and in so doing made a human being with all my attributes, he still had the extra job of creating me, the individual for whom there is *this*.

The difficulty is that, as we argued in chapter 1, as far as the God of the 'super-objective' standpoint is concerned my subjective experience is just another of the objective features of the world, albeit one which he knows as well, or perhaps even better than I. Just because God sees every person's experience as a 'this', he will never appreciate what there is for me, namely *this*. There might not have been *this* and he, it seems, would be none the wiser. It follows that, given the reality of both the subjective and objective standpoints, saying that God created the world still leaves open the question who created me. For there appears to be nothing a deity can add to any of the human beings he has created to make that person I, rather than someone merely like me in every objective respect. If the deity cannot even appreciate the difference between making that person and making I, then the most one can say is that the existence of my subjective standpoint must have come about, in some manner yet to be fathomed, as an accidental by-product of the creation of an objective world. That is the same as saying that I am no part of God's design. God is not my creator. The only solution would seem to be to postulate a god of my subjective standpoint; but that commits me to believing in two gods, not one, neither of whom could have created the other.

9. For the second line of inquiry, we begin by noting a surprising parallel between the fact that the world exists or is actual, and the two inexpressible realities which we called the I-ness of I and the nowness of now. What remains invisible from the objective standpoint is that, amongst all I's there is the unique I, that amongst all nows there is the unique now. Similarly, one may question what it means to say that amongst all possible worlds, there is one unique actual world. What does the actuality of the actual world consist in? The only answer forthcoming – and it is really no answer at all – is that there being a unique world which is actual, amongst all the possible worlds which might have been actual, is the one fact which defines the objective standpoint, just as the fact that a certain person is I defines the subjective standpoint. However, that raises the question whether there might be a third standpoint, which has the same contradictory relation to the objective standpoint as the objective standpoint has to the subjective.

Let us call this third standpoint the ultimate standpoint. From the ultimate standpoint, one might suppose, all worlds are not only equally possible but also equally real. None carries any special mark to distinguish it as being actual as opposed to being merely possible: every world is a possible actual world. If we now ask what it means to say that God created the world, we have first to decide whether God's standpoint is the ultimate standpoint from which all possible worlds appear on the same level, or only the objective standpoint. If we picture God as choosing to create this world out of a pre-existing catalogue of possible worlds, then we are picturing him as occupying the ultimate standpoint. There is nowhere else for God to be, prior to that fateful choice being made. Now there arises the same question about what could be added to any of the merely possible worlds to make it the actual world, as arose when we asked what could be added to any of the persons in the objective world to make that person I. The God of the ultimate standpoint might prefer one particular world to any of the others, might even take a special interest in what goes on there, in the way one returns time and again to one's favourite novel; but that favoured world is no more actual than is the story in the novel.

The only alternative, then, is to say that God's standpoint is not the ultimate standpoint but only the objective standpoint. It follows that God could not have chosen to create this world out of a catalogue of all possible worlds; that is to say, the fact that this world was to be the actual world, that all other worlds were to be consigned to the realm of the merely possible was settled in advance by God's occupation of the objective standpoint of our actual world. If a physical event of creation did take place (say, there appearance of matter or energy where previously there was nothing) that too was settled in advance. If, on this view of the deity, we use the proper name 'God' for the one ultimately responsible for everything that happens in our world, or indeed for there being a world at all, then we must at the same time acknowledge that the selection of our deity out of all the possible deities there might have been – the god who, according to his essential nature decreed that the physical world as we find it should have come into being – is no less inexplicable than the selection of this world to be the actual, objective world.

Either way, then, As a metaphysical theory or hypothesis designed to account for existence or the fact of there being our world, the notion of a selection or choice made by a deity explains nothing. The question this throws into sharp relief is whether logically there could be anything that fulfilled the role of a theory of existence; and, if not, what we are to make of that.

21

10. By now, the reader should have some idea of just what is at stake in pursuing the dialectic of the subjective and objective standpoints. Nothing has been resolved, nor could it be, other than in its proper place. However, it should at least be clear how within its own arena metaphysics brooks no competitors; nor is there any aspect of our thought about the nature of existence or our relation to the world as such which lies outside that domain. Other approaches must stake their claims. What they cannot claim is to be dealing with the same problems, or aiming for the same objective – only, as it were, by a different route. If that route is not pure thinking, then the objective cannot be the same. (That is perhaps not so much a reflection of any pre-eminent status accorded to activity of metaphysical inquiry, as of the sublimity of its ultimate goal.)

If, therefore, these last few questions have left the reader reeling, one need make no apology. By one means or another we intend to stir naive metaphysics from its slumbers. Nor is there any way of entering into the spirit of metaphysical inquiry other than by allowing oneself to be overwhelmed by the sheer impossibility of its questions, and by the reckless audacity with which it throws itself into the task of answering them. Before we rush headlong, however, a degree of moderating caution might be advisable. Like Prometheus, we are setting out to steal fire from the gods, and the same warnings apply to us as we with the benefit of hindsight might have given that Greek hero. First, we had better take pains to establish our right to the treasure we mean to plunder. Proving that claim will occupy the remainder of Part One.

3 Refining egocentrism

1. HAVING done with preliminaries it is time to make a start. – That statement has an air of paradox about it. Our journey is well underway. We have entered the territory of subjective and objective standpoints, and are learning more about our strange new world with every step. What more are we required to do? If philosophy were simply a matter of describing a vision – take it or leave it – the answer would be, nothing. Yet, clearly, something more is required. In a work of philosophy one argues, one aims to persuade. That remains true even though, as we remarked near the beginning of chapter 1, logical argument presupposes the capacity to share a vision. Nor is the goal of persuasion a matter of mere convention. Between what one would like to believe and what is true lies a path that cannot be traversed by a mere effort of will, nor even good will. Vision may guide our steps; but logic supplies the motive power for getting there.

That is the problem. The question of starting point has appeared, to many who might otherwise be sympathetic to our project, the one insuperable obstacle to constructing a metaphysic. Suppose that after an initial survey of the terrain, we locate what looks like a good place to begin. Who is to say that in making that initial move we are not already falling into error? It is no use reassuring ourselves with the thought that if every step had to be justified, including the first, one would never get anywhere. Perhaps there is nowhere to go. So says the sceptic: The need to make a choice at the very start negates any results achieved, for each alternative choice leads to a different theory. Whatever you end up with is simply the outcome of your initial move, and carries with it no less a taint of contingency even if it does not carry any more.

Our response is to proceed dialectically. The remarkable thing about this method is that it allows one to do metaphysics apparently without making any assumptions at all, simply by examining other theories and revealing their inconsistencies, thereby refuting them. That is, of course, an over-simplification. What we carry with us, as we follow the argument on the rebound, first from one view and then another, is not nothing but rather a sense of judgement – of what is logical or illogical, what coheres or does not cohere – that cannot be further articulated. It is a knowing or grasping that we cannot stand back from and make into a theory or an axiom because it is none other than our own selves, the way we see things.

Given that the number of incoherent theories is potentially infinite, however, we still need some principle for sorting the raw material to work on before we can even attempt to get going. A process of elimination, attacking every possible theory and seeing if that led anywhere, could never be completed, for it would take an infinite length of time. Yet now, it seems, we have not been wasting our time with mere preliminaries after all. For what better raw material could one choose than the very attitude of naive metaphysical speculation? It is time to put the pressure on.

2. Forced to confront the contradiction between the subjective and objective standpoints, the naive metaphysician, not surprisingly, sees only a straightforward choice between two theories, the egocentric and the nonegocentric. Some persons will opt for one theory, some for the other. However the numbers work out (and a statistical survey surely has no place in a work of philosophy), it is, or ought to be, a matter of complete indifference which theory we attack first. Since egocentrism has more of the look of a metaphysical theory, however, if for no other reason, it would be better for heuristic purposes to start with that.

Let us suppose, then, that one is drawn towards the egocentric view. I tell myself, 'I exist.' Perhaps for the first time in my life, I am aware that those words mean something. What am I to make of my existence? How am I placed in relation to the world? It seems that the objective standpoint, in its insistence that my being here means just one more human individual added to the world, will not allow such questions to be raised, or, rather, I would get just as good an answer if I asked what I am to make of my neighbour John Smith's existence, or how John Smith is placed in relation to the world. That is surely a hard thing to accept. The world can take or leave John Smith; I cannot entertain the thought that it can just as easily take or leave me. Thus, following what appears the line of least resistance, the naive metaphysician

24

chooses to repudiate the world of the objective standpoint. – Whatever I have to lose, it cannot be as bad as losing my own dear self.

What is it to believe in the egocentric theory? As an egocentrist, one is fully aware that each individual is capable of thinking of herself both from the subjective standpoint, as the axis around which the world of one's knowledge and experience revolves, and equally from the objective standpoint, as just one individual amongst a multitude who share a common world. Regarded as anything more than a useful picture, however, the objective standpoint distorts into philosophic illusion. I am lulled by my experience of living a normal social life into thinking that other persons stand in the same relation to the world as I do, and in my everyday dealings with others I collude happily with this deceptive appearance; but in reality I know that each person I meet is only a character in the story of my world.

3. Now to ordinary persons not corrupted by philosophy, this theory sounds outrageous, and also deeply offensive. To those unfortunates who show by their behaviour that they believe that the world does belong to them we give the name psychopath, and lock them up in asylums for the criminally insane. What precisely is the difference between a philosophical egocentrism and that psychopathic state? Evidently, there must be one, for by hypothesis the philosophical egocentrist continues to live as we all do, showing just as much care and consideration for others as any normal person. This is in itself a remarkable fact which requires some explanation.

The easy answer would be to say that a metaphysical conviction such as egocentrism is not a genuine case of belief. Then what is it? It is not a pretended belief, something one avers but does not truly believe, for that is only another name for a lie; what we mean by 'telling the truth' is just saying what one believes. Nor is the egocentrist's theory something one merely pretends or imagines to oneself; for then anyone who imagined what it would be like to be an egocentrist would automatically become one. It is certainly not merely an inexplicable preference for a non-standard use of words. The egocentrist who says, 'Only my feelings are real feelings,' but continues to show due consideration for the feelings of others, does not intend merely to use the term 'real feelings' to mean the same as 'my feelings'; that would reduce the content of egocentrism to a mere tautology.

This last point was indeed noted by Wittgenstein in a remark in the *Philosophical Investigations* (I/402-3). Finding that he was unable to explain the meanings of the contesting metaphysical claims in terms of the concept of belief, Wittgenstein concluded that the dispute between 'Idealists, Solipsists and Realists' could not have any substance to it, appearances to the contrary, and so dismissed it as nothing more than the result of grammatical confusion. This summary judgement indicates, in the judgement of the present author, the extent of Wittgenstein's continuing implacable hostility both to the idea and the practice of metaphysics – towards the very notion that one should possess the means to describe a metaphysical vision, as opposed to merely giving verbal expression to one's illusions – all this despite the profound metaphysical implications of both his early and late work.

Yet if Wittgenstein's judgement is too swift, what would be the alternative response? The question one ought to ask is, Why should the lack of practical consequences automatically entail that the egocentrist's vision lacks content? Surely, that begs the question by insisting on viewing the egocentrist from the objective standpoint – in looking for signs of the vision in the egocentrist's behaviour – and so assuming from the start that egocentrism is invalid. The correct conclusion to draw is rather that we have been looking in the wrong place. We have to enter, if we can, the egocentrist's mind and see just what it is that the egocentrist sees. (Later on in the book, when we investigate the logical basis of morality, we shall discover a different sense in which the refutation of egocentrism – the proof of the reality of the objective standpoint – does indeed carry 'practical consequences'.)

4. We shall begin by recalling a paradigm experience which, following the example of Descartes, many philosophers have called upon, an experience that first casts doubt upon the status of a world independent of my I. In itself, the experience does not indicate any particular metaphysical theory, but at most delimits a range of alternatives. We are interested, however, in one particular way of taking that original experience; as it were, a vision of the vision. We shall then follow the dialectic of the successive refinements of the vision as philosophy struggles, with greater or lesser success, to find words adequate to express what it seems to see.

The experience might take some such form as this. I am gazing intently at some object; let us say, a shiny red apple, illuminated by the golden glow of a table lamp. The colour fills my eyes, they are engorged with it. Then something strange happens. From one moment to the next, it seems as if the redness and the yellowness are no longer in the apple or in the lamp but in me. Only it is not just the colour. As I continue to look, the very objects themselves seem to dissolve away without a trace; nothing remains of what was supposedly out there. The apple and the table lamp now appear to me as nothing other than

26

images floating in my own mind. As I look round, the same happens to every object I cast my eyes upon.

What caused this extraordinary event to occur? My whole world has completely changed; and yet, in a strange way, everything remains the same as before. Nothing flickered or went fuzzy, no visible sign testifies to the dramatic transformation I have just witnessed. In vain, I reach out to touch the objects around me to reassure myself that they are really out there and not in me; the smooth, hard skin of the apple, the heat of the table lamp and the soft fabric of the lampshade now reveal themselves as mere experiences, just events happening in my mind.

Now one might quickly dismiss this unsettling vision as a momentary mental lapse. Indeed, after a short while the image of an apple becomes an apple again, the image of a lamp is once more a lamp. Everything returns to the state it was in before – or does it? The egocentrist would persuade us otherwise. Think of it this way, says the egocentrist. Say to yourself, I have made a discovery of the greatest importance. I have succeeded in one brief glimpse in catching reality off guard. I have seen beneath the deceptive appearance of a world independent of my I. In reality, all that exists is nothing but the constant flux of sensations, thoughts and ideas that make up the contents of my conscious mind.

5. It would not be much of an achievement to refute what amounts to a first, simple-minded attempt at a metaphysical theory. Such crude subjectivism would be disowned by the more thoughtful egocentrist. The proper basis for a critique – indeed the only way that will yield a result we can use in constructing our own theory – is to allow the original vision of a world in my mind to develop through self-criticism into one that is as far as possible self-consistent and immune from attack. (By the end of the end of chapter 4, we shall see how, ironically, the egocentrist succeeds only too well.)

We begin by noticing that the vision of a dissolving world appears similar to the state of mind which Descartes reached, in the 'First Meditation', by his famous method of systematic doubt: How do I know that there is a world beyond my perceptions, that I am not merely being deceived by an evil demon into thinking so? The egocentrist, however, is far more ruthless in following up the implications of the cartesian method. For it seems that Descartes, despite his avowed aim of questioning everything he formerly believed, makes an unjustified assumption. He never goes so far as to doubt whether it is logically possible for objects to exist beyond his perceptions, that he knows what that proposition means. His only question is whether in fact there are any such objects.

Our simple-minded egocentrist simply does not understand the question. What notion can I have of external objects corresponding with my perceptions? Like everything else I know, it is just an idea in my mind. When one looks at a picture one has some idea of what it might mean to say that the picture either corresponds or does not correspond with what it depicts, or indeed that the object which it is intended to depict really exists; for there is such a thing as comparing the two, the picture with its object. Where logically there can be no comparing the notion of correspondence is empty. (In fairness to Descartes, one should remember that the method of systematic doubt was never meant to extend to doubting the existence of something, I know not what, beyond my perceptions. Whether that something is an external world or only an evil demon, the contents of my mind will always have another side or aspect from the one they present to me. We shall see later that this notion of a plurality of sides in effect defines the objective standpoint.)

6. Let us now try to describe these mental objects. Previously, I believed in the existence of such things as apples and table lamps, trees and houses. Now all that remains for perception are mental images of these and other things. In trying to assert this claim, however, I am embarrassed to discover that I am quite unable to describe my experience other than in terms of the apples and table lamps, trees and houses in which I supposedly no longer believe! One might imagine that one could make a start by talking of variously shaped patches of red and yellow, green and grey, and so on. Yet it soon becomes apparent that such a limited range of concepts proves hopelessly inadequate to describe subjective experience in all its depth and richness .

The embarrassment is soon overcome, however. I can admit that my mind is neither swift enough nor sufficiently acute to devise and employ a sensation language couched purely in terms of such properties as colours and shapes; that I have no choice but to continue using the language which I once used to express my beliefs about an external world. That just means that where I once talked of apples and table lamps I now talk of appearances of apples and table lamps. The images in my mind still have attributes of their own which exist to be described by a hypothetical sensation language, even though they never will be actually so described; just as for the common sense view of the world the grains of sand on the beach do not depend for their

28

existence on anyone's being able to count them all or describe them individually.

We may call the subjectivist view that asserts flatly that the only objects that exist are objects in my own mind simple egocentrism. Having rejected an entire world of independent objects, the simple egocentrist never once questions what could be meant by the notion of a mind, or what kind of thing is referred to by the pronoun 'I'. One thinks of oneself as a kind of ghostly container, with thoughts and feelings floating about inside, into which pours an incessant stream of feelings and sensations. As Hume observed in the first book (Pt IV §6) of his *Treatise on Human Nature*, however, wherever one looks one never sees the I, the container, but only the mental objects it contains. What then could be meant by saying that a given set of mental objects belong in the same container, in the same mind? The only thing I am aware of when I look inside my mind are connections between the various images I find there; for example, between a sensation of red and the memory of having had a similar sensation in the past. Anything added to that is a baseless supposition.

This discovery shatters simple egocentrism. It is as if the implicit dynamic behind the egocentrist's paradigm experience, the mind's power to dissolve every object it touches into mental images, now turns on those mental objects themselves; and with their dissolution mind itself then disappears. Yet, seemingly, all is not lost. The more sophisticated, Humean egocentrist concludes that what we commonly refer to as 'mind' is in reality nothing but the product of a continual process of composition and decay, as mental images connect up or break their connection. Similarly, what I mean by the term 'I' is just the indeterminate bundle of mental objects which connect up either directly or indirectly with a given present sensation or feeling nominated as 'mine'. (The historical Hume, it should be noted, never gives up his belief in the objective standpoint from which the detached philosophical observer views the workings of 'human nature': all praise to his inconsistency.)

7. The difficulty with Humean egocentrism is that as soon as one tries to explain the supposed connection between different mental objects, one is caught in a tight circle. Take the simplest possible case. Suppose that I am now experiencing a sensation of red and also a buzzing sound. Here is red and there is a buzz: but what is the connection between here and there? The buzz is not red, nor does the red buzz. Nor is there, according to this view, any I to act as a link between the one and the other. All one can say is that there is now red and also a

buzz; what connects them is simply their happening in the form of one compound event.

What if the red had occurred before the buzz? There is first red, then there is a buzz, accompanied by the memory of red. The buzz and the memory of red are connected because they occur at the same time, forming a single event; but we still need to connect the memory of red with the actual red that it remembers. It is of course true that a sensation of red can occur together with the memory of a previous sensation of red, but that does not help in any way to connect this particular memory of red with the red that it remembers. The only thing that could connect them is the fact that they occur at different times in one and the same subject, namely myself. However, talk of the subject of experience, of the I, is the one thing the Humean egocentrist cannot allow, since the I is supposed to be defined in terms of connections between its experiences. As a result, the only thing that can be a subject or a mind is something with no identity over time: a momentary coming together of sensations and images.

This bleak conclusion reduces the egocentrist claim that the only objects that exist are objects in my mind almost to absurdity; almost, but not quite. I can continue denying that an independent world exists provided that I also deny that I exist. Still, that is not the same as making the absurd claim that nothing exists. There remains *this*: a momentary constellation of somethings which are neither in the world nor in any mind, which occupy no spatial position and possess no temporal duration.

There is worse to come, however. We still have to ask what it means to say that these momentary somethings have attributes, that they are thus-and-so and can, in principle if not in practice, be described as they really are. Consider again the example of the red and the buzz. What is red? What is a buzz? All terms and concepts, however simple, mean something only in relation to a wider context. One red thing may be compared with another red thing; one buzz with another buzz. On the other hand, a red thing is not blue, a buzz is not a whistle. Yet the red and the buzz of our momentary somethings do not stand in relation to anything else. One is led to argue that the bare experience of red could exist even if the concept 'red' had no meaning, even if there was not even the logical possibility of relating together different red things. Imagine our experienced world in all its original detail, the egocentrist might say. Somewhere in this totality there is a particular red and a particular buzz. Now start taking things away. At no point does the red cease to be red, the buzz cease to be a buzz, even when the red and the buzz are the only two things that remain. – Only now we must ask whether this simple-minded thought experiment tells us anything

30

about real logical possibility, or only about the way our imaginations work; and to that the Humean egocentrist has no reply. (Imagine an artist removing patches of colour one by one from a canvas until there is just one single patch of colour left. Except that the artist herself, her brushes and palette, easel and canvas are themselves part of the painting.)

8. One might call the position to which the Humean egocentrist is driven a 'reductio ad silentium'. If the only reality is this present experience, with no connection with before or after, if all that exists is a momentary constellation of somethings whose attributes cannot be described, then absolutely nothing can be said about anything. Yet remaining silent is no easy thing to do; for the philosopher if not for the mystic. So one continues to talk, inconsistently, about fictions and suchlike – calling it Humean irony.

To reconstruct the metaphysic of egocentrism so that it may, with at least the appearance of consistency, accommodate our notions of a self which persists through time and a world of external objects which the self perceives, requires more powerful tools and materials than Hume allows. For that purpose, we need to borrow insights from Kant's *Critique of Pure Reason*; specifically, from the two 'Transcendental Deductions' and the second edition 'Refutation of Idealism'. (Once again, one should note that the historical Kant is firmly committed to the reality of the objective standpoint; his egocentric epistemology, we would argue, as little entitles him to that belief as it does Hume.)

Kant starts from the basic assumption, which he regards as axiomatic, that I do in fact succeed in describing my experience. I make judgements about how things are, based on how they seem. Not only is there something, a *this,* given immediately in experience (Kant calls it 'anschaaung' or intuition); there must also be concepts available for describing it. Now applying a concept involves an act of recognition: for example, this red is the same colour as a previous red. To do that, one has to connect together sensations of red which occur at different times; they must present themselves to one and the same I. There is no question, however, of reinstating the simple egocentrist's ghostly container of ideas. It is not a fact, contingent or necessary, that where there is intuition and concepts there is an I; rather, it is analytic. The two taken together (as they necessarily must be) make up the entire substance of I; take them away and nothing remains. The I is thus not any kind of object but rather the common element, the 'I think' which is necessarily capable of accompanying every act of thinking, every application of a concept to an object.

Having recovered the I, Kant sets his sights on recovering the notion of a world of objects outside the mind. One might be excused for thinking that such a project, were it to be successful, would mean the rejection of egocentrism. On the contrary, as we shall now see, it merely serves to refine the egocentric theory by ridding it of its distorting, subjectivist element.

Consider again the momentary red and the momentary buzz. It might seem that all one needs to turn this example into one which allows for the application of concepts, and thus for a persisting I, is to make the red and the buzz continue through time. What is wrong with that suggestion? Kant would reply that the subject which utters the words, 'red, red again, red again...', or 'buzz, buzz again, buzz again...' is not actually thinking, is not making judgements on the basis of its experience. It merely detects red and reacts with the word 'red', detects a buzz and says, 'buzz'.

For the sake of argument, however, let us suppose that this primitive subject is continually making very simple judgements, which in some sense do not require thought. Briefly, let us imagine, the red turns to blue, then back again. At the same time, the buzz is replaced by a whistle. One asks: was that blue? was that a whistle? But the question is pointless, for nothing the subject will ever experience could count either way. The only thing it can go on is what it remembers, or seems to remember reporting at the time. The blue whistle might recur several times; then on one occasion, say, blue is accompanied by a buzz. The subject would have no right to say, 'That couldn't have been a blue buzz, because blue always whistles!' Or, rather, it can say that if it likes; it can say anything it likes. Merely to go through the motions of enumerating instances of noisy colours or coloured sounds can never amount to an induction, for each new instance has no sooner appeared than it joins the set of seemingly remembered instances that the induction was meant to verify. – The water flows out of the bucket as quickly as it is poured in.

There is thus not even the logical possibility of our primitive subject ever being wrong about anything, just because everything it says reduces to what seems to be the case at the time. Whatever it says goes, and there is no room for even a shadow of a doubt. Yet making a judgement that could not possibly be wrong is like shooting an arrow at a target, when the target is already attached to the arrow. Just as a target attached to your arrow is one you can neither miss nor hit, so a concept that cannot possibly be misapplied cannot be used to say anything false or true; which is the same as saying that it is not a concept at all. In the imagined experience of the continued red buzz, there are no concepts, no 'I think' – and therefore no I.

32

9. If experience, by definition is something had by a persisting I, then a continuing red buzz is not a possible experience. How far, then, could experience deviate from what we have and still be experience? Kant's answer to this question is very simple. However much variety or order one introduces, the end result will not be a possible experience unless it bears the kind of structure that permits its non-arbitrary interpretation as the perception of a world of objects form a point of view within that world. Sensations, such as the red or the buzz, not only occupy times but are seen as occupying places to which one can in principle return. Thus, on the basis of its experience, the subject makes judgements about the qualities of objects situated at different places, at the same time as it makes judgements about its own spatial position in relation to those objects. By contrast with the fake judgements about the red buzz or the blue whistle, these essentially interpretative judgements commit the subject to believing that things are thus-and-so at places at which it is not now located.

It is this very commitment – to the truth of propositions that can neither be reduced to reports of immediate sense experience nor to any generalizations made up of such reports – that makes the perceptual reports genuine judgements, and thus allows us to regard the I as a genuine subject of experience. Now, it seems, we have everything we wanted: if there is such a thing as experience, then there must be such a thing as an I that uses concepts in judging the character of that experience; if there is such a thing as an I that makes judgements then there must necessarily be a world of external objects – an 'objective world' – which the I perceives. (Note that a two-dimensional quasi-spatial world of relatively stable secondary properties would be sufficient to account for the possibility of false judgement. It is indeed possible to introduce richer conceptions of objectivity, such as the requirement that there be a distinction between primary and secondary qualities: Cf. Evans 'Things Without the Mind'. This represents, in effect, an additional feature grafted on to the original Kantian model, and by no means requires the rejection of egocentrism.)

There is much that Kant says about the way a world is constructed and the subjective requirements for being a subject that is able to do the work of construction – all grist to the egocentrist's mill – which we do not need to mention here. All that is relevant, from the point of view of the refinement of egocentrism, is that the I should possess the concept of space, or something closely analogous to space, in which the I, and the objects of is perception are located; and that what is immediately there for the I should in its intrinsic structure conform to the requirement that the concept of a spatial world have application.

Without doubt the notions used in Kant's account of objective judgement, even in our stripped-down version of it, are doing real work. There are genuine problems to solve about the details of the account, which anyone will discover who attempts to construct different imaginary worlds and tries to work out, case by case, whether and how the requirements of objective judgement are met. At the same time, one may be forgiven for thinking that all this amounts to no more than a conjurer's sleight of hand. For the argument seems to accomplish something quite impossible. How can anyone, starting from the almost totally negative position where all that exists is an indescribable, momentary *this*, where there is no space as such, no world of external objects, no time, no I recover both the I and the world on the basis of the single axiom that there is something to say about something? If any theory is the equivalent of pulling oneself up by one's bootstraps, that is it. Now whenever such an extraordinary move occurs in philosophy, it is advisable to examine one's new, elevated position very carefully to make sure that it is not merely the same old surroundings seen upside down. In the next chapter, we shall raise doubts about Kant's argument which lead, not to a further refinement of egocentrism, but rather to its total rejection.

4 Silencing the egocentric

1. PURSUING our negative strategy for establishing the theory of subjective and objective worlds, we had arrived at the end of the last chapter at a final, Kantian formulation of the first of the two theories to be attacked. According to the egocentrist, my relation to the world is to be comprehended purely from the subjective standpoint. The world is nothing but the world of my possible experience: the ultimate stuff of which the world is made is simply *this*, the indescribable subjective input or intuition upon which I base all my so-called objective judgements.

Now at first sight, this seems to do away with an external world entirely, since all that exists is reduced to the contents of my own mind. However, the Kantian egocentrist has found an ingenious way to retain the idea of a world outside my mind. The simple egocentrist, who believes that the external world has been done away with, fails to see that my having a notion of myself as a subject of experience presupposes that intuition be so structured as to appear as my perception of a world of objects in space. The subjective input cannot be described except in terms of concepts of an external world. We saw that the Humean egocentrist, by contrast, in rejecting both external objects and the self which has experiences, is forced in the end to reject also the very possibility of judgement. Missing the Kantian point, the Humean wrongly assumes that a self or mind could only be a ghostly container of ideas. Kant's argument, then, may be summarized in three statements. First, the only thing that can be a subject of experience, a self or mind, is a being that makes judgements, that describes its experience by means of concepts. Secondly, concepts can only be used to describe something if there is a real difference between

35

getting it right and getting it wrong, between knowledge and error. But thirdly, there is room for error only if the things which the subject perceives appear in space, and not just as a one-dimensional series spread out in time.

Whatever hopes Kant may have held for his 'refutation of dogmatic idealism' (he thought he was attacking Berkeley in the spirit of Descartes: he was wrong on both counts), what his argument actually proves is simply that calling intuition 'mine' logically implies that it has the character of my perception of an external world. In practice, this means that the egocentrist can continue talking about things in the world as we all do, knowing all the while that such talk ultimately relates back to the indescribable subjective stuff, the *this*. Now, it is no objection to the argument that it proves less than one might have expected from its name. We are only considering the argument as employed by the Kantian egocentrist; not some other argument which might be used to prove a stronger conclusion. However, it will be useful to start by considering three elementary objections, corresponding to the three stages of the argument that we have just outlined.

First, why couldn't there be a subject which simply had experiences without thinking or making judgements about them? Why can't a series of experiences just happen, each with a determinate character of its own, even though the subject they happen to is not in a position to make judgements about that character? If they can, why can't that subject be I? Secondly, why must it be possible for concepts to be incorrectly applied? To be red-or-not-red, for example, is surely a concept, yet the law of excluded middle ensures that it may be used to describe anything you like, and the result will never be false. Less trivially, perhaps, the statement, 'Something exists' applies the concept of existence in such a way that that judgement could never be false. Thirdly, why can't a series of stable objects existing in time but not in space serve as the reality external to mind in relation to which concepts may be correctly or incorrectly applied? Why, for example, couldn't a non-spatially located mind whose experiences consisted of an orderly succession of different colours mistakenly describe one of its red experiences as 'blue'? We shall consider these objections in turn.

2. In order to meet the first objection, why there couldn't be a conscious subject which had experiences without making judgements about them, we do not need to go into the question of whether or not it would be right to describe any primitive organism we came across that sought nutrients or avoided harmful agents as having some form of attenuated experience; or whether, at the other end of the scale, a dog

might possess a simple range of concepts, and so qualify as having a mind, even though it never did anything which we call thinking. It would be difficult to deny that non-human subjects do have conscious experience and, given that admission, that such experience whether it be rich or poor must as a matter of logic have its own determinate character. However, when Kant talks of the self or subject of experience he means any being which is capable of having beliefs about the past or future, and which possesses a sense of its identity over time, as we do; a being which is able to raise the question whether its apparent memory of a certain event is correct. (A dog 'checking' where its bone is buried could not be said to be questioning its memory.)

What the simple egocentrist must believe is that a subject with a sense of its identity over time could have a purely temporal experience, an experience which did not appear as the perception of objects in space. Kant's argument refutes that belief. The simple egocentrist fails to realize that the temporally located subject could not have the identity claimed for it, but would disintegrate into individual, momentary experiences, with no connection between before and after. The I think which binds the subjective happenings together into a series of connected experiences is bound up with the use of concepts to describe those experiences as perceptions of one and the same reality; only then can the experiences be said to occur in one and the same mind. The argument is that the only reality which will adequately serve the purpose is a world of objects in space.

Yet, given all this, would it not still be possible for a more sophisticated egocentrist to declare that the reality which, lacking the power to make judgements, I can only call *this* – my subjective experience as it is in itself, in its own determinate character – is what I shall henceforth regard as my self, even though I can never know myself as an I, nor even connect one experience with another? We may reply on Kant's behalf: say that if you like; nothing follows from it. The one thing you cannot say is that the experience you call 'this' or 'self' has its own determinate identity as a series of connected events. In the absence of an I that makes judgements, no glue is strong enough to force the atoms of experience to stick together.

3. The second objection takes the form of two counterexamples. In the last chapter, we said that applying concepts that could not be wrongly applied was like shooting at a target which was already attached to one's arrow. There is neither missing nor hitting, neither wrong nor right. Now, the concept 'red-or-not-red' is made out of the concepts 'red', 'or' and 'not', and so qualifies as a perfectly genuine concept. And

surely one would be right if one said, of a glass of wine, that it is red-or-not-red, even if one would be saying something rather odd. Yet we should be making a statement which could not be false.

This counterexample can be dealt with by distinguishing between concepts that are descriptive, concepts that can actually be used to say something, to convey information however trivial, and those that are non-descriptive. We are deliberately not saying anything about the colour of the wine when we say that it is red-or-not-red; for we do not intend to rule out that it might be blue or green; nor do we mean to imply that one can always be sure of saying when a particular shade of pink counts as 'red'. We do not mean to rule anything out as far as the colour of the wine is concerned, which is why the concept 'red-or-not-red' cannot be wrongly applied to it, and so does not describe it in any way. The necessity of concepts Kant is arguing for, by contrast, is the necessity of descriptive concepts; for the identity of the I in the I think depends upon there being a descriptive content for the I to actually think, a judgement which the subject commits itself to. The discovery that one can put together artificial, non-descriptive concepts does not weaken the argument in any way.

The second counterexample, however, appears on the face of it another matter entirely. What could be of greater significance than the judgement that something exists? Yet, barring the most heroic scepticism, there is no way that such a judgement could be false. Our response is in one respect parallel and in another respect opposite to the one we gave to the previous counterexample. We have seen that there is no thinking, no I, unless the subject thinks thoughts which commit it to something's being the case, something that might turn out not to be the case. In the present example, in thinking that something exists the subject does not undertake any commitment, not because there is no content to commit itself to – we have no sympathy for any view that attempts to block the naive metaphysician's request for an explanation of contingent existence by the simple expedient of denying content to the explanandum – but because as far as the subject is concerned, the content is simply that there is such a thing as content; and to that the subject is equally committed, just as much with every judgement it takes back or deems false as with every judgement it asserts.

4. The third objection asks: what is logically impossible about the idea of a reality, say, an orderly succession of colours, spread out in time but not in space? By reference to such a non-spatial world, one might be said to mistakenly remember a previous red sensation as having

38

been blue, or, alternatively, mistakenly believe that the next sensation is going to be blue, and then find that it is red.

In order to deal with this objection, we must first get rid of the notion that we might stand in the privileged position of being able to observe the temporally located mind which makes judgements about red and blue and other colours, and compare those judgements with the multicoloured reality that its judgements are about. We are asking whether we could conceive of what it would be to have such an experience, and so must adopt the subjective viewpoint of the temporally located mind. Now the peculiar thing about this non-spatial world is that every sensation we experience is one which we have, strictly speaking, never seen before and will never see again. Just because the sensations are identified only by their location in a temporal series, there is no coming back to a sensation previously experienced, as opposed to merely having another one like it, in the way that one might return to an object located in space in order to confirm that one's memory of it is correct. For no amount of similarity between two sensations occurring at different times, or between the patterns in which the two sensations occur, could, logically, ever make them into the same object.

What this means is not, however, that one would have to remain forever in doubt whether one's memory was correct. In the non-spatial world, there is strictly no use for memory. The function of retaining a picture of how things were at different places where we are not now located, so important to us in our spatial world, is indistinguishable in the non-spatial world from a function of merely inventing a picture of how things are at other temporal locations. But supposing one were to grant that in the non-spatial world the past is by definition always just as it seems to have been whenever one thinks about it, could I not still be caught by surprise by a sensation of red which, on the basis of patterns I seemed to have experienced before, I expected to be blue? Let us pretend for the sake of argument that this does happen. My expectation can turn out to have been disappointed only if I remember correctly that it was an expectation of blue and not of red. Yet we have already seen that there is no such thing as memory in the non-spatial world, no difference between remembering correctly or incorrectly. Kant's conclusion therefore stands. A non-spatial world is not something that could be described by means of concepts; there could not be a subject who had experience of a world in time but not in space.

5. The Kantian egocentrist does indeed seem to have the best of both worlds. One retains the metaphysical vision that all that really exists

is the indescribable *this* of my subjective awareness, while at the same time apparently justifying the common sense belief in a world outside my mind. Now the time has come, however, to ask whether egocentrism is in fact true; and, if it is not, how one might refute it. As is well known, Dr. Johnson's reported response to Bishop Berkeley's immaterialism was to kick a stone and declare, 'I refute it thus.' In chapter 15, we shall discover that there is more than a grain of truth in this knock-down argument. (According to our definition, Berkeley's immaterialism is a form of nonegocentrism.) The reader will find that our anti-egocentric argument is also essentially a one-liner. So it would be a good idea to first try out what would seem to be the nearest literal equivalent of Dr. Johnson's kick.

If someone tells me that she is an egocentrist, that the world is nothing but the world of her possible experience, then surely I know without any further discussion that whatever it is that she believes cannot be true. I am certainly not just a character in the story of another person's world. Let me be reduced to nothing in the eyes of others; I still have an absolute reality for myself which cannot be reduced to the possible perceptions that make up the world for some other mind. However, the egocentrist disposes of this argument with ease. 'It's no good your proving the falsity of my egocentrism to yourself; you have got to prove it to me. As far as I'm concerned, you are just a concept that I use to describe my experience, and all your fine words are just sounds in my ears. Why don't you ask yourself how you know that I'm not just a character in the story of your world? Why aren't you an egocentrist? If you could come up with an argument that convinced the egocentrist in you, then maybe I would be prepared to apply the argument to my own case!'

Of course, in saying this, the egocentrist is fully convinced that no such argument could ever be given. – And however certain I may be most of the time that egocentrism is false, are there not also times when I have felt all alone in my world, when everything seemed to be just my own private dream, or nightmare? If this is a possibility I can entertain in my darkest moments, might the possibility not turn out, after all, to be the way things really are?

6. The first question I might put to the egocentrist in me is whether there is any special characteristic that distinguishes between my experience of perceiving an external world, and my experience of having a dream. According to Kant's argument, I exist as a subject of experience only insofar as my experience appears as perception of an external world. Yet so do my dreams, while I'm having them. What grounds do I have for dismissing some apparent perceptions as mere

dreams, while taking others to be genuine? A term one might use here is 'coherence'. The experiences of my waking life cohere, literally, 'stick together', because they back one another up. My home, the town where I live, indeed the whole world appear to me as a relatively constant framework within which all changes take place according to the principle of cause and effect. Every perception is answerable to the knowledge that I have built up from past perceptions. Everything that doesn't fit in is called a hallucination, or else a dream.

Yet is it really necessary that all my waking experiences should stick together as experiences of just one spatial world? Anthony Quinton, in his paper 'Spaces and Times', suggests the following possibility. Every time I go to sleep I 'dream' of waking up in a world which appears in every respect as coherent as this world; and when I go to sleep in that world I once more wake up in this world. The suggestion is not intended to criticize egocentrism, but to show how one might acquire grounds for believing in the existence of another world, spatially unrelated to this one. The problem is that there is no reason why the number should be limited to two. I could find myself regularly visiting three, four or any number of different worlds. What then are the limits to this kind of experience? If every few minutes I fell asleep and seemed to wake up in a world I had never seen before, then my experience would no longer be coherent; there would cease to be any real difference between my perceiving a succession of worlds and my having an endless series of dreams. However, there is no point at which one could draw a dividing line which separated one from the other, which was not completely arbitrary.

The situation we have just described is ripe for the application of an argument which, in ancient times, was known as the paradox of 'the heap'. A few grains of sand scattered on the floor is definitely not a heap. Adding one grain of sand could never convert something that was not yet a heap into a heap. Therefore, by repeating the process, no amount of sand could ever be a heap! The fallacy in this argument lies in the attempt to apply strict logic to a vague term; there simply is no definition of a 'heap', even though we get on perfectly well with the term for practical purposes. Where this form of argument is valid is against any attempt to base an absolute philosophical distinction on a merely relative difference. The egocentrist cannot say that there is an absolute distinction between perceiving a world and having a dream, while at the same time also allowing that someone might experience more than one spatial world, in the way we have described above. There is no number or frequency of worlds at which one could draw the line between a series of worlds and a series of dreams. (We shall consider how one ought to respond to Quinton's thought experiment from the point of view of our two-world theory in chapter 9.)

Kant avoids having to face this difficulty by refusing to allow the hypothesis that one might ever experience more than one spatial world, on the grounds of its prima facie incompatibility with the necessary unity of experience. Perhaps the most sympathetic gloss one could put on Kant's strict view is that, while I am in this world, I can say what I like about the other world or worlds and never be wrong; just as, when reporting a dream, whatever one says goes. According to the refutation of simple egocentrism, if one's memory of something can never be wrong, then there is nothing real to be remembered, correctly or incorrectly. Arguably, not even apparent coherence with the memory reports of other persons who claim to have had similar experiences (Quinton's suggestion) could make any essential difference: what makes my memory of an experience correct is not any number of persons assuring me that it is so, but rather the experience actually having happened at the time I seem to remember it.

The Kantian objection can still be met, however, by allowing events in each world to have the potential to connect in a lawlike way with events in each of the other spatially non-related worlds. If, for example, someone invented a trans-world television camera, then one's apparent memory of events in other worlds would be backed up by listening to the television news reports in whichever world one happened to be in. All the worlds would then be linked together through a single, non-spatial network. The Kantian egocentrist, in the face of Quinton's thought experiment, would therefore seem to have great difficulty in drawing the line at only one spatial world; and if there can be more than one then there is no absolute limit to the number of worlds. Now at some point, the number and frequency of worlds would make it simply impossible to keep up with the trans-world news reports; but this point is not located at any precise place. In that case, according to the paradox of the heap, there is once again no absolute distinction between reality and a dream.

7. With the discovery that reality cannot be defined absolutely, we are already on the slippery slope that will lead to the eventual downfall of egocentrism. But perhaps all is not yet lost. If reality is only a relatively coherent dream, then there is still some distinction to be made between being awake and dreaming, only one that is not absolute. Similarly, no-one would deny that there was a distinction between a heap of sand and a few grains scattered on the floor, although the number of grains required for a heap cannot be defined precisely. Thus, if the egocentrist admits that coherence cannot be

defined precisely, there could still be a difference between a coherent experience and an incoherent experience, between perceiving a world and having a dream or hallucination, even though no sharp line could be drawn between one and the other; a difference which might justify the application of the concept of objective experience.

One ought to remain deeply sceptical about any such admission, however. We saw that Kant's refutation of simple egocentrism turns on the question whether the conditions are satisfied for the existence of a subject or self which applies concepts in order to describe its experience. In a dream world there is no subject in this sense, even if, reporting the dream later, there seemed to be; without judgement, the I think which necessarily accompanies every application of concepts, there is no I. Yet surely the distinction between there being a subject and there not being a subject is absolute, not relative. In which case, contrary to the egocentrist's admission, the distinction between perceiving a world and having a dream must also be absolute and not relative. The argument from the heap therefore applies with full force.

The dream-like quality of the egocentrist's world is revealed even more clearly when one asks, What, ultimately, are the things that the I perceives? What is the I that perceives them? The common sense reply that one perceives such things as trees and houses and people, and that the I that perceives them is just one's own self, a subject located in the world, misses the point of this metaphysical question. The unity of the I in the I think which accompanies all judgements has shown itself to be the unity of a function, a mere capacity for thought, of which no further account can be given. Similarly, there is no explanation of the existence of the immediate, subjective given, the indescribable *this* to which concepts are applied. The power of judgement and the immediate given must both be treated as ultimates, the end point of all explanation.

It is here that the egocentrist parts company with Kant himself, who sought to introduce an unknowable, 'noumenal' subject, the subject as it is in itself, the entity in which the power of judgement is ultimately grounded, together with unknowable noumena or things-in-themselves which come into relation with noumenal subjects to produce the appearance we know as our perceived world. There cannot be appearance, Kant said, without 'something that appears', something of which it is the appearance; and this surely is a powerful argument. For all the difficulties with the notion of unknowable things-in-themselves, it is in one respect far more in accord with the common sense view, that what makes a dream a mere dream is just that its images do not correspond with any actual things outside the world of one's subjective experience, or, rather, that what they do correspond with is only a state of the subject of which the subject has no direct knowledge, a state of that medium or substance in which one's conscious processes are realized.

The strict egocentrist, by contrast, will have none of this. From my subjective standpoint, the notion of any relation between the world as it appears to me, and the world as it really is outside my possible perceptions is meaningless. The whole of reality is just appearance, a world of phenomena, which I cannot question further. To go so far as to ask what the appearance is an appearance of is to abandon my subjective standpoint in favour of the objective standpoint, to relinquish egocentrism in favour of nonegocentrism.

8. The world of the Kantian egocentrist is not a world most of us would care to inhabit; it is a mere spectacle, a succession of images on a cinema screen, robbed of all substance. However, it is not our business to question this vision on aesthetic grounds. The only relevant question is whether egocentrism is a logically self-consistent theory. Its apparent vulnerability to the paradox of the heap implies that it is not. Still, that argument is not finally conclusive. In the absence of an alternative theory, one might argue, a relative distinction between a world and a dream is better than no world at all.

Our main argument, however, is directed towards an even more fundamental assumption. One feature which plays a pivotal role in egocentrism is the principle that there exists a real distinction between true and false judgement, one that does not reduce to whatever is taken to be true or false at any given time. That is how the Kantian is able to refute simple egocentrism, by showing that a world in time but not in space is not something about which one could ever judge falsely. Whatever the simple egocentrist's subject seems to believe at any one time is necessarily the truth; one cannot ever talk of its remembering events in its past correctly or incorrectly. By contrast, the memories belonging to a subject who perceives a world in space are answerable to the future course of its experience; in a spatial world, one can return to places one has visited before. Thus, every judgement becomes an interpretation; nothing is taken simply at face value, but is judged in the light of past experience, and waits to be corroborated by future experience. This is indeed a valid point against simple egocentrism.

The question is whether this argument is consistent with the two metaphysical ultimates which form the basis of Kantian egocentrism: the power of judgement expressed in the I think, and the immediate, subjective given, the *this* which together produce the story of my experience of an objective, spatial world.

44

Now, on its own, the *this* does not dictate what kind of interpretation I should place upon it. That requires the application of concepts, the use of my power of judgement. But suppose it occurred to me to ask myself whether I trusted my power of judgement? To the question whether my experience is perception of a world, or only a dream or hallucination, we have seen that the egocentrist answers that dreams and hallucinations lack the coherence necessary for genuine perception. Coherence is a matter of interpretation, something I have to form a judgement about. However, the one thing I cannot form a judgement about is whether I am not merely making up my interpretations as I go along, so that any false belief can just as easily be deemed true, or any true belief false. This is one possibility I am not allowed even to consider.

Yet surely there is an exact parallel here with what the Kantian egocentrist says about simple egocentrism. The simple egocentrist has to view the subject's memory of events in a non-spatial world as infallible, as incapable of ever being incorrect, since there is no such thing as going back into the past to compare a previous experience with one's memory of it. In an exactly similar way, one might argue, the egocentrist who rejects simple egocentrism possesses no conception of the reality in virtue of which my power of judgement is either reliable or faulty. For that, one requires the objective standpoint, the existence of points of view outside my own system of representation from which that system may be considered as something that either succeeds or fails in putting me in reliable touch with reality, the possibility of subjects whose ways of interpreting our common experience are independent of my judgement. Egocentrism says that there is no such reality; everything there is belongs to the world of my possible experience, the world as seen through my system of representation, as constructed out of my judgements. So my judgement is the sole judge of itself; its authority to evaluate its own judging must be regarded as absolute. In that case, we must say the same thing that the egocentrist said about simple egocentrism: a judgement that cannot, logically, be wrong is one that cannot be right either. There is, therefore, no world for judgements to be about, and no subject to make them. The egocentrist is, for the second and final time, reduced to silence.

So we are back, after a long detour it seems, with the inexpressible vision of the *this*, the unique, self-subsistent reality about which nothing can be said. The attempt to justify talk of a world outside the mind, or indeed of the mind or subject which perceives that world, has come to nothing. Even so, one will go on talking anyway; that is simply to repeat Hume's ironic observation that the demands of the real world soon make one forget one's metaphysic. For our purposes, however, that is not good enough. As we argued in the last chapter, egocentrism is not refuted by the mere fact that its supporters fail to live up to their philosophy. In attacking egocentrism, we cannot rest content until we have destroyed the vision of the one true reality of the *this*. For, so long as that vision remains intact, the whole world stands in abeyance, ourselves included. Our life, or rather my life, everything I seem to do and everything I seem to believe, has no reality or meaning other than what I myself dream into it.

5 Reality of the objective standpoint

1. WE have been grappling with egocentrism, seeking a way to convict the egocentrist of inconsistency. At stake, is nothing less than the world itself. For like a weasel feeding on an egg, the desire to grasp what is immediately real, discarding all but the *this*, the ever-present vision of an indescribable subjective given, sucks all the reality out of the objects of perception leaving nothing but an empty shell, an appearance which is not the appearance of anything. Behind even my own thoughts there is nothing that does the thinking, no mental substance that exists in itself; nor does my power of judgement possess any aspect other than what it judges itself to be, its reality too is made up of its own appearance, the ever-changing content of the I think. There are thinkings and judgings which seem, through an inescapable illusion, to be the acts of one and the same substantial I; there are appearances which masquerade as appearances of one and the same independently existing world. That is all. 'In reality,' says the egocentrist, 'there is no reality.'

As the egocentrist is well aware, that can only be taken as at best a philosophical joke, at worst outright self-contradiction. If all that thought and language take to be real is unreal, then the very phrase, 'in reality' is robbed of all meaning. If the very use of language to describe what I see is sullied by metaphysical illusion, then no philosophical term escapes contamination. Now we saw in the last chapter how the very notion of a world of objects to which concepts may be applied presupposes a distinction between applying concepts correctly and applying them incorrectly, between true and false judgements. But the egocentrist's refusal to recognize any standpoint other than the subjective renders meaningless, and therefore non-existent, the distinction between a reliable and an unreliable power of judgement. I cannot question whether I am perceiving and forming judgements about a world outside me, or only making up my own fantasy world, because the question assumes a non-existent distinction. Thus, in the ruins of the Kantian egocentrist's bold attempt to justify the notion of an external world, we find the true egocentrist silently contemplating the unsayable something that was there all along; refusing to utter a single word lest the existence of the *this* be denied in the very act of acknowledging it.

How do you argue with someone who refuses to speak? What is the point of putting your case, when you know that you're not going to get any response? In our ordinary lives, when someone to whom we need urgently to communicate refuses to acknowledge us, we find ourselves resorting either to persuasion or, in an extreme case, to violence. Perhaps if I say or do something sufficiently provocative, the other will be forced to speak. Yet it seems that the egocentrist cannot be dealt with in this way. If it is in the very nature of the truth that he sees that it would be betrayed in the very act of expressing it, then silence is the only thing he can give me. It is not lack of good will that I have to overcome, but a compelling vision for which silence appears the only valid expression.

There are, however, two very different cases to consider. In the first case, I may be simply unable to imagine what vision the egocentrist sees. There would then be no point in proceeding further; the argument has come to an end and we can only go our separate ways. In the second case, the vision may be one which we both share. I see it too; only I believe its significance to be different from what the egocentrist takes it to be. Which case are we dealing with? We remarked in the last chapter that the egocentrist we have to argue against is none other than the egocentrist in each of us. I too have *this*: it is nothing other than the reality of my subjective standpoint. The task is to account for the reality of the objective standpoint in a way that does not allow the subjective standpoint to slip from one's grasp. If that can be done, then in wiping out the distorted vision of the *this*, we should at the same time be preserving and liberating that vision in a new but harmless form.

To give the requirements for a theory is not yet to give that theory. Indeed, until we have worked through the dialectic, we should not recognize the correct account even if it was presented on a plate. One thing at least is clear: having denounced the Kantian egocentrist's account of the relation between I and the world on the grounds of consistency, there is no way we can get a logical hold on the egocentrist who steadfastly remains silent. For in itself, the *this* is neither consistent nor inconsistent. Logic requires language, the apparatus of concepts and judgements, which the silent egocentrist has given up. However, there is one thing we can do. Behind the egocentrist's refusal to speak lies an assumption concerning the nature of the objective standpoint. It is only because the egocentrist assumes that recognition of the objective standpoint would mean rejecting the subjective standpoint, that he sees no other possible course of action than to reject the objective standpoint, and thus the very medium of language itself. That is the assumption we must now challenge.

2. How might one define the objective standpoint? There is a prejudice, widespread amongst philosophers who identify themselves as belonging to the analytic tradition, that the aim of a philosophical inquiry consists in the definition of some philosophically problematic term; notwithstanding the fact that such an aim is hardly ever achieved in practice. That view goes together with a prejudice against pure metaphysics. What lies behind it is the thought that the only truths that philosophy can uncover are truths about concepts in the widest sense – in effect, the logical consequences of our beliefs about the world, or what for the sake of consistency we ought to believe – the thought that whatever knowledge philosophy might hope to gain, it can never discover or prove sheer facts. As the reader may have gathered by now, the author does not subscribe to this view. It will become increasingly clear that the reality of the subjective and objective standpoints, and their contradictory relation to one another, can only be viewed as sheer facts which philosophical thinking is able to bring to light. Consequently, the only purpose definition can serve in respect of either standpoint is to identify what we are talking about.

What then is the minimum required to identify the objective standpoint? It would be premature to refer to language, as we did for introductory purposes in chapter 1, for we have yet to determine what language essentially is. (We shall begin to discuss language towards the end of this chapter.) Instead, let us assert as a minimal and provisional definition that the objective standpoint is that by virtue of which there exists some point of view on the world other than my own. The objective standpoint is real provided only that the conditions laid down in its definition are satisfied, provided that there is something by virtue of which there exists some other point or points of view.

It must be noted that there are two quite different senses in which other points of view can be said to exist. The most obvious way to take this is to say that there actually exist other conscious subjects in the world besides myself. However, there is a serious flaw in that proposal. If the objective standpoint is a fact, then it is a necessary fact. Its reality is not something one could establish on the basis of observation or experiment, any more than one could establish by examining actual collections of objects the necessary fact that, for example, there always exists a prime number larger than any given prime. Truth in metaphysics, as in mathematics, depends upon proof, not on experiment; and what is established by a process of logical argument cannot be merely contingent. Now it is logically possible that all conscious subjects other than myself should perish; indeed, for all I can prove at this very moment it is possible that they have done so. Yet whatever considerations established the reality of the objective standpoint would still remain valid. In other words, the existence of a point of view other than my own cannot depend on there actually being a conscious subject who occupies that point of view.

It follows that there exist as many points of view as there are places for a point of view to be located; that is to say, an infinite number. If the universe is of finite extent, then only a finite number of points of view could ever be occupied at any one time, unless the occupants were infinitesimally small (the conclusions we shall reach later on in this chapter would seem to count against the latter possibility). As a matter of additional fact, some of these points of view are actually occupied.

We could have made the definition of the objective standpoint even simpler by saying that it is just the sum of all points of view other than my own. Instead, it was defined as that by virtue of which such points of view exist. The reason is this. When I ask myself whether the objective standpoint is real, what I am asking is whether there is something real to be seen from other points of view; whether the world has any sides or aspects different from the aspect it presents to me. The existence of a point of view depends on the existence of an aspect, not the other way round. That is not just hair-splitting. The existence of a point of view is, as we have seen, the existence of a possibility for viewing the world; a point of view can either be occupied or unoccupied. Now the way we necessarily think about possibilities is as something dependent on what is actually the case. For example, the possibility that my desk might catch fire depends upon its actually being made of wood. Similarly, the possibility that someone might occupy the point of view of a person standing in front of me now depends upon the world actually presenting an aspect of itself which it would be possible for someone standing in front of me to see.

We can further illustrate the point about possibility in relation to egocentrism. The Kantian egocentrist wants to say that the world has only one aspect, the aspect it presents to me. My conception of the world is of all that it is logically possible for me to encounter in the course of my experience. What is actual, on the other hand, the reality by virtue of which the possibility of my experience, of my having a point of view on the world, is possible is none other than the immediate given, the ever-present *this* which I interpret as my perception of an external world. In seeking, against the egocentrist, to establish the reality of both the subjective and objective standpoints, what one must show is that the world not only has an aspect which it presents exclusively to me, but, in addition, presents aspects inaccessible to me but accessible to others.

3. The motive for egocentrism lies in its assumption that no account can be given of the objective standpoint which leaves room for the subjective. If per impossibile the objective standpoint were real, says the egocentrist, then my subjective standpoint could not also be real. In terms of aspects, what the egocentrist believes is that were I to admit that the world had any aspects that it presented to other points of view, then I should have to deny that the world had any aspect that it presented exclusively to me. For I can imagine simply slicing off the latter aspect as a self-contained reality, not connected with anything else. Nothing in my self-contained world provides any material that would enable me to form the conception of aspects of reality presented to others; just as nothing in the aspects of reality presented to others would enable them to conceive of the existence of an aspect presented exclusively to me. The subjective standpoint gives my world, the objective standpoint gives the world of others; but these are two worlds, not one. As far as my subjective standpoint is concerned, the world of others does not exist; as far as others are concerned, my world does not exist. Now the one thing that it is absolutely impossible for me to deny, says the egocentrist, is that my world exists. Even if I am denied language, there is still the ever-present *this* which makes up the stuff of my own private reality. The world of others, the objective standpoint, therefore cannot exist.

Our aim is to discover what is wrong with this strangely compelling argument. First, however, we must prove the reality of the objective standpoint, at least to our own satisfaction if not to the egocentrist's. The proof can only be hypothetical, since it will rest on the condition that there are such things as concepts and judgements; something that the egocentrist, in remaining silent, steadfastly denies. The question we have to ask is this. On the assumption that we are not condemned to perpetual silence, what are the necessary conditions for the existence of a subject matter with respect to which something can be said, a reality to which concepts may be correctly or incorrectly applied? How must the world be if there is such a thing as making a false judgement about something?

The simple observation that brought the egocentrist's attempt to justify the use of concepts and judgements down in ruins – our one-line refutation of Kantian egocentrism – was that the egocentric subject's power of judgement is the one thing against which that subject cannot allow for so much as the existence of a question. There is no place in the exclusive reality of my subjective world for the fact that my power of judgement is reliable rather than unreliable. For there are no facts which, as an egocentrist, I am not, in principle, in a position to judge; and to judge that my power of judgement was unreliable would amount to self-contradiction. (I can judge that my judgements are inconsistent; but then I am relying on my ability to judge consistency.) In effect, the necessary assumption of reliability is a judgement that cannot ever be wrong. However, a judgement that logically cannot be wrong is one that cannot be right either. One must always be able to separate the reality that makes a judgement true from that of a subject's taking it to be true; otherwise there is neither falsity nor truth, neither missing the target nor hitting it.

What kind of reality is it, in relation to which my power of judgement might be said to be either reliable or unreliable? There is only one possibility: it must be a reality which I alone am not in a position to judge. Yet if I do not have the authority to judge it for myself, and if the reliability of my power of judgement is something that can be judged at all, then the authority I lack must pass to others. It must in principle be possible for someone other than myself to come to a rationally justifiable judgement about it. Therefore, there exists a reality that others can be in a position to make authoritative judgements about but I alone am not; or, as we put it at the end of the last chapter, 'a point of view outside my own system of representation from which that system may be considered as something that either succeeds or fails in putting me in reliable touch with reality'. That is to say, reality presents aspects to others which it does not present to me; there is something by virtue of which there exist points of view on the world besides my own.

4. We said that this proof of the reality of the objective standpoint is only hypothetical. One has to assume that there are such things as concepts and judgements, something the silent egocentrist denies. Now this limitation is directly linked with the question whether there can be an account of the objective standpoint that leaves room for the subjective; whether the contradiction between the two standpoints can in some sense be reconciled. We are not yet in a position to say to what

extent such a goal is attainable; first, we must learn a lot more about the nature of the objective standpoint. What we can say now is that, were the egocentrist to admit the possibility of a reconciliation between the two standpoints – that is to say, some point at which they could be seen to meet despite their contradiction, or some way in which each can still hold back from mutually destructive conflict – then the egocentrist's only motive for remaining silent, for denying the existence of concepts and judgements, would have been undermined. For it was only to preserve the reality of the subjective standpoint against the threat apparently posed by the objective that the egocentrist took such a heroic course in the first place. We should then be in a position to regard the proof of the reality of the objective standpoint as to all intents and purposes absolute. If no opponent can be found to question the existence of concepts and judgements, then it ceases to be a mere assumption and becomes instead our fundamental principle.

As a merely hypothetical proof, the argument for the reality of the objective standpoint does not require any further additions. However, there still remains the question of how others could ever be in a position to make authoritative judgements about the reliability of my power of judgement. The first question is just what it means to say that another person can have such authority over me. In what does the other's authority consist? How am I able to express recognition of that authority?

At first sight, the very idea seems impossible. Take the simple case where I make a judgement that something is blue and the other corrects me: what we are both clearly looking at, says the other person, is not blue but mauve. If I accept the correction, then it seems I have judged that the other is a better judge than I, either about the difference between blue and mauve in general, or at least on this particular occasion. That the object we are looking at is mauve becomes my judgement. Or suppose instead that I reject the other's correction, and judge that the object is blue and not mauve. Later, however, I come to reconsider my judgement; either on the basis of memory – having, say, come across other objects that I should definitely call 'mauve' – or after returning to give the original object a fresh look. I now judge that I made a misjudgement when I said that the object was blue. Perhaps it was the unfamiliar surroundings, or a lapse of memory, or my hangover; or maybe I have no explanation to give and cannot understand how I could have made so palpable an error. Once again, I have judged that the other was right to judge my judgement wrong.

This is one of those occasions in philosophy when one is prompted to exclaim, rhetorically, 'How could it be otherwise?' How can the other have authority to judge my powers of judgement if I can still reject the other's corrections? Yet how, if I accept the other's corrections, can the other's judgement retain its authority, if my acceptance is necessarily my judgement? The answer is that the training of my powers of judgement, the bringing into line of my judgements with the judgements of others does not reduce to the judgements that I make. I am not in a position to judge the authority of others in general to correct my judgements, even though every time I accept a correction I make a judgement. One might say, the authority of the other is no mere empirical fact about the world I happen to find myself in – as if I came to discover that the reports of others can sometimes be a more reliable source of knowledge than judgements based on my own sense perception – rather, it is a necessary condition for the very possibility of there being such a thing as my judgement.

5. The ground for the other's authority over me lies in the fact that the other is given something, a basis for judgement, that I am necessarily not given: a point of view outside my own judging, the operation of my own system of representation. How then does the reality of my existence as a subject who makes judgements and employs a system of representation present itself to others? What are the criteria by means of which others are able to judge whether my powers of judgement are operating reliably or unreliably? We must separate here the question of fact from the question of principle. As a matter of contingent fact, I find that I possess a body, that I perform actions, and that I communicate with others by means of language. All three provide others with the raw material to pass judgement on my powers of judgement. But how do these facts contribute to that assessment? what part does each play? For all we know at this stage of the argument, one or more of these facts may be redundant, if not in practice then at least in theory. The only way to find out is to investigate the matter logically: to ask in what sense, if any, it is necessary that I possess a body, or perform actions, or communicate with others by means of language. In asking those questions, we shall be making our first steps towards an account of the nature of the objective standpoint. I shall be discovering just what it is that I, as a subject cast into the objective world, essentially am.

If others are to pass judgement upon the reliability of my powers of judgement, then they can do so only if they are able to observe me. It would seem to follow that I must necessarily possess a body for as long as I continue to exist as a thinking subject. For if I existed only as a disembodied voice, the only basis for telling whether my correct judgements resulted from observation and rational thought rather than guesswork, or whether my incorrect judgements resulted from my own misjudgement rather than from judging soundly on the basis of incorrect evidence, would be what the voice said. If I seemed to get things right more often than could be explained by guesswork, and told a consistent story about my lapses of judgement, then one would have to assume that I did possess a body, even though no-one had yet identified it; a body whose observational and mental capacities could in principle be investigated.

That does not, however, count as an argument against the belief that each of us possesses a soul which leaves the body when we die, and goes to live in another world. For the soul might be just another kind of body, invisible to human perception and so far undetected by our scientific instruments, but visible to, say, angels, or else alien beings who possessed far more refined organs of perception than our own. So long as there exists a point of view to which my soul-body presents an aspect, then one may continue to speak of a reality in relation to which my powers of judgement might in principle be judged to be either reliable or unreliable. However, the possibility of becoming disembodied can no longer be used to prove the soul's immortality. If I must always exist as some sort of body, a space-occupying substance whether visible or invisible, then the logical possibility remains that, even if I should survive the death of this physical body, my soul's invisible body may eventually wear out or be destroyed.

6. There are two more questions to consider: whether I am necessarily a physical agent, able to manipulate things and get about the world; and whether I necessarily possess a language that can be used to communicate. (We shall return to the question of agency from a different angle in chapter 10 and following.) Suppose that I were to become totally paralysed, so that there was no outward indication of whether I was conscious or unconscious, whether I was thinking and making judgements or only drifting along in a half-awake, dreamlike state. If I was having thoughts, there would be no way others could determine whether my powers of judgement were reliable or unreliable; at least by the methods we now employ. Yet surely, one might think, my judgements would still present an aspect to other points of view, for there would be processes going on in my brain – call it a brain language – which others could read if only they possessed sufficiently advanced scientific instruments. Is that correct?

Now, under normal circumstances, the only way we can translate a language is by observing the actions of speakers of that language in relation to their environment. Consider the role played in our interpretation of a subject's utterances by the simple actions of pointing to things, or walking over to an object, or picking it up. Nor would there seem to be any way to test the hypothesis that, for example, 'niap ni ma I' meant 'I am in pain', if the subject could not rub the affected spot, or show any discomfort, or take any steps to remove whatever was causing damage to his body. Surely, translating a brain language would be an impossible enterprise; a lump of grey matter cannot point to things, or rub its painful parts.

Imagine then that someone drilled a peep-hole in my skull, revealing flickering images like a silent film of my surroundings or of things that others might expect me to be thinking about, perhaps in reaction to what they were saying; or, better still, a running text – in 'English'. This might become a normal occurrence. I and other mutants like me might spend several hours a day paralysed, during which time anyone could look through the peep-hole to find out what we were thinking or read off our replies to their questions. If a sceptic were to raise doubts about whether the brain images were not being systematically misinterpreted, or whether the running text was not English at all but some unknown language only typographically similar, no-one would listen; so long as the practice of brain reading retained a high degree of coherence with our ordinary communications.

However, let us suppose now that one of the mutants whose brain language has hitherto displayed a high degree of coherence with ordinary discourse fails to recover from her paralysed state, and moreover that the subject's beliefs seem to become increasingly irrational as time goes on. How long would it take before a doubt could be allowed to arise? How long would we continue to play this game? Surely that is all it would be, or, for that matter, ever was. (Remember the paradox of the heap: whether the subject is actually thinking cannot be taken as a vague question, however uncertain we may be of the answer.) It is true that brain reading might not only provide us with entertainment but would also serve a useful communicative purpose. However, whatever purpose it did serve could only be judged to be achieved by the standards of rationality of our normal discourse, within which there is a way of dealing with any doubts that might arise. In other words, brain reading could only ever be a parasitic activity.

7. Yet couldn't what happened sometimes not happen always? Could we not envisage circumstances in which producing words was the only game that was played, where there was no higher communicative standard from which it fell short? Consider a different thought

experiment. Let us imagine that there exists a race of intelligent trees, who communicate by flexing their bark and making creaking sounds; that is all they do. Their civilization is not very advanced; they talk about such matters of immediate concern; the weather, the comings and goings of the animals in the forest and so on. One question is what we should say if we came across such beings, say, if someone noticed that the creaking of certain trees sounded like English if one listened closely. However, we already know the outcome of that thought experiment. Whatever use we made of such a discovery, the activity of listening to trees converse with one another, or of conversing with them could only be parasitic on our own interpersonal discourse.

Let us, for the sake of argument, look at the matter instead from the trees' point of view. The trees are to conceive of themselves as making judgements about their world. As to what that entails, however, the same applies to the trees as applied in our case: we have to ask under what circumstances one tree might have the authority to correct another tree's judgements. Formally, the condition of a point of view outside another subject's system of representation appears to be satisfied. I remark, 'There goes a jay,' and my tree-neighbour says, That's not a jay, that's a blackbird.' Yet the substance of that condition is surely not met. Correcting someone's judgement is more than a matter of merely making her agree with one's own judgement or getting her to step in line. For the question inevitably arises who is in a better position to judge and what one should do to get into that position; who is better qualified and what training she received; what steps have been taken to verify this particular judgement. It takes more than mere agreement in judgements to give meaning to a language: in addition there has to be a physical and not simply verbal practice of verifying whether judgements are correct or incorrect. Indeed, if the concepts used are to have a genuine point rather than grouping together arbitrary collections of particulars, there must arise, somewhere along the line, practical as well as theoretical consequences of applying a concept incorrectly. In the light of this, whatever the trees are doing, we cannot say that they are making judgements; and they cannot 'say' it either. The hypothesis of a tree language is incoherent.

8. The supposed judgements of a subject who does not have the power to perform non-linguistic actions do not present an aspect, qua power of judgement, to other points of view. That is so whether or not the passive subject produces images or noises that look or sound like a language, nor even if we find it useful to treat those images or noises as if they were a language. The pattern of neurone firing in its brain

presents the aspect of a pattern of neurone firing and nothing else. It follows that there is no reality in relation to which its power of judgement may be evaluated as either reliable or unreliable. The subject does not apply concepts or make judgements. Now we began with my imagining that I might become totally paralysed. Surely I would know that I was thinking, even if no-one else did? The answer, according to the argument against egocentrism, is that I would not be thinking; I would not be exercising a power of judgement. If I am the only person who could ever know, then my power of judgement must be regarded as ultimately beyond criticism; which we have already seen is the same as saying that it is not a power of judgement at all.

On the face of it, this conclusion is not easy to swallow. What should we say, for example, about a totally paralysed doctor who not only recovered her ability to speak and act when her illness had passed, but showed that she had listened closely to her case being discussed and had spent the time thinking out her own detailed conclusions about it? It seems highly paradoxical to say that, while the doctor was paralysed, something occurred in her brain which was not thinking and judging, but that when she recovered from her paralysis that something retrospectively became thought and judgement. If that were the case, then a cause could occur after its effect! The solution to this puzzle requires that we discard our prejudice in favour of atomism: we have to recognize that certain kinds of object, amongst them such things as thoughts and judgements, are what they are, in their very essence, only in relation to a wider diachronic context. Supplying the missing components for that context can, under certain circumstances, bring it about than an object of this kind existed in the past.

9. The last question we have to discuss is the exact reverse of the question of a passive thinker or a passive language user. Could there exist a race of intelligent mutes, who applied concepts and made judgements, but who simply had not acquired any form of language, and indeed were incapable of learning one? Once again, the question is whether the power of judgement possessed by such a mute presents an aspect to other points of view; whether any other individual could ever have the authority to judge the reliability of its power of judgement.

Consider the following example. We have been following a mute as it makes its way through a dense forest. Suddenly, it plunges down into a hidden pit, its arms and legs flailing the air. We could not but draw the conclusion that this mute had believed that the ground beneath its feet was safe to tread on, and that on this occasion its power of judgement failed. On second thoughts, however, we might realize that had this incident occurred to someone who could communicate, it is just possible that he might have told us that he had known the pit was there all along, and had jumped into it deliberately. Should we remain forever in doubt? The moral of this tale is not merely that the interpretation of any action, no matter how apparently loaded with meaning, can still be overturned if one takes what the agent says into account. It is of course an immediate consequence of the rejection of atomism in favour of holism that whatever interpretation of a person's actions one reaches on the basis of an finite amount of data, it is still logically possible to describe further data that would overturn it. In our story, however, the absence of language means that no authoritative judgement could ever be made concerning the reliability of our subject's judgements. Even if one could alter a mute's behaviour by bringing things to its notice, that would not amount to criticizing its judgement; criticism cannot be effectively targeted where there is no way for the subject to answer back.

Still, might one not hold out the prospect of reading its brain language? Might the actions of the mute not supply the very thing that was missing in the previous examples? Suppose there occurs a pattern of neurone firing in the mute's brain, which represents its belief that the ground is firm. Just as with its actions, our interpretation of this pattern as that belief, rather than the different belief that there was a pit, can still be overturned if the subject turns out not to have been a mute, and tells us that it knew all along that there was a pit there. Nor, for reasons have already been rehearsed, would it make any difference if one could peep into the mute's skull to see the words, 'That ground is firm' written there.

10. The imagination rebels when confronted with arguments such as these, which claim to prove logically that there could never be a race of intelligent trees or intelligent mutes; or that a totally paralysed person could never exercise a power of judgement. We have considered some of the reasons why a subject who makes judgements must not only have some sort of body, but must also be an agent, and be capable of communicating with others. In doing so we have taken the first steps towards defining the place of the thinking subject within the objective standpoint. No quality or state has any reality unless it is able to present an aspect to the objective standpoint. The same must therefore apply in the particular case of thinking subjects themselves, even at the cost of drawing strict limits to the kind of being that can be a thinking subject. If that principle appears to contradict our commonsense intuitions, then we must teach ourselves to have different intuitions. That is the cost of keeping the egocentrist outside the gates of our philosophic citadel.

6 Mind and body

1. ASSUMING I am not condemned like the egocentric to perpetual silence, then, as a subject who necessarily presents aspects to points of view other than my own – as an occupant of objective standpoint – I must have a body, be a physical agent and language user. This is a significant result. We must remember, however, that at present it remains purely hypothetical. We have defined a term which for all we know has no application. If there is such a thing as an objective standpoint, then certain other things follow, consequences whose validity we have no independent means of checking. If I am able to apply concepts or make judgements, if I possess a power of judgement whose reliability can come into question, then others must have the authority to question it, and so must occupy points of view other than my own from which the working of my system of representation may be evaluated. Yet who is to say that the egocentric is not ultimately right, that there is nothing for the philosopher to do but forswear all judgement, and silently take in what there is to be seen? We shall make no progress until we can justify the leap into the objective world to which our talking commits us. Until then, we remain suspended between the subjective and objective standpoints without any stable footing; refusing to stay silent, but unable to justify that refusal.

This would be a good time to call again on the naive metaphysician, to ask what our companion on the journey thinks of all this. At the beginning of chapter 3, faced with the contradiction between the subjective and objective standpoints, the naive metaphysician took the line of least resistance and embraced egocentrism. However, developments since then have shown that egocentrism is not the easy option it seemed to be at the time. The only other course of action which then presented itself – any questioning of the law of non-contradiction seemed unthinkable – was to embrace nonegocentrism. However, it takes a certain tough-mindedness to repudiate the subjective standpoint altogether, and one might readily forgive our companion for not being ready to make that hard decision. Yet what other alternative is there?

2. The naive metaphysician, to our surprise, is ready with an answer: 'Why don't you just admit that the world is made out of two fundamentally different kinds of stuff? There is the kind that, as you say, can be described by means of concepts, judged, talked about, the kind that presents aspects to different points of view. In addition, there is the kind that cannot be described in any way but can only be simply felt or had, the subjective side or aspect of conscious experience which, unlike the objective side we can all talk about – the pain or tickle, the sound of a buzz or sensation of red – exists or is real only for the subject whose experience it is, presents an aspect to only one point of view. In the world of objective stuff and subjective stuff, each of us has our own subjective stuff, our own *this*. Animals have it too, of course, although for some animals we may lack the concepts to describe, objectively, their feelings or experiences on their behalf in the way that we are able to do for one another. What could be simpler, or more in accord with what we all believe, prior to any acquaintance with philosophy?'

The suggestion, in short, is that we comprehend the relation between the subjective and objective standpoints in terms of a dualism of subjective and objective substances. Now objective substances are familiar enough. They are the things that exist, that are what they are, irrespective of one's point of view. A tree is a tree, wherever it may be and whoever happens to be perceiving it or thinking about it; a pain is a pain, whether it is in me or in someone else. By contrast, the subjective substances are very strange indeed; one wonders whether the naive metaphysician has fully appreciated just how peculiar they are. My *this* exists, is what it is, only for me; your *this* exists only for you; my neighbour's cat's *this* exists only for it. Yet how can existence, the sheer difference between being and not being, be qualified in this way?

The account of the subjective and objective standpoints which the naive metaphysician has stumbled upon, simply by assembling materials that were ready to hand, is in fact a sophisticated philosophical theory. Nor is it an accident that it should have appeared at precisely this stage of the argument. In essence, it is the dual aspect theory for which Thomas Nagel has argued, within a framework of

61

multiple standpoints. (The basic moves needed to set up the theory are to be found in 'What Is It Like to Be a Bat?' It is further elaborated in *The View From Nowhere*.) It is important to bear in mind that in what follows we shall be sticking to our own definitions of the subjective and objective standpoints. The subjective standpoint has been defined in such a way that there can only be one – my own. Subjective aspects, in the plural, can only be, in our terminology, subjective substances, not subjective standpoints. The crux of our disagreement with Nagel lies here.

Note also that we have taken the liberty of stating Nagel's theory in our own way. He would no doubt prefer to talk of subjective attributes rather than subjective substances, but in the theory under consideration this does not amount to anything. Nagel would also be the first to agree that what he has given is only the first gesture towards a full account. (In the aforementioned book he describes it modestly as 'probably nothing more than pre-socratic flailing about', p. 30. As we shall discover that what disables the theory is his 'continued attachment to the metaphysics of substance and attribute', ibid., this seems an apt diagnosis.)

3. According to our account of the objective standpoint, no mental attribute or state has any reality as a subject matter for judgement, if it does not present an aspect to points of view other than my own. For so long as I exist, it is necessary that I exist as some kind of physical body, upon whose states, whether physical or mental, others are in principle able to judge with authority, and so correct my judgements concerning those states. One way of expressing this is to say that there is nothing in the mind which does not have an objective correlate in a body: every feeling, every mental image, every thought imprints itself, is projected upon a body, so that its qualities can in principle be read off by those who are suitably placed to observe the body, to interpret its speech and actions, or if need be to investigate its innards.

Now it is one thing to say that everything in mind is correlated with some aspect of body, so that the self must always possess a body, and quite another to go on to assert that everything in mind is itself a bodily state or attribute, in other words that the self is nothing but body. For example, the twinge of pain I feel in my thumb presents an aspect to me, to my subjective standpoint, and also presents an aspect to the objective standpoint, in the words I am now uttering, or in my behaviour, or in the states of my brain which an alien scientist or angel might be able to read and interpret. The question is, are the subjective and objective aspects merely views of two objects closely connected with one another, a non-physical mind and its physical

62

body, or are they different views of one and the same physical object, a body which is in some sense identical with mind?

The way we have presented this question may have given the impression that the identity of mind and body is something that still has to be proved, since the identity does not follow logically from the premiss that mind and body are necessarily correlated. Two things connected together, however intimately, are still two things and not one thing. The reality of the objective standpoint gives only a necessary correlation between mind and body; so establishing their identity requires something extra. It would seem that the onus is therefore on the supporter of identity to produce the necessary proof.

However, the identity theorist need not be forced on the defensive; for she can argue with equal justification as follows. The supposedly non-physical mind of the dualist is in fact completely parasitic upon the states and attributes of body, since it possesses no states or attributes in its own right, independently of body. Every property that it has, everything it is in itself, is imprinted or projected onto a body, and is capable in principle of being fully accounted for by observing and investigating that body. Now even my shadow has properties in its own right, for example colour and size. By contrast, my non-physical mind is an invisible, perfect double which not only goes wherever my body goes, but does not have a single attribute which does not project onto body; other than the purely negative attribute of being non-physical. Why on earth should anyone believe in such a thing? Surely the onus is on the dualist to prove the existence of a non-physical mind, and not on the identity theorist to prove its non-existence.

Put in these terms we seem to have all the makings of a philosophical dispute that could never be resolved. Both sides have a case, there is no doubt about that. The trouble is that there appears nothing further to which one might appeal in order to decide the onus of proof: to determine whether it is up to the identity theorist to prove identity, or up to the dualist to prove non-identity. Yet surely that should have been obvious from the start. We must be missing something. Let us begin by asking what is it the dualist seems to see, that convinces him that the identity theorist must be wrong.

4. The sticking point for our dualist is the thought that the mind or consciousness, unique amongst the things that make up our world, is not only something in itself but also something for itself. Take away the attributes of mind – that which can be described and judged, all that is projected onto the objective standpoint of body and accountable in terms of bodily attributes – and no thing or object, no substance in itself remains. Yet what mind is for itself is something over and above

its mere attributes; it is not an object in this sense, it is beyond all such accounting. For all that, the for itself is, the words 'for itself' refer to something rather than nothing. What then is it? how do we know that there is such an 'is'? One struggles for some other language, something more discriminating, but the problem is not one to be solved by inventing more words. Nor, lacking anything positive to say, can one fall back on the facile expedient of a purely negative definition – as if we could move a single inch closer to what the for-itself is by listing all the infinite things it is not.

What is it, then, that we think we are looking for? what does my imagination tell me? I watch my neighbour's cat, and think: 'There is something for it, beyond all that I could ever know from the outside, even taking it apart, brain function by brain function, cell by cell, molecule by molecule.' I imagine entering its head, seeing through its eyes. I realize immediately that any attempt to put this into practice would be futile; I do not have to experiment with vivisection in order to discover the simple fact that I can never get inside the cat's mind. Even if I were to undergo the experience – which is logically possible – of leaving my own body and entering the body of a cat, I would still be imprisoned within my own point of view. Whatever there was for the cat would still be as far away from me as it is now.

Whence the conviction that there is something for the cat, something beyond all that I can look into or take apart? It seems as if the question would not even arise were it not for the fact that there is one for-itself which is given to me, whose point of view I am already inside. Now of course no question would arise for me if I didn't exist; but it might appear in this case that my belief concerning what is for the cat actually depends, in a logical sense, on what I know about myself, what there is for me. The dualist's belief that there is something that cannot be accounted for in terms of body would then ultimately rest on my unshakeable cartesian knowledge that there is something I refer to when I say, 'I'. (We shall see shortly that this is not Nagel's view.)

5. Let us investigate this possibility. 'I accept all you say,' says our dualist, 'in criticizing the simple egocentrist's cartesian account of how I am able to know the contents of my non-physical mind. Whatever is in my mind I can know only by exercising a power of judgement whose reliability others must in principle be in a position to judge. Ultimately, my mind keeps nothing to itself; everything that is in it is projected in some manner onto the physical world. However, Descartes was right about one thing. There is one fact I know about my mind that cannot be judged from the objective standpoint: my pure unmediated awareness of my own existence. This is not knowledge of

the existence of my living body, which anyone can come to know, but knowledge of that indescribable something that makes the possessor of a body with the all physical attributes of my body me, rather than merely a perfect double whom other persons would in principle be unable to distinguish from me. That something has, I admit, no positive attributes of its own; but it does have one negative attribute. By hypothesis, it cannot be physical, since everything physical that I have, my double could have also. That is all I mean by calling it non-physical.'

Now at first sight this last admission seems to contravene the principle that one cannot extract anything positive out of a pure negation. The dualist is only able to tell us what the for-itself is not, not what it is. However, the dualist disagrees vehemently. One positive fact about the for-itself has emerged, a fact of primordial significance: when I look inside myself and see what is there to be seen, what I find myself looking at is none other than what makes the sheer difference between my existence and my non-existence, between there being a world for me and – nothing.

The clarity of the refined cartesian vision soon clouds over, however. When I, as a dualist, try to express what that something is, which is responsible for making me the unique individual that I am, all I can do is point into myself and say *this*. Now suppose I consider again what it means to say that some other person or animal possesses a for-itself, a non-physical mind. The only answer is that there is something which is *this* for her, or for it, just as mine is for me. Every conscious subject has a *this*, the subjective side or aspect of its conscious experience which is only for that subject. Yet now it occurs to me that if every conscious being has a *this*, then so too would my perfect double; let us say, the Klempner that God might have created instead of me. (We shall investigate further the question of doubles or 'doppelgangers' in chapters 7 and 10.) By hypothesis, the *this* has no properties to be described, which means that my *this* and my double's *this* are the same; there is nothing to distinguish one from the other. Nor would it serve any purpose to say that the two thises must in some respect be different simply because mine is mine and my double's is my double's; that is precisely what is in question. I am trying to envisage a world without me but where my double exists in my stead; but the two worlds appear in every respect identical.

It follows that my *this* fails to do what it was meant to do, which was to distinguish me from my double. If my *this* is to perform successfully the function of distinguishing me from my double, then I cannot allow that my double has *this*. Does any person or animal have *this* besides myself? The only ground for denying that my double can have *this* is that the very thisness of *this* consists in the fact that I am the one who has it. In that case, only I, amongst all conscious beings, can have *this*. That in turn must mean one of two things. If every conscious being has a non-physical mind, then *this* is something I have over and above my non-physical mind; my having a non-physical mind is not, after all, what accounts for my awareness of my own existence. On the other hand, if my possessing a non-physical mind is equivalent to my having *this*, then I am the only conscious being in the world who possesses a non-physical mind.

The conclusion to which the dualist is driven is far from the one originally envisaged. The dualist wanted to say that every conscious being has the same inner stuff as I have; but the argument from my indubitable sense of my own existence will not allow such a generous result. Let us not mince words. I am the only person who can lay claim to a real mind. Everyone else is just a zombie, a complex physical organism – with or without non-physical parts added on – lacking that essential extra something that I have. Of course, this point is still only ad hominem. The dualist might acquire the taste for solitude. However, there is a further logical objection which the dualist cannot evade. If the *this* has no properties, then it has no number and no identity. I cannot say that there is one *this* in me, for there is no distinction between my having one *this* and my having a thousand thises. Nor can I say that the *this* that exists now is either the same or different from the *this* that existed one second ago, for there is no distinction between its identity and non-identity through time. Nor, finally, can the sense that I have *this*, the pure, unmediated awareness of my own existence, be any form of belief or judgement, because it would then have to be a judgement that could not possibly be wrong; which means that it could not be right either. As a sense, it is not the sense of anything real; and the sense of something other than what is real is no different from the purest illusion.

6. In the light of these results, the dualist will do everything possible to avoid making the fatal cartesian move. I must set my face against the overwhelming temptation to regard my existence as having any special role to play. For the philosophically emancipated dualist, such as Nagel, the case for a non-physical mind rests rather on the impossibility in general of extracting from the objective standpoint the concepts required to characterize experience as it is for certain conscious subjects. Now we already possess the concepts needed to describe one another's conscious experience. So it may seem to us that there is nothing in the human for-itself that cannot be extracted by means of language. Once one abandons the privileged cartesian

starting point of my own existence, the idea of an insolubly non-objective and hence non-physical residue seems to get little grip. With animals it is different. As our companion the naive metaphysician pointed out at the beginning of the chapter, common sense requires little prompting to recognize that whatever it is that animals have in their minds, we may in many cases lack the concepts to describe. We have already raised the question of what there is for a cat. Nagel prefers to talk about a bat. Bats are more different from us in the way they perceive than cats, and so seem to provide a better example of experience that we can never describe. There is something it is like to be a bat, for example, to perceive by means of sonar detection, that human beings it seems can never know. Vivisection will never get down to what there is for the bat.

One needs to be clear, however, on just what kind of possibility is in question. It is conceivable that I could periodically change into a bat; then I would know what it was like! By contrast with my fantasy of seeing through the eyes and mind of my neighbour's cat, we are talking here only about coming to enjoy the kind of experience had by animals of a particular species. The logical barrier that prevents me from seeing the very for-itself of this particular cat does not apply in the latter case. It might be argued that being of the natural kind human precludes as a matter of metaphysical necessity one's turning into a member of some other natural kind. (That is the upshot of David Wiggins' account of the role of sortal concepts in individuation in *Sameness and Substance*.) Yet it is hard to make the case for sheer logical necessity: It would take a lot to show that one could not, as a matter of logic, cease to be human without ceasing to be. What I should say if I discovered that I had the ability to turn into a bat – say, that I periodically showed increasingly bat-like tendencies – was that either I had turned out not to be of the natural kind human or that there was no such natural kind, that the word merely denoted an outward form of the natural kind bat-human.

Let us waive this objection, however. Let us suppose that the emancipated, Nagelian dualist's case has been made out: there is something subjective, for example in bats but by implication in us too, which we have no right to assume will ever be understood, in its very essence, in terms of physical concepts. A nagging question still remains: how am I to expunge my residual cartesian intuitions?

7. Nagel is very well aware of this problem, and in chapter IV of *The View From Nowhere* makes strenuous attempts to 'account for [the] philosophical "flavour"' of his thought, 'I am *TN*' (p. 64); or, as the present author should say, my thought that I, the possessor of this

subjective viewpoint on the world, am the objective self known as Klempner. When one examines Nagel's account of the objective self, however, one finds no less than three different explanations of the thought, each consistent with a different metaphysical theory.

First, there is the thought that 'I am the world soul in humble disguise' (p. 61), a thought which is, however, 'available to any of you' (ibid.). Each of us 'ordinarily view[s] the world from a certain vantage point, using the eyes, the person...as a kind of window' (ibid.). Now these words could be interpreted by an absolute idealist in a nonegocentrist manner (according to our definition) to mean that each of us in some sense partakes of the one absolute mind, as that mind indulges itself in the illusion of being this person or that. Nagel's assurance that 'there need not be only one such self' (ibid.) might be interpreted in this spirit to mean that the absolute mind, the one objective self, divides up into fragments in the process of indulging itself in the illusion of finite existence: I am no more the objective self than you are.

When Nagel comes to describe how the concept of the objective self is formed, however, his account at first corresponds exactly to one which would be given by the Kantian egocentrist: Klempner is my empirical self, a mere component of the world; whereas I am the transcendental ego. But Nagel is quick to reject 'solipsism' (p. 63, note 3): 'The objective self that I find viewing the world through TN is not unique; each of us has one' (p. 63). In the blink of an eye, the Kantian egocentrist's transcendental ego is now reinterpreted (paralogistically, the egocentrist would argue) in a nonegocentrist manner: each of us is, or has, a transcendental ego.

The upshot is that Nagel's 'strange sense that I both am and am not the hub of the universe' (p. 64) turns out to be one available either to the absolute idealist, or the Kantian egocentrist, or the plain nonegocentrist. Thus, for the absolute idealist, the thought is that l am the absolute mind, the one objective self, but also play hide-and-seek with myself, or undergo a process of self-alienation that leads me into the illusion of being Klempner and other finite selves. For the Kantian egocentrist, the thought is that I am both the transcendental ego and the empirical Klempner. For the nonegocentrist who is not an objective idealist, the thought is that the concept of a transcendental ego that Klempner possesses leads him to think of himself qua transcendental ego as the hub of the universe, while at the same time he realizes that he is just one transcendental ego among others who think of themselves in the very same way. – It should be apparent by now that there is no substitute for recognizing the reality of my subjective standpoint: the best explanation our emancipated dualist can give of such a thought as, 'I am Klempner' must in the end be an attempt to explain it away.

8. Both Nagel's emancipated dualist and our refined cartesian dualist started out with the intention of expressing the reality of the subject's viewpoint on the world. Instead, the emancipated dualist has been led to deny the reality of my subjective standpoint; while the cartesian dualist, in trying to explain the nature of my subjective standpoint, became trapped in a logical quagmire. What went wrong?

The fatal error may be traced back to an inflexible ideal of the task of metaphysics; a notion enshrined by Aristotle, but originally given impetus by the pre-socratics. That task is thought to be the comprehensive description of all the different logical types of entity that exist or have being; a kind of philosophical taxonomy modelled on the biological classification of living organisms into species and genera. This model works well when we are only concerned with explaining, for example, the different logical categories of things and properties of things: say, concrete things such as trees and abstract things such as numbers, or essential properties of a living person such as being human, and accidental properties such as having long hair. A lot of philosophy can be done simply by analysing these kinds of categorial distinctions. The problem is the dualist has greater ambitions. If all the logical types of entity that exist for the objective standpoint are grouped together, then the group as a whole might in some sense be said to represent the reality of the objective standpoint. By analogy, the dualist thinks, the reality of the subject's viewpoint on the world must consist in the existence of at least one type of entity that does not belong, that remains invisible to the objective standpoint. The for-itself seems just such a candidate.

Unfortunately, the emancipated dualist has been unable to find a place for my unique for-itself in this scheme, and so is led to embrace nonegocentrism, to deny the reality of my subjective standpoint. For the refined cartesian dualist, by contrast, the only entity that can belong to the category of the subjective has, in the light of the arguments used in criticizing simple egocentrism, turned out to be one that has no attributes, the *this*. Only the cartesian dualist is then dismayed to discover that not only do 1, as sole owner of the *this,* become the only real for-itself, but the *this* itself refuses to obey logic. It is not an entity to be classified, and nothing this dualist can say will turn it into one.

9. What should we say, finally, about the identity theory asserted in opposition to refined cartesian dualism? One begins with the familiar

observation that the same things can be seen from different points of view. For example, it was an astronomical discovery that the morning star and the evening star were one and the same: the planet Venus. Following that analogy I imagine my mind to be like a room, containing various objects of furniture each with its own distinctive features. The very same things, the very same mental objects that I see from the inside an observer interpreting my mental states can 'see' from the outside. The observer does not of course see them the way I see them, for the outside view is always complicated by the window frame. It is not surprising then that something which I feel, say, as a stab of pain, the observer sees only as a pattern of pain behaviour, or, if we indulge in science fiction (bearing in mind the strictures of chapter 5) a pattern of neurone firings in my brain. It is still true that my stab of pain possesses no attribute which is not in some manner projected onto the physical world of the observer. Even so, my pain has a completely different way of being present to me from the way it is present to the observer, even if this difference cannot by hypothesis be described as a difference in the attributes which my-pain-for-me and my-pain-for-the-observer possess. The difference is simply the thisness of my pain for me, the fact that I am the one actually feeling it and not the observer.

The cartesian dualist, however, remains unimpressed by this explanation. The very same metaphor of the room and its furnishings can equally well be used to justify the dualist's view that the thisness of my pain is a logically separate entity from what any mere observer can see: there really are two pains, and not merely one pain seen from different points of view. For I may with equal right think of the window which gives the observer access to my mental states as only an opaque screen onto which the physical correlate of my non-physical *this* is projected.

What then, one might ask, is the difference between identity and non-identity? The answer is none: there is no difference between the realities contemplated by our identity theorist and dualist, corresponding to the difference between looking through a window and looking at a screen. We are in both cases dealing with the very same conception of the *this* as one of the kinds of entity which make up the world, as a constituent of reality, which we attacked when we examined the cartesian dualist's attempt to define what it is that gives me my sense of my own existence. Clearly, whatever logical difficulties are faced by the dualist apply with equal force to the identity theorist. Quite independently of those criticisms, however, one can say now that if it is equally valid to assert that the *this* is identical with body, as to assert that it is non-identical, then one must conclude that it is not the kind of thing that can be either. That is to say, both theories have at their core the same incoherent content; both are equally false. Whatever the *this* is, it is not an entity of any kind, it is not a constituent of reality; we must find some other way to express the reality of the subjective standpoint.

7 Reality of the subjective standpoint

1. WITHOUT meaning to, we have become entangled in the mind-body debate. A dualism of subjective and objective substances seemed a natural move in the face of our determination to recognize the reality of the objective standpoint while maintaining our hold on the subjective, but that move has led nowhere. The *this* refuses to be treated like a substance, nor can any sense be made of its identity or non-identity with any other object. However, we have by no means left the debate behind. While traditional cartesian account of self-knowledge espoused by the simple egocentrist was ruled out from the start by its failure to account for the possibility of false beliefs about one's mental states, we still have to face the more radical, emancipated dualist such as Nagel who refuses to make any deductions at all from the proposition, 'I exist.' In the light of the egocentrist's enforced silence, what alternative is there indeed but to embrace nonegocentrism, to reject altogether the claim of my unique subjective standpoint to be an irreducible reality in its own right, apart from the objective?

For one who has struggled to find a place for cartesian subjectivity, this conclusion appears so simple and so obvious, one wonders why one didn't think of it before. All the labour of trying to reconcile the subjective and objective standpoints, of trying to untie the Gordian knot is just wasted effort. For if my subjective standpoint is no more than an illusion, then the conflict between the subjective and objective standpoints is itself only apparent. I imagine that there is something in me which is incompatible with the objective standpoint, but all I really see is an insubstantial apparition, which disappears in the light of philosophical reflection.

I am almost tempted to agree with the nonegocentrist; until I realize that, unlike a momentary apparition, the *this* does not disappear, but remains with me all the while. Before, I saw it as something real; now I am supposed to see it as an illusion. What, then, is the reality of the illusion? What is the illusion an illusion of? To say that something is an illusion implies, first, that it is something in its own right; and, second, that there is something else behind it which it covers up or distorts. Those implications must be followed up. Having cut the knot, one still has to pick up the pieces. In philosophy, it is one thing to declare that you reject something, say, on the grounds that reflection has shown the impossibility of making logical sense of it, or simply because rejecting it solves some difficulty; but when the thing still appears to be real it becomes quite another matter to work out a theory which will make that rejection intelligible. In the absence of such a theory, simply uttering the words, 'I reject...', however strong one's reasons for doing so, accomplishes nothing.

2. In this chapter, we shall seek to refute nonegocentrism, by showing that it is in principle debarred from explaining the so-called illusion of my subjective standpoint. However, in order to do that it is first necessary to find a description of the appearances that both parties can agree on: an account of the experience I call my 'incommunicable sense of my own existence' and the nonegocentrist calls 'illusion'. Now, my opponent has far less interest in reaching such an agreement than I have. For if we cannot even agree that there is something we are arguing about, then the nonegocentrist will feel all the more justified in calling whatever I think we are arguing about an illusion; whilst I should not be in a position to demand an explanation of what the illusion is in itself and what lies behind it.

Thus the argument has two distinct stages. In the first stage, the task is simply to secure the nonegocentrist's agreement on the facts of the case. Each of us has a sense of our own unique existence which, on elementary reflection, we are capable of seeing as something that does not present an aspect to the objective standpoint. Further reflection shows that this something cannot be the subject matter of true or false judgements, and hence cannot be described in language.

If the nonegocentrist can be persuaded that this incommunicable sense of one's own existence does appear in each of us, then the argument moves on to the second stage. The nonegocentrist declares that if there is such an appearance, then it is nothing but sheer illusion: once we have gathered together everything whose reality can be expressed in the form of judgements, or which can at least be meaningfully judged to exist even if we are not in a position to determine its specific nature, there is nothing real left over that remains invisible to the objective standpoint. Even though when I look inside myself I seem to be aware of something I call *this*, there is in fact nothing that the word 'this' refers to or in any way indicates. Against that negative claim, it will be shown that the nonegocentrist is incapable of explaining how there could be such a thing as the mere illusion of a *this*. The only alternative for someone who takes the goal of metaphysics seriously – who wishes to account for the whole of reality and not just a part of it – is to take the incommunicable sense of my own unique existence as a sense of something real, even if that is the only thing that can be said about it.

3. One way to express the appearance of there being something in me that makes me the unique individual that I am, but which I cannot communicate to anyone else, is to describe a possible situation which I should feel compelled to view as one where a perfect double possessing all my physical and mental attributes exists, but where I myself – with that peculiar emphasis only I can grasp – do not. In the last chapter, we considered the thought that God might have created a Klempner who, lacking *this*, was not I. One difficulty with this thought that was pointed out in chapter 2 is that God does not appear to be in a position to choose either to create or not create my subjective standpoint, since all that exists for God's objective or 'super-objective' standpoint is some unique individual with Klempner's physical and mental attributes. Waiving that difficulty, however – supposing, let us say, that *this* came about but might equally well have not come about as a completely accidental by-product of the process of creating Klempner – it would be only too easy for the nonegocentrist to retort that not enough had been said to make it so much as appear, at least to those who have not yet been initiated into this metaphysical vision, that there are two possible worlds to consider, a world with *this* and a world without *this* – as opposed to only one.

Rather than try to focus one's mind on that difficult counterfactual possibility, consider instead the following thought experiment. Unknown to me, an evil scientist has over the past few weeks been growing an exact duplicate of my body in a vat, on the basis of genetic information from one of my own cells. Its muscle and fat distribution have been carefully controlled to match mine. The lines on its face which indicate my characteristic moods, and the scars on its body which tell of the minor accidents that have befallen me, have been etched into its skin tissue. By means of a brain scanner the scientist has even succeeded in programming the brain of this artificial being, using up-to-the-minute information, to be the exact duplicate of my own. Every experience I have ever had that has made any kind of permanent impression on me is imprinted in its memory. This Frankenstein's monster is none other than my perfect doppelganger. As a coup de grace, the scientist plans to secretly substitute the artificial being for me. Perhaps I shall go out on my daily walk, and my doppelganger will return to greet my wife, and then go on to live the very same life I would have lived. The question is, What, if anything, would my doppelganger lack that I now possess? It turns out that this question appears to have two quite different answers, depending on whether it is I or another person, for example my wife, who is asking it.

For my wife, the question whether my doppelganger has been substituted for me turns, prima facie, on the history of the man who returns to greet her. My doppelganger is different from me because, even if we matched one another cell for cell and molecule for molecule, we should still have different pasts. The man standing before her now is not the man she married. Nor would she lack philosophical backing for this stance, and against what would seem to follow from Locke's account of personal identity, that mere temporal continuity of apparent memory would suffice to make the doppelganger the man she married, were the original Klempner to be destroyed at the moment when the doppelganger was brought to life. (For example, cf. David Wiggins' insistence on the condition of spatio-temporal continuity of the physical basis for memory in *Sameness and Substance* ch. 6.)

The question whether a substitution has taken place may indeed turn out to be one which neither she nor anyone else will ever be able to answer. For one may suppose that the day after the switch the scientist's laboratory was burned down, not only killing the scientist but erasing every trace of the experiment. In that case, there would be nothing in the whole universe, barring a recording angel, which testified to the substitution having taken place. The difference between my doppelganger and I would depend solely upon undiscoverable facts about the past.

By complete contrast, when I ask the question what distinguishes me from my doppelganger, it seems that the answer stares me right in the face. As I comb my hair before going out, I gaze at my reflection in the bathroom mirror and wonder – musing perhaps on my mortality – Is this an experience I shall ever have again? And when I return safely from my walk, I shall surely know the answer without having to make any further inquiries. Yet what if I returned to find my wife doubting me? How could I persuade her? The fact is, there is nothing I could do or say that my doppelganger would not do or say also. I must conclude from this thought experiment that there seems to me to be something in me now which, independently of any facts about my past which others might or might not discover, makes me the unique individual that I am for myself, but which I can never communicate to any other person.

4. It is true that, given a few moments to reflect about the story, my wife might well come to reject the prima facie view, and insist instead that facts about the past cannot be the only thing that distinguishes me from my doppelganger. There must be an inner self that belongs to me alone, one which is necessarily different from the inner self of my doppelganger. The explanation for her conviction is surely that she has first imagined how things would be if she had been replaced by her doppelganger, and then put herself in my shoes. From the point of view of psychology, this capacity for sympathetic projection is fundamental to all human relations other than those of blind antagonism or sheer indifference. As far as metaphysics is concerned, however, such a move cannot be logically justified. For in making the claim to necessity, in asserting that there must be something in me which is of the same nature as what she seems to find in herself, my wife would in effect be appealing to the refined cartesian dualist notion of an indescribable subjective entity, a constituent of reality non-identical with physical body about which nothing can be said other than that it exists. This is no longer describing appearances but giving a theory, and, moreover, one which we have already shown to be incoherent. As far as appearances are concerned, my view and my wife's view of the thought experiment remain completely different.

The reader may have begun to perceive that this raises intense difficulties for our grasp of the reality of other selves; but these must be deferred until their proper place. As we remarked in chapter 2, the question of the relation between self and other is the central problem arising from the dialectic of subjective and objective standpoints. For now, we shall merely note that for all my wife may believe about her ability to discern the indescribable something that distinguishes me from any mere copy, she will never seem to see the unique I that I seem to see. It may indeed be said that her love for me involves a faith in my revelation of an inner self to her, which cannot be analysed in terms of the concepts of knowledge or perception, and which cannot be justified by pointing to any specific events in her experience. Even by the standards of religious faith, however, such a belief would seem to be completely irrational. For religion does at least give grounds for forming some expectations about the future. Yet, by hypothesis, my wife will enjoy or suffer the very same experiences with my doppelganger as she would have done with me.

Note that it would be logically consistent to hold that each person is born with a non-physical soul which, for those beings such as angels with the power to perceive souls, always remains distinguishable, not only numerically but in the very uniqueness of the substance of which it is constituted, from the soul of a manufactured copy of that person (assuming that a copy could have a soul), or indeed from the soul of someone physically indistinguishable born and grown up in the normal way. It might even turn out to be the case that the content of mental states is realized not in states of the brain as scientists now believe, but rather in states of the subject's soul: in which case the requirement that the subject's mental states present an aspect to the objective standpoint would be met by acknowledging the possible existence of individuals with the perceptual capacities of angels. A consequence of either view would be that, unless difference in soul substance was found only in the souls of physically indistinguishable persons – surely a dubious ad hoc move – there would be just as many different types or species of soul substance as there were souls; a notion which echoes in a strange way Aquinas' notorious view that angels, lacking 'matter' and therefore incapable of being individuated by spatial position, could only be distinguished at all if each corresponded to a unique Aristotelian 'form'. The existence of souls is not, however, a belief to which the emancipated dualist need subscribe, cf. Nagel: 'it seems likely that in a rationally designed world the mental properties would be at least supervenient on the physical' (*The View From Nowhere* p. 48. Supervenience would not entail psychophysical reduction if the 'necessary identity between the mental and physical process...proceeds through the intermediate link of a more basic term, neither mental nor physical, of which we have no conception' [ibid.].)

For the nonegocentrist who does believe in souls, on the other hand, we have to use a modified version of the thought experiment. Since, by contrast with Aquinas' angels, we must always allow for difference in spatial position as a way of individuating souls – the number of soul-bodies, like any facts about their states, necessarily presenting an aspect to the objective standpoint – there can be no logical barrier to the creation of two souls out of the very same species of non-physical soul substance. But now the evil scientist need only team up with an evil angel who has the power to make duplicate souls indistinguishable in substance from the originals. My doppelganger now has not only all of my physical and mental attributes, but a non-physical soul which even an angel could not tell apart from my own soul.

5. How does the nonegocentrist react to the story of the doppelganger? A nonegocentrist intent on resisting me every step of the way will simply deny that she reacts to the thought experiment in the same way that I do. 'You may imagine,' says the nonegocentrist, 'that you would simply know the answer to the question whether you had returned home safely, but I imagine no such thing. All I can think of is that, were circumstances to arise which raised doubts about my identity, I should seek to discover the answer to the question whether I had been replaced by my doppelganger by undertaking the very same kinds of investigations as any other person would do.'

Yet is the nonegocentrist being really honest in saying this? If one tries to fill out the details of the story from the first-person point of view, it becomes increasingly clear that a person who possessed no sense of conviction that he would be immediately aware of being the same person and not his own doppelganger is a very unusual individual. If the switch did take place, then somewhere on my walk I was either killed or taken prisoner. The person who is I either is no more, or else is locked up somewhere. The person who returns to my home is not I. If I do find myself returning home, then surely I know that neither of these things did happen. That, at least, is how it seems to me anyone with an inner life comparable with mine must view the thought experiment on a first encounter with it, however much he may alter his convictions as a result of philosophical reflection. One would put it to the nonegocentrist that she is not being honest in claiming to describe how the sense of her own existence appears to her, but instead is merely repeating a considered philosophical position according to which the appearance can only be illusory.

The argument could simply come to an end here, with the nonegocentrist stubbornly refusing to admit to sharing my initial reaction to the story of the doppelganger. All one can say about this is that the very possibility of disagreement in metaphysics depends upon some kind of shared perception and understanding. The fact that there might exist human beings with whom one could not discuss certain metaphysical questions no more casts doubt upon our being able to discover answers than does the fact that there might exist Martians with whom one could not discuss those questions. However, a nonegocentrist might react to the thought experiment in a more constructive way. She may point out instead that the so-called appearance of my inner self to me reveals a fatal ambiguity, when the thought experiment is pursued a little further, which shows that it

78

cannot be the mere appearance it purports to be. Suppose that I return from my walk, not suspecting that anything untoward has happened. A week later, a stranger calls at my door and asks me how I am getting on. 'What do you mean?', I ask innocently. 'Well, of course I knew you'd say that!', says the stranger, and then proceeds to tell me the details of the experiment. Gradually, as more and more evidence is presented to me, my initial total scepticism turns to disbelief, and then to the growing sense of horror that I might not be the same individual who set out on his walk on that fatal day. Thinking about this new chapter in the story, my sense of absolute certainty that I would know that I was the same person without having to make any further inquiries begins to crumble. Perhaps I would be persuaded in the end that I was my own doppelganger. 'Now,' asks the nonegocentrist, 'does there still seem to be something in you which proves that you are the same unique individual, even in the face of conclusive evidence to the contrary?'

This extension of the thought experiment, contrary to what the nonegocentrist intends, only strengthens the original conclusion. If what has just been described were to happen to me, the appearance of my incommunicable sense of my own continued existence would surely remain undiminished, even though, under pressure from evidence which was presented to me or which I discovered for myself, I might come to espouse the belief that I was not the same individual who went out on the walk. In telling the story of my life, I should recount the apparent memories of 'my' former existence with an undaunted sense of conviction, despite the fact that I now acknowledged that these memories in some sense really belonged to someone who is now dead, or else to the unkempt, barely recognizable individual languishing in a prison cell beneath the scientist's laboratory.

It is true that I might still try to explain these events to myself by telling some story about a soul which left my original body and entered this one. However, that would be a theory whose explanatory power I could count on only for so long as it remained logically unverifiable. For, as we have seen, one can take the story one step further, and suppose that my very soul had been removed or destroyed by an evil angel and replaced by one with the very same substance and mental contents, leaving my sense of my continued existence unaffected. My stubborn belief that there would then have to be a soul of my soul, which left my first soul and entered the second, is no more than a picturesque expression of my unshakeable sense of my own continued identity. That is the way things seem, even if one has no explanation to offer for it, and even if it flies in the face of all the evidence. No-one would deny that this seeming, this appearance leads to highly paradoxical consequences. Yet as an appearance it is not altered or diminished in any way by them.

6. Enough has been said now to establish the reality of the appearance of my incommunicable sense of my own existence. There are many questions still to be answered about the degree to which this appearance depends on certain stable features of one's inner life; for example, what happens in the case of gradual or sudden memory loss. How much, indeed, does the inner life of a being with an incommunicable sense of its own existence have to be like our own? We shall merely note these problems, and move on. Now that we have established that the appearance of a sense of my continued existence can survive conclusive external evidence to the contrary, the question of how far one could alter internal conditions without destroying the appearance is only a matter of detail. A different set of questions relates to the consequences of the fact that my subjective standpoint belongs to a being who exists for the objective standpoint. These must be deferred until we come to discuss the essential attributes of the subjective standpoint in chapter 9. We shall then have to decide how we are to treat such cases as multiple personalities, or the case of a single person with multiple bodies.

We have now reached the second stage of the argument against nonegocentrism. The nonegocentrist who is still with us concedes that there is such a thing as the appearance of an incommunicable sense of my own existence, but denies that the appearance can depict anything real. If the appearance were veridical, then there would have to exist something that was not the potential subject matter of true or false judgements, a reality that did not present an aspect to any point of view other than that of the subject. The failure of the attempts of both refined cartesian dualism and the mind-body identity theory set up in opposition to it to reconcile the existence of my subjective standpoint with the objective standpoint of language shows that such an incommunicable subjective reality cannot exist. Its appearance must therefore be an illusion. Having stood by this claim, however, the nonegocentrist still has to answer the question of what kind of reality is possessed by the illusion in itself, and what is the nature of the reality that lies behind the illusory appearance, by virtue of which we are able to say that the appearance fails to depict the way things really are.

The nonegocentrist's strategy for answering these questions is the same in both cases. 'Forget how the illusion presents itself to your own introspection, and concentrate instead on how you would describe the nature of the illusion as it appears to someone else, and how you would describe that person's actual situation, which he is unable to see clearly because the illusion distorts it or covers it up. Once you have done that, you can go back and apply the results to your own case.' Now it is difficult to quarrel with this advice, for the very reason that the reality of the objective standpoint means that every judgement I can make about myself, and in particular about any illusion I may be under, can also be made by others about me. Since the kinds of judgement that others can make about me are the same as the kinds of judgement I can make about them, it follows that there is no kind of judgement that I can make about my illusion that I cannot make about the same illusion when it occurs in others, and vice versa. Everything that I can say about others, no more no less, applies to myself also.

Having secured that principle, the nonegocentrist has no difficulty in finding a way to account for the illusion of an incommunicable sense of one's own existence. It is part of the very nature of what it is to be a being capable of self-reference, a being whose conscious experience has the logical form of a standing potential for self-consciousness, to view its own existence in a fundamentally different way from the way it views the existence of other persons or things. I do not discover my own existence – for all that I may discover about myself – in the way that I discover the existence of others, for it is there right from the start. I do not locate myself in my own map of reality, the compendium of all the things I have encountered in the world or facts I have found out about the world, in the way that I locate anything that is not myself: my existence is logically equivalent to there being a map of reality for me. The illusion of an incommunicable sense of my own existence arises, according to the nonegocentrist, out of an inevitable misinterpretation of these logical facts, a faulty inference which every self-conscious subject cannot help but make, and which it is the business of philosophy to correct.

7. Let us see in more detail how, according to the nonegocentrist, the illusion does arise. A subject acquires his conception of the objective standpoint in the process of learning to use language. In mastering the ability to communicate with others, I learn that I am an object of reference for them in the same sense that they are objects of reference for me. I also learn that I am an object of reference for myself. As an object of reference for others, my status is that of a being whose existence is contingently given, a living body whose continued identity is subject to various causal factors that others are in a position to investigate. By contrast, as an object of reference for

myself, my existence is not contingently given. I do not find myself amongst the things that make up the world, for I am doing the seeking; nor do I follow my own continued identity through space and time, for my body is not separated from me by any distance that would enable me to stand behind it and track its movements and changes. (If I possessed two bodies, one body could indeed observe the movements of the other; but that would be no different in principle from observing myself in a mirror: cf. chapter 9.)

Now when we are confronted by a thought experiment such as the story of the doppelganger, these two pieces of knowledge, the knowledge of how one figures as an object of reference for others and the knowledge of how one figures as an object of reference for oneself, come into conflict. The fact that one does not discover one's own existence in the way that one discovers the existence of others is misinterpreted as a form of infallible knowledge which no-one can ever controvert. For example, the doppelganger's artificially induced memories of its former life are, as far as we are concerned, just false beliefs. Yet the doppelganger cannot help but view them as if they were absolutely genuine. Whether it can ever be persuaded to alter its beliefs will depend on whether we are able to get it to grasp its situation in the way that we see it. The potential for doing so is already there, in its understanding of language and the conception of the objective standpoint that goes with that understanding. Even so, the doppelganger's sense of identity with the person whose memories it has acquired remains as clear and as vivid as the memories themselves. As an item of supposedly infallible knowledge, that sense of identity is indeed incommunicable; the doppelganger is aware that it can never persuade us to believe what it thinks it knows with absolute certainty. Once we have made it acknowledge its error, however, the doppelganger will come to view that sense of identity as we do: as just an illusion.

So far, the account has gone very smoothly; but there is still one thing missing. The whole point of the explanation was that, having worked out what I should say about any person, I then go on to apply the account to my own case. Yet when I try to apply the account to myself a baffling paradox arises. According to the objective standpoint, we are all in the same boat: we are each of us uniquely placed with respect to our own existence, simply by virtue of our performing acts of self-reference. Of each of us it is true to say that we do not find ourselves amongst the things that make up the world, nor do we follow our own identity through space and time. Now, I am one of the persons in the boat, by virtue of the fact that I exist as a being capable of self-reference. It is therefore true to say of me that I am uniquely placed with respect to my own existence. However, this last proposition appears to have two quite different meanings, depending upon whether it is I or someone else who utters it. Said by another person, the proposition, 'You are uniquely placed with respect to your own existence' appears as a straightforward instance of the general principle that applies to all of us. But when I utter it, a peculiar thing happens. If I am uniquely placed with respect to my own existence, then in answer to the question first prompted by the thought experiment, How does the nature of my existence compare with that of others?, I have to reply that I do indeed differ from all other persons in being uniquely placed with respect to the existence of the one and only person who is in question: myself.

As far as I, the person asking the question, am concerned, the fact that I am uniquely placed with respect to Klempner's existence is not included in or in any way accounted for by the fact that A is uniquely placed with respect to A's existence, B is uniquely placed with respect to B's existence...Klempner is uniquely placed with respect to Klempner's existence. I am not 'in the same boat' as everyone else. Whilst I may allow that any other person is fully justified in applying the nonegocentrist's explanation of the illusion of an incommunicable sense of my own unique existence to me, I cannot apply it to myself. The fact that I exist, by contrast with facts that either I or others can know about me, or with the fact that A or B exist, is a fact with respect to which I am uniquely placed, and is for that reason and in that sense incommunicable.

8. One can well understand that someone who has become used to thinking within the framework of nonegocentrism will react to this argument with sheer incredulity: how could it ever work? how can I set myself apart from others in this way? There is nothing to say to those who simply refuse to consider on principle any philosophical view tainted by egocentricity. For those who only need more words to grip the idea, however, consider the point from philosophical logic that I can only think the content that my own I-thoughts have for the person thinking them. This statement expresses two logically connected propositions, one which stresses the word 'I' and one stressing the phrase 'my own'. Only I, and no-one else, can think the content that my own I-thoughts have for me; and I can think the content only that my own I-thoughts have for me and not the content that the I-thoughts of others have for them. (The I-statements of others do have a content for me, but it is a content equivalent to one I would express by means of the second- or third-person pronoun.) Interestingly, Gareth Evans, who makes this point (*The Varieties of*

Reference pp. 209–12), rejects any implication that this feature of self-reference prevents me from forming an objective conception of my own existence in the world as merely one subject amongst others. Rejecting egocentrism, he sees nonegocentrism as the only possible alternative.

Let us, however, look at this point about content in relation to the paradox of the boat. A nonegocentrist might say, 'You and I are still in the same boat, I cannot think your I-thoughts and you cannot think mine!' But what does that mean? That my unique placement with respect to Klempner's existence is a fact strictly in addition to Klempner's unique placement with respect to Klempner's existence follows from the surplus of content of my own I-thoughts over thoughts about me expressed impersonally. To say that the fact is additional is to say that there is something more to reality just because it contains that fact than there would be if it did not contain that fact. (We do not need to define what a fact is; the minimal notion of something that makes a difference to reality is all one needs.) What then should I say, for example, about my wife's unique placement with respect to her existence? Isn't that the same? I grant that I cannot express a certain content, namely the content that the corresponding I-thought has for her. It follows immediately, however, that I cannot say that there exists a fact strictly in addition to her unique placement with respect to her existence corresponding to the fact, strictly additional to Klempner's unique placement with respect to Klempner's existence, of my unique placement with respect to Klempner's existence. I cannot say that, not because her 'strictly additional fact' merely eludes all my attempts to express it – as if there were something whose existence I could still acknowledge, even though I lacked the means to indicate that acknowledgement – but because for me there simply is no such fact. What I am permitted to say is that for her there exists an additional fact; but that is not to assert the existence of that putative fact, any more than my assertion that for her God exists commits me to the existence of God.

We remarked in chapter 6 that our definition of the subjective standpoint as necessarily singular was the crux of our disagreement with Nagel. For him, my inability to think the thought that my wife would express by, 'I am uniquely placed with respect to June-Allison's existence' falls under the general rubric of facts described by means of concepts I shall never be able to grasp, together with systems of explanation that I, with my own limited mental capacities or with the limited mental capacities of a human being shall never be able to comprehend, and also with facts accessible only to beings with different modes of sense-perception such as bats. But the argument is not: I cannot think her I-am-uniquely-placed thought, therefore the thought cannot be true, but rather: I cannot meaningfully say that there is something in virtue of which her I am-uniquely-placed thought is either true or false, over and above that in virtue of which the thought that June-Allison is uniquely placed is true. In order to say that, I should have to be in a position to have her I-am-uniquely-placed thought, i.e. I should have to be her. Yet I am apparently able to assert that there is something in virtue of which my I-am-uniquely-placed thought is true, over and above that in virtue of which the thought that Klempner is uniquely placed is true. What enables me to do this is not, however, an ineffable power of metaphysical intuition but simply the acknowledged fact of the irreducibility of 'I', the surplus of content of my own I-thoughts over thoughts about me expressed impersonally.

9. My inability to communicate, to get others to see the fact that I exist as I see it is not infallible knowledge of an invisible inner something which makes me the unique individual that I am. Nothing makes me the individual that I am other than the fact that my history traces back to a child born of certain parents, and conceived at a certain time out of a particular sperm and egg. (Cf. Kripke *Naming and Necessity*, pp. 112–3. At any point along this line the substitution of a duplicate could conceivably take place, up to and including the very moment of conception.) Insofar as I believe that I possess an infallible knowledge of what really makes me me, contrary to whatever historical evidence may turn up, then I am indeed under an illusion. That is not, however, the illusion that the nonegocentrist had in mind. What the nonegocentrist's account of self-reference purports to show is that the very vision of an incommunicable sense of my existence is illusory, and not merely that I am under an illusion when I seek to base any claim to infallible knowledge of my own identity upon it.

Starting from the external viewpoint of the observer, the nonegocentrist carefully examines all the facts which explain why a person should have such a vision, and then concludes that everything that a person says in trying to give expression to the vision can be fully explained without having to assume the added existence of anything actually seen which the observer is unable to see. Since it has already been established that the vision is incommunicable, anything said about it obviously cannot be meaningful. So the illusory vision I seem to see is nothing in itself but an impulse to make nonsensical assertions! What we have discovered from the paradox of the boat is that I cannot seriously entertain the thought that that is all my incommunicable sense of my own existence amounts to. If someone explains to me the reason why I am under the visual illusion that, say, a pencil half immersed in a glass of water is bent in the middle, then I learn that what I seem to see does not correspond with the way things really are. It would not be an adequate explanation of my illusion merely to account for my saying such things as, 'Look at the bent pencil.' Yet that is in effect the kind of explanation that the nonegocentrist is offering.

Anyone who approaches the problem of the relation between the subjective and objective standpoints must ask the same question: how am I to place my existence within the context of the reality of the objective standpoint? For each of us there appears, within us, something that renders problematic our own relation to the world as conceived from the objective standpoint; an appearance which becomes especially vivid when we consider certain thought experiments. We seem to see something that no-one else can see, a *this* that remains invisible from the objective standpoint.

Still, one is not infallible; perhaps what we seem to see is in reality different from the way it appears. Then the nonegocentrist comes along and offers an account of our relation to the world which claims to justify this suspicion. The appearance of the *this*, my incommunicable sense of my own existence, is an illusion. In fact, the nonegocentrist has done no such thing. For the only explanation the nonegocentrist is able to give does away not only with the purported object of this vision, the indubitable fact of my existence and identity as it presents itself exclusively to me, but also the vision, the seeming as well. In rejecting the reality of the subjective standpoint, the nonegocentrist has failed to satisfy what we described at the beginning of this chapter as a necessary condition for saying the words, 'I reject,' in the context of a philosophical argument: to provide an account which makes that rejection intelligible. For the nonegocentrist's explanation of the illusion of a subjective standpoint fails to capture the one thing that alone could make it intelligible as an illusion: the existence in me, the existence in each one of us, of a seeming which we cannot but take to be an awareness of our own existence as that fact presents itself to ourselves alone.

8 A two-world metaphysic

1. ON account of the reality of the subjective standpoint, each of us must say, 'I exist in addition to the world.' So I must say. The existence of I is a fact only for I and for no other possible individual; not even an omniscient deity. That is a truth of logic, not psychology. For an account of how the act of self-reference generates the illusory appearance of my subjective standpoint can in principle be understood by every conscious subject except the one asking the question: myself. That is one issue about which I cannot suffer others to speak on my behalf; and I can speak on behalf of others only so far as saying what they must say, not so far as meaning what they would mean by it.

I am the sole witness to the fact that there is *this*. That is what the egocentrist wanted to say, but could not, because in the absence of the one condition for there being such a thing as applying concepts or making judgements, the egocentrist is disbarred from making any statements at all. Thus our proof of the reality of the objective standpoint is placed finally on an unconditional basis. On pain of self-contradiction, each of us must recognize the reality of our own subjective standpoint simultaneously with the objective. With that recognition, the egocentrist's only motive for remaining silent and refusing to acknowledge the objective standpoint is brushed aside.

Yet to secure finally the objective world hardly seems fair compensation for having to embrace, on the basis of a single thought experiment, the paradoxical view that mine is the only subjective world. It is true that the sense of paradox, if it does not point to a fault somewhere in one's reasoning, indicates only that an idea fails to fit one's current mental parameters. In time, mental parameters can be altered. The real difficulty, however, is that relying on purely negative

87

argument, as we have done up till now, has serious defects as a method of doing philosophy. There is a danger of proving results that we simply do not understand. To call the relation between the two standpoints a metaphysical contradiction, as we did in chapter 2, is merely to give one more negative characterization.

Indeed, as we saw in chapter 6, the *this* cannot be regarded as any kind of entity or constituent of reality, for there is nothing in reality with which it could be meaningfully said to be either identical or non-identical. Yet what other way is there for it to be real? Either something belongs to, is part of reality or not. Unless we can find a way to avoid having to assert simultaneously that the subjective standpoint is both real and unreal, we shall have more than a mere paradox on our hands.

2. What we are seeking is an adequate form in which to express the reality of the subjective standpoint, a logical structure through which its special manner of being real, its similarity to and contrast with the objective way of being real will become manifest. What would suffice to show that a proposed form was adequate would be that it did not lead to the logical contradiction of calling the subjective standpoint both real and unreal, while at the same time preserving the univocity of the concept 'real'.

Finding a form to express the reality of the subjective standpoint is, moreover, something we must be able to do in advance of reconciling the conflict between the subjective and objective standpoints. The question of reconciliation might, after all, turn out to have a negative answer; we should then be left with an insoluble philosophical problem. In the absence of an adequate formal expression for the reality of the subjective and objective standpoints, however, we should not even be able to describe ourselves intelligibly as being in such a predicament.

Now the reader will recall that we took the first step towards explaining what is meant by the reality of the subjective standpoint back in chapter 2. The very possibility of distinguishing a metaphysical contradiction as something that can be actual or real – that can be realized in the nature of things themselves – from a logical contradiction which cannot be true on pain of absurdity, lies in the fact that whereas a logical contradiction involves conflicting statements, a metaphysical contradiction involves conflicting realities. Since the subjective standpoint lies beyond the public domain of language, its reality cannot consist in the truth of any statement. So the conflict between the subjective and objective standpoints is not the kind of conflict that obtains between contradictory statements.

As a first step, can we say more accurately how the subjective standpoint differs from the objective in this regard? An immediate implication of what we have just said is that the reality of the objective standpoint, by contrast with the subjective, does consist in (and indeed consist wholly in) the truth of certain statements. There is no mystery about which true statements are in question, any will do. For we established in chapter 5 that the objective standpoint is real on condition that there is such a thing as judgement or the application of concepts. For example, if 'grass' and 'green' express concepts, then the assertion, 'Grass is green' is a judgement, and the truth of that judgement entails the reality of the objective standpoint. (It is quite consistent with this view to maintain that there is more to what is objectively real than could ever be captured by any finite number of judgements; for this more is essentially more of the same.)

We cannot, however, use a similar means to express the reality of the subjective standpoint. The truth of the statement, 'I exist,' or the statement, 'I have a pain in my thumb,' entails the reality of the objective not the subjective standpoint. For within the domain of language, my use of the pronoun 'I' is understood in a relative sense, as referring to the one uttering it, a person given to himself in the same way that all other referents of 'I' are given to themselves. My incommunicable sense of my own existence may indeed be said to involve the conviction that 'I' has an additional, absolute sense of which only I am aware. Only it must be remembered that 'I' is not then functioning as a word in a language, but merely as an inarticulate, inner pointing gesture, no different from the word *this*.

3. Another thing we know about the reality of the objective standpoint is that it consists, by definition, in the existence of things that present aspects to points of view other than my own. To exist, to be a thing or an entity in that sense, is to be a constituent of objective reality. As my beliefs about things are expressed in statements which others have the authority to correct, there is clearly an essential link between saying that the reality of the objective standpoint consists in the existence of things, and saying that it consists in the truth of statements about things.

It is at this point that there arises the temptation to represent the reality of the subjective standpoint as consisting, by contrast, in the existence of things which present an aspect only to one point of view, things about which no judgements can be made. Thus we saw in chapter 6, the fatal error made by both the refined cartesian dualist and the opposed identity theorist was to attempt to exploit the notion of reality as the domain or totality to which all existing things belong in order to express the special nature of the subjective standpoint. In this totality, there would exist objective things which present aspects to many points of view, and also subjective things each of which present an aspect only to one point of view. The dualist asserts the existence of non-physical, subjective somethings correlated with the states of physical body, but which are real only for the subject. The identity theorist denies that there exists anything apart from physical things, while allowing that I can have a point of view on the subjective aspects of my own physically realized mental states which I share with no-one else, from which they appear, just as they appear to the dualist, as indescribable somethings.

These somethings are thus treated in both theories as entities which belong to that part or region of reality which I know as my subjective standpoint. The failure of the two theories to distinguish what were set up as directly opposed positions reveals that their notions of the peculiar, one-sided thinghood of these subjective constituents of reality are completely empty. The reality of my subjective standpoint cannot be understood either in terms of the existence of a special class of non-physical entity visible only to myself, or in terms of a special class of physical entity, such as a brain, which possesses an additional internal quality or aspect which only its owner is in a position to enjoy.

The reality of my subjective standpoint means that the objective standpoint can never, so long as I exist, exhaust the totality of what is real. However, the admission that the subjective standpoint cannot be taken to consist in the existence of a special class of subjective entity obliges us to heavily qualify that statement (It will be qualified further when we consider in chapter 10 what it could mean for my subjective standpoint to cease to exist.) The most obvious way to interpret it would be to say that the totality of what is real must include not only the objective standpoint but in addition my subjective standpoint. We now know that such an interpretation is wrong. If there did exist a totality which included both the objective and subjective standpoints, then the subjective standpoint would, after all, have to be thought of as involving the existence of a special class of subjective entity. Reality would then exist as a single domain divided into two halves: on one side would be objective things, and on the other side subjective things.

In the face of the admission that the *this* which constitutes my subjective standpoint is not an entity or in any sense a constituent of reality, only one conclusion is possible: there is no such thing as the totality of what is real. The reason why the objective standpoint cannot be taken to exhaust the totality of the real is that the discovery of my subjective standpoint undermines the very project of trying to comprehend the real as a totality. Since, as we noted in chapter 6 in connection with Aristotle's taxonomy of ways of being, that project has been central to the activity of metaphysics from the very beginning, that is a very significant result. The radical position we are forced to take gives us all the more reason for seeking a different perspective on the arguments which led up to it, one that might provide some sort of check on their validity, or on our interpretation of their outcome. Only then can we go on to canvass what alternatives there might be to viewing the real as a totality, in our attempt to work out the form in which to express the reality of the subjective standpoint.

4. We shall shortly be re-examining, in the light of the critique of totality, the fatally misleading metaphor of the room seen from the inside and from the outside, as a picture of my mental states as I and others stand towards them. In preparation for that, let us first consider another metaphor. One way of thinking about the claim that the subjective and objective standpoints cannot be added together to form a totality, is that either one or both is so large already that it simply will not tolerate any further addition. We can represent the egocentrist as saying that the world of my subjective standpoint, the world of my possible experience, fills up all the available logical space that could be occupied by reality, so that the existence of things or facts accessible only to points of view other than my own is inconceivable. The nonegocentrist makes a parallel claim on behalf of the objective standpoint: since everything real can be explained from the objective standpoint, including the appearance in me of a subjective standpoint, there is no logical space left in reality for the inclusion of a real subjective standpoint corresponding to the appearance.

We shall not repeat the reasons why both these metaphysical positions are wrong. It suffices for now to interpret the outcome of the dialectic in terms of the concept of logical space. The egocentrist's subjective reality is not big enough; but acknowledging the reality of the objective standpoint still cannot make reality any bigger. The nonegocentrist's objective reality is not big enough; but acknowledging the reality of the subjective standpoint still cannot make reality any bigger. There is no space where the objective standpoint could be added on to the subjective standpoint, nor is there space where the subjective standpoint could be added on to the objective. In that sense, both the egocentrist and the nonegocentrist are equally in the right. What they both overlook, however, is the possibility of acknowledging the reality of both the subjective and objective standpoints without adding them together to form a totality.

Both the refined cartesian dualist and the identity theorist started off by acknowledging the reality of the objective standpoint; each erroneously believing that a formula had been found which provided the sole means for expressing the reality of the subjective standpoint, simply by adding a subjective something onto the world of the objective standpoint; neither realizing that their competing formulae are no sooner stated than each transforms into its opposite. Let us now see how this diagnosis works in terms of the metaphor of the room and its furnishings, which represents my mind and its contents.

The objective standpoint tells me that what I see before me is a reality to which others in principle have access: the mental furnishings I see from the inside others can see or can come to see from the outside. Suppose that I try now to put myself in the place of someone outside the room and, on that person's behalf, ask, Is there a way that the furnishings look to someone inside the room? Is there someone who sees the furnishings from the inside? Of course I, the person inside the room, know the answer already: but the question is what form that answer should take. According to the refined cartesian dualist, the only way the furnishings could be seen from inside the room is if there exists a non-physical mind which cannot itself be seen from the outside, whose sole function is to perceive the furnishings directly. According to the identity theorist, on the other hand, the subject's mind is none other than the room itself, which others can see. Its having an inside which appears to the subject as such is taken care of by the fact that it is the kind of complex material structure, say, the brain of a human being, which appears to itself as an inside and to others as an outside.

Both the dualist and the identity theorist are trying to explain my incommunicable sense that there is something given to me alone, over and above my body which others are able to observe: the fact that I exist as that fact presents itself exclusively for my enjoyment. Both explanations fail for the very same reason. From the objective standpoint, an inside added on can be any inside. Every person has his or her own inside. But which of all the insides added on to the outsides of all the persons that exist is my inside? Where is the fact given to me alone that determines that one of these persons is myself? Clearly, this fact cannot simply be the fact that I possess an inside; it has to be the fact that I possess *this* inside. Yet neither the dualist nor the identity theorist has anything more to tell me than I already knew at the start: that I, just like everyone else, possess an inside. If I start with this inside, then however vehemently I assert my identity with an outside, I remain on the inside. If I start with an outside, then however vehemently I assert the existence of an inside non-identical with the outside, I remain on the outside. As far as relating the subjective and objective standpoints is concerned, talk of identity or non-identity is equally futile.

5. In order to justify the claim that the subjective and objective standpoints are each too large already to tolerate any further addition, we have just given the example of attempting to add something to the objective standpoint. Giving insides to beings who possess the outsides of beings such as myself cannot be interpreted, as both the refined cartesian dualist and the identity theorist wish to do, as adding on a subjective something that which can exist side by side with objective things, to form an all-encompassing totality comprehending both the subjective and objective standpoints. For everything added on to the objective standpoint automatically becomes just another objective thing. Talk of insides and outsides fulfils no purpose other than to obscure the fact that what I am trying to add on is not the existence of a being such as myself but my very own existence.

Now one could just as well have justified the above claim by observing that no addition to my subjective standpoint would suffice to meet the objection raised against egocentrism in chapter 4, that it cannot account for the possibility of false judgement. The only way an egocentrist can interpret the necessity of recognizing the existence of other points of view is in terms of a phenomenological investigation of the necessary structures to be found within the world of my possible experience, structures which enrich or expand it, even while they impose additional restrictions on what is to count as genuine experience. This necessity, as we noted parenthetically in chapter 3 in connection with Evans' account of primary and secondary qualities, would be relative to some further requirement on top of the minimal notion of objectivity required by the Kantian egocentrist, so its status within an egocentrist metaphysic is in any case dubious. (One would hesitate to call any actual practitioner of phenomenology, for example, the Husserl of the *Cartesian Meditations,* an egocentrist according to our definition. Yet arguably that is precisely what his methodology commits him to, despite his attempt in the 'Fifth Meditation' to establish a plurality of transcendental egos.)

Setting aside the question of the questionable status of this additional phenomenological necessity, however, merely to recognize that my experience must in some sense include the experience of communicating with other persons in a common language, or the experience of having my judgements corrected by others, is not to add on an objective reality that can exist side by side with my subjective world. In submitting to the corrections of others, I remain the sole authority on the reliability of my judgements, including my judgements concerning the credentials or expertise of others. In effect, anything added on to my subjective standpoint automatically becomes just another feature of the world of my subjective standpoint, the world of my possible experience, vulnerable to exactly the same fatal objection as before.

6. These two observations taken together suggest a second way of thinking about the claim that the subjective and objective standpoints cannot be added together to form a totality. On the face of it, the reason why a subjective reality cannot be added on to the world of the nonegocentrist to compensate for the deficiencies of the objective standpoint, is very different from the reason why an objective reality cannot be added on to the world of the egocentrist to compensate for the deficiencies of the subjective standpoint. When we look closer, however, we discover that these two reasons share a common logical structure. Both the subjective and objective standpoints may be said to possess a characteristic shape. In both cases the shape is so firmly engrained that, as in legend of Procrustes, who racked or decapitated his unfortunate guests to make them the right size for the beds that had been assigned to them, each of the two standpoints compels anything one tries to fit into it to adopt its own shape. Whenever we attempt to force the two standpoints together, either one or the other must give way, depending on which standpoint we take as our fixed starting point, our Procrustean bed.

The two incompatible shapes can best be pictured in terms of the notion of symmetry. From the objective standpoint, my relation to the world has the same logical status as any other person's relation to the world. Although each actual view of the world is different in terms of its content, these differences cancel one another out: every difference is, logically speaking, equally different. The object of all these different views, the world itself, is always the same from whichever direction one approaches it, and is in that sense perfectly symmetrical. By contrast, from my subjective standpoint, my relation to the world is fundamentally different from every other person's relation to the world. I am the very axis around which the world revolves. This imposes an ineradicably asymmetric shape on reality: every direction from which one might approach the world other than the direction from which I myself approach it lies at a greater or lesser remove from the world's axis. The reason why the subjective and objective

94

standpoints cannot be added together is simply that there is no compromise between symmetry and asymmetry; there is no way we could form a totality while preserving the characteristic shapes of the two standpoints.

7. There are, admittedly, limits to understanding abstract metaphysical concepts in terms of such concrete notions as filling out a space or having a certain shape. Still, anyone who feels uncomfortable with the idea of such analogical thinking should remember that, in metaphysics, one is not simply trying to construct arguments or prove things. Logic is a vitally important tool; but it is not our only tool. There would be nothing to apply our logic to if we were not engaged in a struggle to formulate a coherent metaphysical vision. The logical guarantee of bare consistency does not suffice to render intelligible to us the concepts that we have to use in the process of fleshing out that vision. That is why any hold that we can get on them is welcome.

That hold seems, at the present stage, still very tenuous; but we have made some progress. We now know just what we have let ourselves in for, in acknowledging the reality of both the objective and subjective standpoints. And we are better placed than we were before to search for ways of grasping that dual reality, which offer a genuine alternative to the discredited notion of totality. It would be a good moment, therefore, to return to the question raised at the beginning of this chapter: how can the subjective standpoint be real without being a mere component of reality? In other words, what is the form in which the reality of the subjective standpoint should be expressed?

The most immediate conclusion one can draw from the rejection of totality is that the subjective standpoint is real, not by being a component of a larger reality, a single domain containing both the subjective and objective standpoints, but because it is itself a reality, complete and in its own right. The objective standpoint is another reality. Together, they are two; although strictly speaking we cannot talk meaningfully of their being together, or being added up to make two. We cannot say this, simply because every act of counting presupposes a domain within which the counting game makes sense. There are five apples in the basket; there are nine planets in the solar system; we do not know how many galaxies there are in the universe, but we at least think we know what it would mean to count them. Now there are two realities, the subjective and the objective – but in what? There is no answer to that question because we have already admitted that each reality is too large to be in anything. (It would be facile and quite obviously missing the point to say that there are two realities in this book or in our metaphysic!)

Clearly, this use of the concept of number pushes at the limits of intelligibility: it simply has no precedent. No other example of counting can be appealed to in order to provide an analogy for a two which we cannot even think together as a one. In view of what we have said about the contradiction between the subjective and objective standpoints, that is perhaps not surprising. Rather than question the use of number here, it might be more fruitful to ask what the subjective and objective standpoints have in common, as we put it earlier, which justifies our using the same word 'reality' in both cases. Is there any prospect of explaining the subjective standpoint in terms of the attributes it shares and the attributes it does not share with the objective standpoint? We have already seen that the reality of the subjective standpoint consists neither in the truth of subjective statements nor in the existence of indescribable subjective objects. As we have repeated many times, there is nothing that can be said about what goes to make up the subjective standpoint other than that it is *this*. How could anything of so little substance possibly be a reality, a world?

8. For the Kantian egocentrist, the subjective standpoint is the only reality, a world totally self-sufficient: everything that is true, is true of the world of my possible experience; every object that exists, belongs to the world of my possible experience. Now it may well have seemed that, in the course of rejecting egocentrism and coming to recognize the reality of the objective standpoint, we have allowed everything substantial, every truth, every existing object to be taken away from the egocentrist's reality, leaving only the bare *this* as the marker for the empty space that remains. Indeed, in the face of our refutation of Kantian egocentrism the silent egocentrist admitted as much, only refusing to allow that there could be any other world in which truths and objects could find a home.

For us, that is a misleadingly one-sided view. For we have an objective world. One may admit that nothing can be said about the reality of my subjective standpoint other than that it is *this*. But like the cup half-empty and the cup half-full, there are two opposite ways of taking that statement. The first way is the one we have just considered: the subjective standpoint is completely devoid of substance, pure emptiness relieved only by a mute pointing gesture. There is another way of taking it, however, which leads to a completely different picture. Instead of asking what is left over when one subtracts all that can be described in language, one should ask instead what the *this* adds, over and above all that can be said in language.

The keyboard I am now using to write these words is, to take an example, an object that belongs to the world of the objective standpoint. It is also an object that is given to me in a way that it can never be given to any other person; even if that person could so arrange things that he had the very same view of the keyboard as I have, even if that person was my own doppelganger. From the objective standpoint, the possessive 'my' has of course a relative sense, referring to whoever happens to utter it. Yet it also seems to me – and this is an appearance whose reality as an appearance I cannot deny – that I can mean it in an absolute sense, a sense that I cannot communicate to anyone else. As we said earlier about the absolute sense of the pronoun 'I', its only function is that of a mute, inner pointing gesture, intended to indicate to myself my incommunicable sense of my own existence. Yet that mere gesture is sufficient to transform the keyboard into one which is *this* keyboard, not in the relative sense of the keyboard which some person – who happens to be me – is indicating on a particular occasion, but in the absolute sense which places the keyboard within the world of my subjective standpoint.

What then is the relation between the keyboard in front of me and *this* keyboard, in the unique and incommunicable sense in which I, the absolute, not the relative I mean it? Are they the same object, described in different ways, or are they different objects? The question seems straightforward enough; but as soon as we try to answer it we run into paradox. Talk of two worlds or realities, the subjective and the objective, immediately suggests that the objects must be different: there is the objective keyboard that exists in the objective world, and in addition my subjective keyboard that exists in my subjective world. Yet if there are two keyboards, then I myself am not, after all, perceiving the objective keyboard, nor does it have anything to do with the being I refer to as 'I'.

Suppose one tries to avoid this conclusion by saying that the absolute, subjective I perceives the subjective keyboard, while the relative, objective I perceives the objective keyboard. Now either the objective I is identical with the being I refer to as 'I', in which case the objective keyboard is my subjective keyboard, contrary to the initial hypothesis, or, alternatively, the objective I is not identical with the being I refer to as 'I', in which case once again neither it nor the objective keyboard it perceives has anything to do with the being I refer to as 'I'.

Nor would it serve any purpose, other than to create still further confusion, to distinguish the fact that the keyboard is there in front of me from the fact of my perceiving that the keyboard is there. There is of course no difficulty in allowing that one and the same keyboard can figure in two different kinds of fact, even though one fact concerns a person's experience while the other does not. However, since both facts may be construed either as facts about my subjective world or as facts about the objective world, we now have four facts, not two.

The only way out of these difficulties would seem to be to reject the hypothesis of two keyboards. Yet now it appears we cannot stop there. If there is only one keyboard, however it is described, then it seems there can only be one world that the keyboard is actually in. If that world is my subjective world, then by a similar process of reasoning no objects that I have anything to do with can belong to the objective world; which is tantamount to saying that as far as I am concerned there is no objective world. I find myself once more tempted to embrace Kantian egocentrism; all that prevents me from doing so this time is the thought that there is the empty *that*, the bare form of the objective standpoint, stripped of all content: a vision of a universe where all that exists is the world of my possible experience and the noumenal something of which it is the appearance; a position which indeed has little to recommend it, since it can only explain false judgement in terms of a virtually empty notion of 'failure to correspond with what noumenal reality determines appearances to be'. (One should add that this solipsism is not the position taken by the historical Kant or by Schopenhauer, both of whom believed they were justified – in the author's view wrongly – in viewing the world of my possible experience as merely one amongst many: for Kant, each experienced world corresponds to one of a plurality of noumenal subjects; for Schopenhauer, each corresponds to a physical brain.)

If, however, rebounding from that alternative, we say instead that the one and only world that my keyboard is in is not the subjective but the objective world, then by repeating that process of reasoning, my subjective world cannot after all contain anything other than an empty *this*, and we are back exactly where we started.

9. Despite these difficulties, we should persist in trying to find a way to justify the thought that my subjective standpoint can be viewed as a world of objects, and not a mere inarticulate pointing gesture. For we are exploring new territory, and it would be surprising if we did not make several false moves before finding the correct route. Now a first, unthinking reaction to our initial failure might be to say that the question whether the objective keyboard that anyone can see in front

of me is the same as or different from *this* keyboard, in the sense intended by the absolute, subjective I, is no more intelligible than the question of identity or non-identity which our refined cartesian dualist and identity theorist argued over, in trying to decide the status of such things as my mental state of perceiving the keyboard.

That would be completely wrong. We have seen that there is no such entity as the subjective quality or aspect of my mental state of perceiving a keyboard as that state presents itself to me alone, of which one could intelligibly ask whether it is a state of a non-physical subjective substance inside me or only a state of my objective, physical brain. When I talk of this keyboard, however, I do not intend to refer to an imaginary subjective object but only to the very same keyboard that anyone else can see. Yet, in the face of the difficulties of the last section, how could that be? – Where we fell into error was in letting ourselves talk too freely of two worlds, forgetting that this is a two which does not add up to a one, forgetting that the two worlds stand in a contradictory relation to one another, each staking a claim to the whole of reality.

Each world, one might say, claims possession of one and the same keyboard; only, in pulling in opposite directions, the two worlds attribute to it contradictory properties. The keyboard is the keyboard in front of me, the keyboard which a person is indicating to others on a particular occasion; but it is also *this* keyboard, in the sense which I cannot communicate to anyone else: the keyboard grasped in relation to *this*. This contradiction, like the contradiction between the subjective and objective standpoints themselves, is metaphysical, not logical. Indeed, it is now clear that the contradiction between the two standpoints is realized in every single object, however far removed in space or time; for no spatial or temporal boundary could be drawn beyond which objects ceased to be subjectively mine. Thus, my subjective standpoint which contains nothing in itself other than a mute, empty *this* takes objects from the world of the objective standpoint and makes them its own. In the process of doing so it adds nothing to them, and yet it changes them utterly.

10. It is not only objects which are transformed by the subjective standpoint. In addition, the spatial proximity of objects ceases to be relative and becomes absolute. That is because the absolute spatial position of every physical thing is fixed by its relation to the absolute I. For example, Nottingham is nearer than London for someone living in Sheffield, but further away for someone living in Plymouth. But as regards the Nottingham and London which belong to the world of my subjective standpoint, my Nottingham and my London, there is no

such relativity. For as long as I continue to live in Sheffield, Nottingham is absolutely nearer than London. If I were to move to Plymouth, then London would become absolutely nearer than Nottingham.

There is an intriguing remark apparently to a similar effect in Wittgenstein's *Zettel*: '"Put it here" – indicating the place with one's finger – that is giving an absolute spatial position. And if someone says that space is absolute he might produce this as an argument for it: "There is a place: here"' (§713). Wittgenstein is describing a speaker and hearer pair; but there are many speaker and hearer pairs, and at any one time only one includes the person who is myself. As far as that pair is concerned, the object being indicated may or may not be nearer to one person than it is to the other. If it is, say, nearer to me, then in the world of my subjective standpoint it is absolutely nearer. If, on the other hand, one considers that same speaker and hearer pair from the objective standpoint, then no absolute spatial position has been indicated: all one can say in this case, as in every other case, is that the position known as 'here' is relative to the occasion of utterance. For finite beings such as ourselves, indexicals such as 'here' and 'there', 'this' and 'that' are no doubt indispensable; the falsity of Leibniz's principle of the identity of indiscernibles shows that we cannot secure reference to places and things that occupy them in purely general terms. (Strawson argues against Leibniz' view, and in favour of the necessity of demonstrative reference in ch. 4 of *Individuals*, setting his discussion within the context of reference to particulars by a speaker and hearer pair.) Yet to make the point Wittgenstein appears to be making requires something extra: the recognition of the reality of my subjective standpoint.

11. In the light of the transformations of both objects and spatial relations brought about by the subjective standpoint, we can look again at the metaphors or analogies which we used earlier to explain why the subjective and objective standpoints cannot be added together to form a totality. It was said that each standpoint is too large to be added to, since it fills up all the available logical space that could be occupied by reality. It was also said that the characteristic shape of each standpoint, its symmetry or asymmetry, necessarily imposes itself on the other, depending on which of the two standpoints one takes as one's fixed starting point. In both cases, we were dealing with the subjective and objective standpoints as understood by the egocentrist and nonegocentrist respectively. This in fact introduced a certain distortion, since neither the subjective nor the objective

standpoint has exactly the characteristics which the egocentrist or nonegocentrist respectively attribute to it.

Now at last we are in a position to offer an explanation without distortion. The two standpoints are each too large, because each contains the same objects; and you cannot add an object to itself. Nor is there any way in which their different shapes would permit them to be fitted together, since there is no compromise between viewing spatial proximity as absolute and viewing it as relative. The subjective and objective standpoints, we may say in summary, order the very same things in incompatible ways; these orderings are not imposed from without but appear to each one of us as intrinsic to the things themselves – there is no escape from being here and at the very same time somewhere neither near nor far. Yet even saying that is not to say the one thing that stands in the way of totality. Every incompatible ordering would finally fit together in the whole were it not for the existence of my unique ordering, my subjective standpoint.

We have said much about the subjective standpoint, but have not yet explicitly answered the question of the form in which its reality should be expressed. The reader will recall that our task was not to reconcile the subjective and objective standpoints, something which we are not yet in a position to do, but only to find the terms in which the question of reconciliation may be intelligibly posed. It should be clear by now, however, that nothing in fact needs to be added to what has been said already. The subjective standpoint transforms all objects, making them mine. In so doing, it imposes an ordering on the world which gives an absolute sense to spatial proximity. But this transformation, this imposition take place only insofar as the world appears to me in that guise, in the light of the incommunicable sense of my own unique existence. I cannot express that appearance to anyone else, and yet I cannot deny its reality as appearance. It is indeed a reality constituted by its own appearance, a subject matter which is not the subject matter of any possible judgement. For as soon as I make judgements about objects, the world ceases to be my world, objects cease to be my objects, the absolute I is replaced by the relative I.

In short: the subjective standpoint is a world every bit as rich and detailed as the world of the objective standpoint. Yet its reality hangs by the slenderest possible thread. It is real because I take it to be real, and only for so long as I take it to be real. By the slenderest possible thread the objective world is held at bay, yet no power in the universe can break that thread, so long as I exist.

Part two

"All truth is simple." – Is that not a compound lie?'

Part two

9 Attributes of my subjective world

1. OUR investigations have reached a watershed. The break with the traditional idea of totality means that from now on we shall be dealing with a two-world metaphysic in its most radical form: a dual reality which cannot even be thought together as one. Whereas previously we talked of subjective and objective standpoints, we may now with equal right talk of subjective and objective worlds. For each standpoint is indeed a universe complete and in its own right, and not part of some larger whole. Both worlds have equal right to be called real, yet neither world can be added to the other to make a single all-encompassing reality, for each claims the very same space occupied by the other.

This space, we now know, is not mere logical space, conceived by analogy with physical space, as it appeared in the opposed visions of the egocentrist and the nonegocentrist. It is physical space. For we have discovered that the subjective and objective worlds contain the very same objects: the subjective standpoint takes all its objects from the objective world, having nothing extra of its own to contribute other than the bare *this*, which makes spatial proximity absolute, and all objects mine. We found that the property of being *this* or being mine stands in a relation of absolute conflict with the property of being the object to which the person now speaking is pointing. The former is defined in relation to the absolute I of my subjective world, while the latter is defined in relation to the relative I of the objective world.

Thus, in pulling objects in opposite directions, the contradiction is realized and maintained with a tension that never once relaxes: no object escapes, nor can any be torn asunder. To acknowledge the reality of this contradiction, its realization in things themselves, is to concede that there can be no hope of an end to the conflict: there is no compromise between viewing the world from the standpoint of my absolute I, and viewing my relative I from the standpoint of a world of other relative I's. Having conceded that much, however, we have taken only the first step towards an account of the relation between the subjective and objective standpoints, an account which would in some way reconcile the two perpetually conflicting worlds, allowing each to press its claims without destroying the other, so satisfying the demand for an adequate metaphysic.

2. Our predicament illustrates a recurring feature of metaphysical thinking. Once the materials for a problem have been assembled, we can, by working backwards, say what form a solution to the problem should take. In doing so, however, we find that we must make use of some central concept or concepts of which we have at best only a very partial grasp: as if we ourselves cannot yet enjoy the fruits that our inquiries have yielded. A good example of this is F.H. Bradley's repeated use, in Book II of *Appearance and Reality* of the formula: 'For what is *possible,* and what a general principle compels us to say must be, that certainly is' (p. 196). The unsolved problem for Bradley is to understand in specific detail how the contradictions in appearances are 'transformed' in the Absolute into something that is not contradictory, as his general argument claims to show they must be; while all he can offer is a general account, based on analogy with the unbroken wholeness of 'immediate experience', of how they might be.

The concept of metaphysical contradiction plays the same central but problematic role in our system as the transformation of contradiction plays in Bradley's. While we can, in working backwards, report the kinds of thing that one would be justified in saying about the concept, if only one could secure its meaning and validity, we do not yet have any certain sense whether what the course of the argument obliges us to say is meaningful; even though we know in the abstract that it must be. That is something that can be fully known and appreciated only with the benefit of hindsight; when, as in our case, the subjective and objective standpoints have finally been reconciled – if indeed such a thing is possible. (Bradley remained sceptical about the prospects for the philosopher ever having such explicit knowledge of the Absolute.)

Now, someone who was determined, despite all setbacks, to follow the way of the nonegocentrist or egocentrist might try in a similar way to recast our refutation of nonegocentrism or of egocentrism as a problem to be solved, arguing that some loophole can and must be found, if only one looks hard enough. In the end, it is only our rock bottom sense of what is feasible that decides that it is futile to base ones metaphysic either on a power of judgement that never once dares to enter the world, or on an illusion of an I that I can never grasp as such. We have made our decision, and must now follow the argument wherever it may lead. If someone thinks than an alternative decision would lead to more fruitful consequences, our response is simply, 'Go ahead and try.' The attitude of the metaphysician, in the face of the limitations of the human mind and its susceptibility to error, can only be pragmatic: the true metaphysic is the one that works.

3. The project that will occupy the remainder of this chapter is to work out the consequences of a two-world metaphysic for the essential attributes of my subjective world. What qualities must the world of my subjective standpoint possess, as constitutive of its very nature, at all times? What are the boundaries of my subjective world, the limiting conditions beyond which it ceases to be identifiable as my subjective world? The answer to that question will lead us beyond an account of the form of the subjective standpoint, the assertion that it is a world in its own right, to the delineation of its actual shape or structure.

The most fundamental condition for being my subjective world is to be the world of a being who exists for the objective standpoint. Every essential attribute that I possess as a member of the objective world corresponds to an essential attribute of my subjective world. Now we saw in chapter 5 that a subject who makes judgements can be identified from the objective standpoint only if that subject has a body of some kind, is able to express its beliefs in language, and is capable of acting on those beliefs. Only on those three conditions can the reliability of the subject's power of judgement be a subject matter for other persons to form judgements about; only then does the existence of the self as a thinking subject present an aspect to other points of view. It follows that my subjective world must be the world of a subject who has a body, uses language, and performs actions. It is clear, however, that all these conditions could be satisfied by a being who was very different from a human being. The question is, how different?

A second question is how my subjective states, my pleasures and pains, my tactile, auditory or visual sensations, or my beliefs and desires as objects of my introspection, can appear both in the subjective and objective worlds. How am I to explain, for example, the relation between *this* pain in my thumb and the objective pain which presents aspects to other points of view, without reverting to either to either a dualism or identity of subjective and objective stuffs? The answer is implicit in what has already been discussed at some length; it remains only to render that answer explicit.

Finally, a third question arises, which appears to raise a serious obstacle to accepting the fundamental condition that my subjective world is the world of a being who exists for the objective standpoint. Back in chapter 1, we saw how the question of my own death appears to sever once and for all any intelligible relation between the subjective and objective standpoints. From the objective standpoint, I am a being who necessarily possesses a body of some kind, so long as I continue to exist. As we argued in chapter 5, even if my visible, human body is not essential for my continued existence, my disembodied soul body must still present an aspect to other points of view; it must be made of some kind of material which other subjects, if only alien beings or angels, could perceive. Yet all forms of material body are capable in principle of wearing out or being destroyed. For material is necessarily composite: anything that occupies space can always be thought of as being broken down or fashioned into other forms. From the objective standpoint, therefore, death can never be a logical impossibility. From my subjective standpoint, by contrast, my death seems inconceivable. To represent my death to myself as a possibility in relation to my subjective world, I first have to represent a world where all objects are mine, where spatial proximity is absolutely determined in relation to my absolute I, and then represent the result when the absolute I is taken away. Only this is something it seems I cannot do. How then is the apparent logical contradiction between the possibility of my death and its impossibility to be admitted without falling into absurdity?

4. Returning to the first question, How different might my experience have been from the experience of a human being, while still satisfying the three conditions for a subjective world? Since there necessarily exist points of view other than my own, it is ruled out that I should ever have been, or should ever become God; if by the term 'God' one understands a ubiquitous being who grasps the world from all possible points of view. The standpoint of such a deity is necessarily objective (or 'super-objective') not subjective; whether or not that is a coherent notion is something we shall need to investigate when we consider the form and attributes of the objective world.

To say that I could not possibly grasp the world from all points of view, however, leaves open the possibility that I might possess more than one, perhaps many, points of view. The simplest case would be if I existed as two separate bodies, all of whose knowledge and perception was shared by a single mind. The connection we are envisaging is closer even than total telepathic communication, as that notion is popularly understood, since the two bodies would not only perceive and know as one, but would speak and act as one also.

One question which this raises is how, if I were to acquire a second point of view, a second body, I should know that I was not merely hallucinating. Certainly, my experiences to begin with would be very confusing. My situation would in some respects be comparable to the confusion suffered by someone totally blind from birth, whose sight is restored by an operation. However, in time I should learn to co-ordinate the actions of my two bodies, in just the same way that I am now able to co-ordinate the movements of my right and left hands. If, on the other hand, the two bodies lived in different parts of the world, or even on different planets, I should find myself living a radically double life. The only way it seems I could ever be certain that one or other of my apparent experiences was not a permanent hallucination would be if the two bodies met up; although I could undoubtedly acquire much evidence in advance that pointed towards that conclusion; for example, if this body were to visit countries or planets that the other body had been to, or if this body acquired mental or physical skills that the other body had learned, or, best of all, if I was able to achieve certain objectives by co-ordinating the actions of my two bodies at a distance.

The question would, however, always have an authoritative answer as far as the objective standpoint was concerned. For even if no human being could ever know the answer for certain, it would still be possible in principle for some intelligent subject, say, an angel who could take in different planets at a glance, or an alien scientist who possessed the skills or forms of perception required to uncover the causal basis for the co-ordination of the movements of the two bodies, to determine whether or not the two bodies were indeed bodies of one and the same agent.

5. We are now in a position to answer a question postponed from chapter 4, arising out of Quinton's thought experiment of a being who regularly travels between two apparently spatially unrelated worlds. There is no doubt that the description of the experience – say, of seeming to wake up in the second world as soon as one falls asleep in the first – is coherent; the question for us is how the experience is to be interpreted within a theory of subjective and objective worlds. We suggested on behalf of the egocentrist that the objection that while I

am in this world I can say what I like about the other world and never be wrong could be met by having a trans-world television network, whose news reports I could check against my apparent memory of events in the other world. That move will not work for us, however. To begin with, if I was the only person who seemed to travel between this world and the other world, then no-one else could ever have the authority to correct my judgements about the other world, or judge their reliability: as far as others were concerned, the trans-world television news reports would appear merely as an inexplicable phenomenon, whose significance only I was in a position to judge.

A better prospect seems to be offered by a variant which Quinton considers to the thought experiment: that a number of persons travel to the other world when they go to sleep and meet up there. At first sight, this does seem sufficient to settle the question of the real possibility of spatially unrelated spaces: surely in such a case a philosopher would have no right to insist that the spaces must be spatially related, despite the fact that the 'most thorough geographical investigations' ('Spaces and Times' p. 143) failed to discover the location of the other world? We shall argue, however, that merely adding other trans-world travellers does not supply sufficient material to justify such an interpretation: for the requisite authority to correct one another's judgements would still be lacking.

Suppose for the sake of argument that we do claim this authority. In the world we are now in, call it world 1, there exist certain investigative procedures for resolving disagreements about events that happen in world 1. In addition, there are shared beliefs concerning events in world 2, based wholly on memory; in this case, resolution of disagreements ultimately depends on taking a majority vote. How are we then to conceive of the truth of our beliefs about world 2? What is it that we conceive ourselves to be agreeing on? There are two alternatives. Either we regard at least some of the ways of establishing truth in world 1 as capable in principle of being extended to verify claims made about world 2, even though in practice we are unable to do so; or we rule out that possibility on principle. In the latter case, the truth of judgements about world 2 reduces to the most consistent story that can be told on the basis of some maximal set of memory judgements about world 2 concerning which there is minimal disagreement. We ought then logically to regard world 2 as having the status of a collective dream or hallucination; although in practice that would be no easy thing to do, for it would seem as if, in travelling back and forth between one world and the other, we had to keep changing our minds as to which was the real world and which was the dream. (It would be pointless to define truth in world 2, from

110

our present vantage point in world 1, as what we would be able to investigate were we now in world 2; for that involves appeal to a counterfactual whose meaning cannot be given prior to resolving the very question at issue.)

In the former case, belief in the possibility of extending the investigative procedures available to us in world 1 entails, at the very least, belief in the existence of an answer – albeit one we might never know – to the question, Where is world 2 now? Refusal to acknowledge the legitimacy of that question would amount to a belief in magic: any hocus pocus that seemed to corroborate one another's memories about world 2 (even inexplicable trans-world TV news reports) would do equally well. If, then, the two worlds are to be regarded as equally real but spatially unrelated, no-one who shares my predicament, who like me has to wait to be magically whisked away from one world to the other, can have the authority to correct my judgements, now made in world 1, about events in world 2. The only being who could have such authority would have to be conceived of by analogy with the angel or alien being of our previous thought experiment: either a being who could take in spatially unrelated worlds at a glance, or else a being who possessed the mental powers and forms of perception required to investigate the causal connections between the spatially unrelated worlds. In either case, the world in which such a hypothetical being perceived and acted would not be our spatial world or worlds but rather whatever quasi-spatial or non-spatial reality was the ultimate source of spatial appearances.

6. Returning to our previous thought experiment, the admission that I might come to possess more than one point of view on our spatial world obliges us to qualify what was said in the last chapter about the imposition of an ordering on objects, through my subjective standpoint, which renders spatial proximity absolute. If I possessed two bodies, for example, then what was nearer to one would be further away from the other. Being nearer or further as such would have to remain relative spatial properties. On the other hand, provided that my bodies were in the same geographical location, they could still determine the absolute spatial property of being nearer to a second geographical location than to a third. In principle, however, my bodies could be as far apart as any two objects in the universe; furthermore, we have allowed that having just two bodies is the simplest possible case of multiple viewpoints. How then could any form of spatial proximity be defined as absolute in relation to my absolute I, if my point of view could, in principle, be scattered across the whole universe?

The answer is that so long as I possess a subjective world, so long as my point of view on the universe is limited in some manner or other, it will always be possible to define some complex notion of spatial proximity which is rendered absolute in relation to my absolute I. Even if nearer and further as such, or nearer-to-a-given-geographical-location and further-from-a-given-geographical location remain relative, the set of all my different viewpoints will always determine a unique orientation which differs from the orientations of all other subjects, in virtue of which the sum of all my relative proximities to objects, that is to say, the conjunction of all true statements of the form: a is nearer to __ than it is to__, b is nearer to __ than it is to__, c is nearer to __ than it is to__, where a, b, c etc. are my scattered bodies, would be rendered false if any substitutions were made throughout of names of bodies which were not my own for 'a' or 'b' or 'c' etc. This orientation, which is an absolute feature of my subjective world, becomes merely relative when viewed from the objective standpoint. For every subject has its own unique orientation: in the objective world, there is no such fact as the fact that the orientation of the set {a,b,c...} is not merely an orientation but my orientation.

Note that the necessity that I should be an agent and not a passive observer sets further limits to my subjective world beyond the requirement that my point of view should not be the ubiquitous viewpoint of a deity. I could not have existed as a body capable only of perceiving objects, nor as any number of such bodies. Nor would it suffice, in order to have a point of view at a certain location, merely to have a detached sense organ situated there, which relayed information back to a main body located somewhere else. I am where my body is, the body which acts, and not wherever my sense organs happen to be. Thus, if it is possible that my point of view might be scattered across the universe, then that could only happen if I existed as a multiplicity of bodies which collectively thought and acted as one agent. It would not be enough merely to possess sense organs located in various parts of the universe, and just one active body here in this room. (One interesting question of detail which this raises is under what circumstances the sending of an unmanned space probe to another planet would become a form of space travel: according to our account, this is perfectly feasible.)

By contrast, it is by no means necessary that each of my scattered bodies be capable of making itself understood to the local language-using inhabitants of whichever planet it happened to find itself on. I possess language by virtue of the fact that I have learned to speak a language and at least one of my bodies has the means to make itself

112

understood to other users of that language. My leg or my foot, as it were, do not have to speak for themselves: I speak for them (though of course I might still contrive to use them to tap out a code and receive the coded messages of others if unforeseen circumstances, say, a disabling accident, made it necessary to do so).

7. Just as a single self-conscious subject might occupy two or more bodies, so one and the same body might be occupied by two or more self-conscious subjects. The autonomous subjects would each have their own experiences and their own memories which none shared with any of the others, and would exist intermittently, each in its own time. For example, I might find that I was aware of waking up to live a normal life on Tuesdays, Wednesdays and Fridays; while I learned from the reports of others that another subject owned my body on Mondays, Thursdays and Saturdays; while a third took it over on Sundays. However, things are not quite as simple as that. Would it not, after all, be possible for me to remember, perhaps with feelings of acute embarrassment, what my alter ego did last Saturday, for example, as actions which he did while I passively observed? Why indeed should I not enjoy – or suffer – special access to the experiences of each of my alter egos, without having to identify my subjective world with theirs?

Before we can answer that question, it is first necessary to clear up the following point. It is sometimes claimed that continuity of memory is not sufficient for personal identity, since a person might under certain circumstances come to disown categorically his past life. For example (it might be said), remembering that Klempner was once deeply in love with a certain person does not necessarily entail my remembering that I was deeply in love with that person. It is not simply that I no longer feel any trace of that emotion; nor even that my feelings are now a distant and fading memory. It is rather that the emotion that Klempner felt belonged to a person whom I, in the very different circumstances in which I now find myself and after all the changes I have been through, can no longer identify as having been mine: I have thrown off that burden from my past, and no longer accept responsibility for what 'I' did then.

However, two issues are being confused here. It may be the case, although this would be difficult to prove, that the subject of praise or blame, pride or regret, the person as that notion is understood in our society, has an identity which depends upon something more than mere continuity of awareness or memory, together with the objective conditions which that entails. One might claim that taking responsibility for my past actions involves a positive act of self-identification; of recognizing my memories as truly my own, my past actions as not merely the actions performed by the former owner of this body, but as actions that I did. Yet the very possibility of explaining such dramatic discontinuity in my sense of personal identity depends on a prior identity, the apparent continuation, through all my changes, of one and the same subjective world; and it is this that is the more fundamental notion.

In the case of split or multiple selves, a new element is introduced, namely the fact that only one agent can be in control of my body at any one time. That would seem to raise the possibility that the alter egos could all be subject to the same experiences, even though they had to take turns to be the agent. While waiting for its turn, an alter ego could only passively observe the actions of the subject controlling the shared body. Now it might seem that such a possibility is ruled out by the requirement that each conscious subject must at all times be capable of being identified as such from the objective standpoint; it must be an agent and language user so long as it actually exists as a conscious thinker of thoughts. If I were able to gain special access to the experiences of my alter egos, that could not, as a matter of logic, be through my directly sharing their experiences, but only through some process of communication between one agent and another. However, we still have to reckon with the case of the paralysed doctor, discussed near the end of chapter 5. While my experience of the activities of my alter ego last Saturday could originally only have had the logical status of a dream or hallucination, it would still be possible for me, on regaining control of my body, to transform the experience retrospectively into one which, at that actual time, was the subject matter of my thought and judgement; to bring it about, through my present acts of judging, that certain conscious thoughts existed in the past.

8. Our second question concerned the status of my subjective states, my thoughts, feelings and sensations, within my subjective world. How does the two-world metaphysic differ in its approach from either refined cartesian dualism or the opposing identity theory? The reader will recall that our cartesian dualist, unlike Descartes, conceded that the entity which I refer to, say, as a pain will always be correlated with objective happenings from which all its qualities could in principle be inferred by others. However, the objective bodily state of pain which others are able to identify, and the indescribable thisness of my pain as it is for me remain two separate things: one physical and the other non-physical. The identity theorist then seemed to contradict the dualist by maintaining that the indescribable thisness of my pain

114

and the objectively identified pain were only different aspects of one and the same physical state. If both these positions are wrong, or indeed, as we argued in chapter 6, if they are only nominally different versions of the very same false theory, what then is the true account?

It may seem at first that this is an impossible question to answer. If one allows, as we have done, that there is such a notion as the thisness of my pain, my pain as it occurs within my subjective world, then it would seem that there is no third alternative between either identifying it with my state of pain as it occurs in the world of the objective standpoint, or refusing to make such an identification. What other choice could there be between identity and non-identity? If I talk about an object x and then about an object y, then surely another person always has the right to ask me whether x is the same object as y or not.

The clue to solving this puzzle may be found in what we discovered in the last chapter about the way ordinary, spatial objects exist both in the objective world and in my subjective world. We gave the example of my computer keyboard, which was found to possess the contradictory properties of being both the keyboard to which the person now speaking is pointing, and also *this* keyboard. Although the properties are, in a metaphysical sense, contradictory, there is only one keyboard. It possesses the first property as an object to be found in the objective world, and the second property as an object belonging to my subjective world. Yet because the subjective and objective worlds cannot be added together to form a single totality, there is no standpoint from which the conflict between viewing the keyboard in relation to my relative I, as something which I can indicate to others by the act of pointing, and viewing it in relation to my absolute I, as an object whose thisness I cannot communicate to anyone else, could be seen to be only apparent and not real.

Now this is exactly what we should say about the thisness of my pain. One and the same pain, that is to say, a physical event in the brain accompanied by a characteristic feeling in a certain part of the body, occurs both in the objective world and in my subjective world. However, that in no way vindicates the identity theory, since the two worlds cannot be thought together as one. As in the example of the keyboard, the properties of being *this* pain and being the pain suffered by the person now speaking remain in perpetual contradiction. Nor, however, can the admission of two worlds be seen as a vindication of dualism. For the dualist's claim presupposes that the objects said to be separate and not identical, the state of my non-physical mind and the state of my physical body, must exist in one and the same world for the claim to make sense.

From the vantage point of a two-world metaphysic, it is possible to explain the error made by both the refined cartesian dualist and identity theorist, as the result of a running together of two very different senses of 'subjective'. In one sense, we may distinguish between a person's subjective mode of access to her own mental states, and the objective mode of access which others possess. Clearly, a self-conscious subject's awareness of her own mental states arises in a completely different way from an external observer's awareness of those same states; that is indeed one of the defining characteristics of the mental. The precise nature of this difference is a question for the philosophy of mind. The point which is relevant to us is that the distinction between the subjective and objective modes of access to mental states operates wholly within the objective standpoint. In investigating the nature of the mental, for example, in confronting such issues as Nagel raises concerning the possibility or impossibility of mental-physical reduction as such, no reference need be made to the subjective standpoint.

The subjective standpoint, as opposed to the subjective mode of access to one's mental states, becomes an issue only when one moves from the philosophy of mind to metaphysics proper. As we saw in chapter 7, it was the possibility of explaining, purely from the objective standpoint, the unique nature of a person's subjective mode of access to her own consciousness which persuaded the nonegocentrist that the subjective standpoint can only be an illusion. Yet if the appearance of my unique subjective world cannot be dismissed in this way, then I must recognize a distinction between the way my subjective mode of access presents itself to the objective standpoint, and the way it figures in my subjective world. From the objective standpoint, the pain suffered by the person now speaking is known to that person by his subjective mode of access, a fact which any other person is in a position to recognize. From my subjective standpoint, by contrast, the thisness of my pain is something I cannot communicate to anyone else. That is not because pain is a subjective phenomenon, however, for I can no more communicate the thisness of the keyboard which I am now using to type these words. The mistake made by both the refined cartesian dualist and identity theorist is in confusing my subjective mode of access to my pain with its thisness, with the incommunicable property which it possesses when I grasp it from my subjective standpoint.

9. The third question which an account of the attributes of my subjective world has to answer is how the possibility of my own death is to be accommodated. In the last chapter, it was said that no spatial

or temporal boundary can be drawn beyond which objects cease to be mine: in populating itself with objects from the objective world, my subjective standpoint is in no position to pick and choose – it has to take them all. The subjective world of objects that spreads outwards from this point of reference, the place where I now stand, thus appears as having a past that stretches back to a time before my birth and a future that projects forwards to a time after my death.

When my absolute I represents to itself the possibility that my daughter, for example, might outlive me, my daughter does not lose the incommunicable property of being *this* human individual, even though at that future time I am no longer there to call her *this*. Nor, in the world that my absolute I represents as continuing after my death, can any object come into existence which does not trace its ancestry back to objects which are *this*. Indeed, the objects in my subjective world which existed yesterday or will exist tomorrow are located in a map whose co-ordinates are fixed by the place where I now stand, not the place where I stood yesterday or the place where I shall stand tomorrow. Any story I can now tell about what might have happened or what might happen to the objects in my subjective world at any time, however far removed in the past or future, makes use of those same co-ordinates.

Yet it is no less true to say that my subjective world cannot exist without me. I may tell a story about my own death in terms of the co-ordinates of my subjective world as it exists now, but when I think about what it would take to make the story true, I find that I am not after all thinking of *my* death, but only the death of some person with my attributes. It is not sufficient for my death that a person whom I trace back through space and time to the person standing here, in these shoes, should die. It is not the death of my Klempner that I am now trying to focus my mind on, a person whom I locate in future states of my subjective world alongside *this* keyboard or my Sheffield: it is I, the absolute I that I am trying to think of as ceasing to exist. At that future time, there will no longer be such a place as here, no such thing as being *this* or mine. There will be no setting of co-ordinates in virtue of which objects in the past or future are represented as being *this* or mine. However, that is the one thing it seems I cannot represent to myself in terms of the map whose co-ordinates are fixed by the place where I now stand. While I can think the death of my Klempner, the ceasing to exist of a person whom I locate at future times within my subjective world, I cannot think the death of I, the sole and irreplaceable foundation for the existence of my subjective world.

10. The fact that, as a material being, Klempner is subject to death and decay just like all other living things, is a fact about the objective world, and, since the two worlds share all the same objects, a fact about my subjective world. By contrast, the possibility that I, the absolute I should die, as opposed to the death either of the objective Klempner or my subjective Klempner, the thought of the sheer contingency of my subjective world, is something I cannot in any way comprehend. Yet if I cannot think of the existence of the absolute I as contingent, then it would seem to follow that I must think of it as necessary. I can never cease to be. However, that seems to contradict the principle that every essential attribute which I possess as a member of the objective world corresponds to an essential attribute of my subjective world. There would seem to be just two alternatives, if we wish to avoid this contradiction. Either I am wrong in thinking that I must be like all other conscious beings in being subject to death and decay, or I am wrong in thinking that I cannot conceive of the ceasing to exist of my subjective world.

Let us consider the first alternative. One might argue that, on pain of logical inconsistency, I must regard the inconceivability of the death of I from my subjective standpoint as proving, via the principle of correspondence between the subjective and objective worlds, either that I am the one conscious being that cannot die, or else that the death of my living body must necessarily lead to my reincarnation. Reincarnation would only solve the problem, however, if the reincarnated being retained a memory of its former existence; otherwise there is no basis for the continuity of my subjective world. Since I do not now remember any previous reincarnations, I must conclude that before the birth of this body, the absolute I did not exist. But the problem of how I am to represent, within my subjective world, the non-existence of I before my birth, the birth of my Klempner, is exactly the same as the problem of how I am to conceive of the non-existence of I after my Klempner's death. It is therefore no solution to say, either that my living body cannot die, or that after my death I shall experience my first reincarnation.

What about the other alternative? Is it possible that I am wrong in thinking that I cannot conceive of the ceasing to exist of my subjective world? It might be claimed that this thought does rest on a simple fallacy. For it would be obviously fallacious to argue that the physical universe could not cease to exist, on the grounds that every possible state of the universe must be the state of something and not the state of nothing. On the contrary, while there are many possible states of the universe, states in which it exists in some form or other, as something, there is in addition the possibility that it should cease to

118

exist, that it should cease to be something. Similarly, one might argue, there are many possible states of my subjective world; and in addition there is the possibility that my subjective world should cease to exist. Why aren't the two cases parallel in this way?

The reason why the cases are not parallel is that, while the possible situation in which the universe ceases to exist is not a possible state 'of' anything, the possible situation in which the absolute I ceased to exist would have to be a possible state of the objective world. For if it is not necessary that I should live, then it is contingent; and surely the only circumstance it can be contingent on is the continued existence either of a living human person, or of a soul, identifiable from the objective standpoint. The difficulty in conceiving of how my subjective world might cease to exist lies in the fact that, as soon as I think of my death from the objective standpoint, I have left my subjective world behind. Just as the existence of a person with my attributes in the objective world in no way explains why there should exist my subjective world, so my thought of the ceasing to exist of that objective person fails to connect in any intelligible way with the putative event of my subjective world ceasing to exist. The contingency of my subjective world, if it is contingent, is absolute and inexplicable.

If neither alternative is acceptable, then there must be a third we have overlooked. Earlier it was said that in order to represent my death to myself as something that happens to my subjective world, I first have to represent a world where all objects are *this* or mine, where spatial proximity is absolutely determined in relation to my absolute I, and then try to represent the result when the absolute I is taken away. The problem is not in conceiving of what would be left behind after the absolute I was removed: there remains the objective world, a world of objects which are no longer *this* or mine, where all spatial properties are once again relative. The real difficulty is in conceiving of what it could possibly mean to take the absolute I away, when there is no objective ground for its being there in the first place. I might, for example, imagine that my absolute I has existed for just one second, or that it is regularly taken away and then returned to existence, in both cases without my noticing. When I pretend to myself that I am representing such a possibility, however, I am not actually thinking of anything at all. Thus, the reason why my subjective, absolute I, the foundation and sole support of my subjective world cannot be destroyed is not that it somehow possesses the power to resist death, but rather that its continued identity through time is purely imaginary. Only something that continues through time can cease to exist. Yet my subjective world, as a reality

119

constituted by its own appearance, only appears to continue; and that appearance itself is something which neither continues nor fails to continue. My subjective world can never die, can never cease to continue, for with every new moment it is as if it had never existed, and will continue no longer than that very moment.

10 Non-continuity of my subjective world

1. WITH the non-continuity of my subjective world, we have yet another paradox on our hands, a result at first so unbelievable that it casts serious doubt on the arguments leading up to it. My absolute I, we are told, has never existed and will never exist but only exists now. Yet that seems impossible. With every moment that I am conscious, I am aware of myself coming from the past and going towards the future. My experience possesses an unbroken flow which links past, present and future together in a way that cannot in any way be halted or split asunder, or analysed in thought into static elements, without reducing my existence to a meaningless jumble of fragmentary feelings and images. The continuity of my awareness, the flow of conscious experience, cannot be denied without absurdity.

There are three sources to this objection. The first two derive from long-standing problems in the philosophy of time. The problem about the flow of experience goes back to the paradox of Zeno's arrow, which cannot be said to move because at every instant it occupies exactly the space it occupied when at rest, and therefore must also be at rest. The duration of now, on the other hand, is a problem first raised by Augustine, in his attempt to define a notion of the present which we are able to live through, which is not a mere knife-edge separating the future from the past. All we need say in response to either of these problems is that, in asserting that the absolute I only exists now or in the present, we have not made any attempt to define the present or measure its duration – and for the purposes of this book need not do so – other than to say that it is the time during which an appearance actually appears. An experience ceases to be now just when the question meaningfully arises whether one's

121

apparent recollection corresponds to the what really occurred at the time.

The third source of the objection rests on a confusion between the subjective and objective standpoints. The extended temporal continuity of my awareness, the connection of my past self to my present self through memory, is a fact not about my absolute, subjective I but rather about my objective, relative I, the individual known as Klempner. As a direct consequence of this, it is necessarily also a fact about the individual in my subjective world I call my Klempner. My continued existence, my survival as a subject of experience is a subject matter for judgement, a fact which I show in the continuity of my speech and actions, and which others discover in constructing their map of reality. If this is one objective fact I myself cannot be said to judge in the strict sense, that is only because it is a presupposition of my being capable of any rational judgement; but I am aware of it all the same, and can reflect on that awareness. And because my Klempner is the same object as the objective Klempner, I discover that same continuity of awareness as an object of reference within my subjective world.

As for my subjective world itself, however, the articulated whole that is brought into being through my subjective standpoint, it has already been established as one if its defining characteristics that it is not the subject matter of any possible judgement; and therefore not even the judgement that it continues. All that can be said about my subjective world, as a reality distinct from the objective, is that it is *this*. If I were to go on to say that the *this* existed just one second ago, I should be saying more than one is logically permitted to say about a reality constituted by its own appearance, for that would be to claim, absurdly, that the present appearance of a past *this* corresponds with a real *this* existing in the past.

Yet after one has said all that it is logically correct to say, there remains the feeling that, having sought to maintain the real appearance of an incommunicable sense of one's own existence in defiance of the nonegocentrist, we have had the rug pulled from under our feet. From my subjective standpoint, all that I, the absolute I, have to call my own is something that I cannot be said to possess, for a possession is something one keeps for some length of time. Nor do I succeed, when I utter the words 'my subjective world', in referring to the same thing as I referred to a moment ago; for a moment ago there was neither my subjective world nor an absolute I, but only the objective world and an individual like me struggling to express what seems to lie at the very limit of meaningful expression.

2. Later, we shall test this result with a thought experiment not unlike the story of the doppelganger which we used to defeat the nonegocentrist. In the new thought experiment, the non-continuity of the subjective world will come to the fore. First, however, let us pause for a while to reflect on our pessimistic conclusion, in order to see if there is not an alternative way of looking at it; one in which we might after all take some grain of comfort. For it is not uncommon in metaphysics to find that an apparently extreme position has a flip side: a way of grasping it which is in one sense equivalent, but in another sense completely opposite from the way it first presents itself.

Sometimes the inversion can happen in the blink of an eye. I now know that there is nothing to my existence as I alone sense it but a momentary light, which is just as soon extinguished. From the point of view of my subjective world, the word 'I' is no more than an unmeaning cry of protest against the objective order. I exist, therefore...nothing. The cry has hardly passed my lips, when the I that asserted its absolute unique reality is no longer. – What is it then, one might ask, that we strive for in all the desperate measures each of us takes to preserve the existence of our bodies, our objective selves? A human life is valuable as such; mine is a human life, and therefore possesses as much value as any other; as much, but no more. Why should I especially fear my death?

There are three separate issues here. In many cases, death involves suffering, and my own suffering matters to me, not just because I believe suffering in general to be a bad thing, but because my suffering is mine. Pain would not be pain were it not for the fact that, for all the persons to whom its existence gave cause for distress, there was one individual whom it actually hurt. My desire to avoid death as such, on the other hand, is something which I possess in common with all conscious living things: that indispensable spring of action which biologists call the survival instinct. There is, however, a third element: the fear that my subjective world might be taken away from me. In the light of the non-continuity of the subjective world, this fear may now be seen to have no object, and therefore no content. While my subjective world is given to me during this present moment, it is not something which I may logically be said to keep or possess; nor then, as a matter of logic, can I ever lose it or have it taken away.

3. Since antiquity, philosophers have striven to prove that the fear of death is irrational. Our result has little impact on the two traditional views, either that death is not to be feared because our essential selves or souls do not really 'die', as Socrates argues in Plato's *Phaedo*, or, in complete contrast, that there is nothing to fear from

death precisely because there is no subject that suffers the dissolution of our material bodies, as the atomist Epicurus argued. Neither argument is addressed to the metaphysical illusion that my subjective world might be taken away.

The first view assumes only the instinct for survival, our unquestioned desire to keep on living, to enjoy more of the same. Contrary to physical appearances, human beings do survive the death of their material bodies. While it is natural that human beings should take precautions against untimely death, philosophical reflection teaches us that what we call death is only a transition to a state where we are more truly ourselves. The second view, on the other hand, is intended to demolish the picture of death as something which, like pain or injury, one suffers or which changes one for the worse. If we do really die, then that is not something that happens to us, something we go through. But all fear for ourselves can only have for its object things that might happen to us. Whatever it is that we do fear, therefore, we are wrong in thinking that it is death.

Now the problem with the first view is not that it seems to evade the question of death. If there is no such thing for us as real death then there is no such question. Nor, so long as we are specifically addressing the fear of death, is it any objection to this view that making my soul indestructible allows for the possibility of a time before my soul came into existence. Whatever philosophical problem is still posed, as we noted in the last chapter, by my non-existence before birth, it is not something for which fear is the appropriate emotion. The difficulty is rather that forever is a very long time. The thought that these few years of one's life on earth are but the beginning of a journey indefinitely prolonged ought to give rise to a fear far greater than the fear of death.

The problem with the second view is simply that it appears to rest on a non-sequitur. For the middle term required to establish its conclusion, the premiss that fear for oneself can only be fear of things that might happen to one, surely proves too much. For example, a dying author could not fear – out of legitimate vanity and not or any altruistic motive – that a few years from now her reputation will be destroyed by hostile critics. The destruction of a reputation can only metaphorically be described as happening to a person who exists in the past (it is certainly not in any sense something which happens to her mortal remains, although if there must, in the literal sense, exist a concrete subject to which the destruction of dead person's reputation happens, these would be the only candidate). If this is a legitimate fear, as it seems prima facie to be, then no reason has yet been supplied why I should not, purely for my own sake, fear to contemplate a future world without me in it – a future where, for example, I am no longer around to defend my views – even though the coming to pass of such a world will not be something that happens to me.

4. The two traditional arguments against the fear of death, though of limited interest in themselves from our point of view, serve to set the stage for two more recent views which are of special relevance, those of Heidegger and the early Wittgenstein. The Wittgenstein of the *Tractatus* gives voice to just what the Kantian egocentrist would say about the prospect of my death (although the structure of the Tractarian metaphysic remains, arguably, ambiguous on the question of nonegocentrism versus egocentrism): 'So too at death the world does not alter, but comes to an end' (6.431). The context of this remark is a sequence of remarks to the effect that ethical questions relate to the aspect that the world presents as a whole, and not to facts that make up the world. Thus, in the previous numbered remark, 'If the good or bad exercise of the will does alter the world, it can alter only the limits of the world' (6.43). We are fully justified, however, in considering the remark about death on its own merits, without reference to the Tractarian view of ethics. One might say that the transcendental ego, the I whose identity through time is the transcendental condition for the unity of the world of appearances, is free to view the death of the empirical Klempner as just another event in the world; but in doing so it necessarily represents to itself a possible course of future experience which projects beyond that event. By contrast, there is no such event as the ceasing to exist of the transcendental ego itself, for events can only happen in the world: there is no way I can represent to myself the ceasing to exist of the world of my possible experience.

The difference this makes to Epicurus' account of death is dramatic. The objection that I might still fear to contemplate a future without me in it is met by denying the very existence of such a future. However, it should be clear that the Kantian account of the transcendental ego and the empirical Klempner, implied in Wittgenstein's remark, is quite unlike our own account of the relations, either between the absolute, subjective I and the relative, objective I known as Klempner, or between the absolute, subjective I and my Klempner. While the absolute I has no identity from one moment to another, the transcendental ego must continue through time in order to fulfil its role as the non-empirical condition for the unity of the world of appearances: at every moment the transcendental ego perceives the spatial world from the point of view of the empirical subject within which it finds itself located. This contrast between the absolute I and the transcendental ego reflects the vastly different amounts of work that the two notions are required to do. Whereas for the Kantian egocentrist the weight of the whole world, the world of my subjective standpoint, rests on the transcendental ego, the absolute I of our two-world metaphysic adds nothing to a world already given from the objective standpoint. Thus it is that the death of the transcendental ego would be equivalent to the destruction of the whole world, that whose existence is the necessary condition for the truth or falsity of any thought, while, by complete contrast, the absolute I possesses nothing that death can take away.

5. The other account of death of special interest to us is Heidegger's struggle, in *Being and Time,* to formulate what it is to grasp my death as mine, and not just another death that happens in the world (Division 2, ch. I). If only the objective standpoint is real, then my death is just another death that happens. If only the subjective standpoint is real, then my death cannot be something in the world at all. To ask Heidegger's question is therefore to recognize, at least implicitly, the reality of both the subjective and objective standpoints. The fact that Heidegger does not explicitly endorse a two-world theory thus makes interpretation from our point of view especially difficult – leaving aside the fact that interpreting Heidegger is difficult anyway. Nevertheless, it is possible to pick out the salient moves.

We have seen that the absolute, subjective I cannot, literally die. Yet the absolute I that dies with every passing moment is the subjective I of one particular individual who will die just once; and that death, which I represent in the objective world as the death of Klempner and in my subjective world as the death of my Klempner, retains a special significance to me which it has for no other person, and which no other death can claim: if there were no Klempner at this very moment then there would be no absolute I. Now one way to put the question of the reality of my subjective standpoint is to ask what I can do to actually acknowledge the unique significance that my own death has for me, something which goes beyond the emphatic, but futile repetition of the tautology, 'My death is mine'; and it is this project that Heidegger undertakes.

In our everyday lives, whatever importance we may attach to the act of thinking, our thoughts remain wholly occupied with mundane questions, questions which the objective discourse we share with others is equipped to answer. Yet there comes a time when we are forced to direct our attention towards the fact of our own unique existence as such: when we become aware of the certainty that we are going to die. Traditionally, the thought of a day of judgement served as a call to conscience: the realization that it matters at every moment what I choose to do in a way that transcends any advantage I might gain or lose in this life. For Heidegger, the source of this call, far from being something outside my life as the traditional view presupposes – the eternal Judge who rewards and punishes – is only my comprehension of that very life as a totality which results from what I choose to do, rather than the life of some person which is given to me as a fact. Thus, my acknowledgement of my death as mine calls me to undertake a life of 'authentic' action: I shall strive at all times to act in such a way that my actions flow from my own decisions, my own unique existence, and are not decided merely by the mundane consideration of what a person like me should do, in the circumstances in which I find myself.

It should be clear from what we have said about the reality of the objective standpoint, however, that this is something which is quite impossible. How I am to exist, what course of action I am to undertake at any moment, is, for the very reason that I can explain myself to others and make them aware of the issues facing me just as I am myself, only a matter of mundane, objective knowledge: any reason I may give for my actions is a judgement, which others have the authority to correct. That I exist remains an issue only in the specific context of the contemplation of my death as mine. There is nothing I can do to express my recognition of the reality of my subjective standpoint, the uniqueness of my death, other than to embrace the metaphysic of subjective and objective worlds.

6. We shall now test the view that my subjective world has no identity over time. Consider the following variation on the doppelganger thought experiment. We are back once more in the laboratory of the evil scientist. This time, however, the scientist has found a way to dispense with the time-consuming process of growing a duplicate body in a vat. Instead, everything is done with a body-duplicating machine. The original is made to divide like an amoeba into two identical copies of itself, the additional mass for the two bodies being supplied by a mixture of chemical compounds kept in a reservoir. Thus I imagine myself watching, in fascination and dread, as the scientist orders one of the nearby lab assistants to stand in the duplicating chamber. The door is closed and the machine starts to hum. Moments later, the door opens to reveal two identical lab assistants in identical white coats, who turn to one another and smile. 'As you can see,' says the scientist, 'I have no difficulty in obtaining extra staff! Now here's something you might ponder,' the scientist

continues as the two assistants advance towards me. 'Tomorrow morning, I am going to do the same to you. The duplicate standing on the left will be set free. The other I intend to keep for my medical experiments.' As I am led away to my cell, struggling, just one thought is on my mind: shall I be the one on the left? shall I go free? or shall I find myself on the evil scientist's operating table?

Our approach to this thought experiment will be guided by the principle that all questions of self-identity, just like any other matter for judgement, must, if they have answers at all, be capable of being answered from the objective standpoint. Now the interesting thing about the idea of matter-duplication is the way it seems to pose a real problem for our concept of self-identity which the first thought experiment did not. If I am captured, and replaced by a duplicate of myself which has been grown in a vat, there seems little doubt which is the original and which is the copy. From the objective standpoint, the person who returns home is not me. Yet in the case of matter-duplication, each duplicate has an equal claim to be me.

One thing we cannot say is that one person is identical with both the resulting duplicates. If x is identical with y, and also identical with z, then, according to the logic of identity statements, y must be identical with z. The duplicates, however, despite their perfect similarity at the time when they first came into being, are two and not one: they are not the same individual. There is more than one way to avoid logical contradiction; the question is which is the most appropriate. For example, one might choose to replace the notion of the identity of a subject over time by a suitably defined notion of similarity. There is no logical objection to this; the question is rather whether we are prepared to accept the moral consequences of this wholesale redefinition. Thus Parfit argues in ch. 12 of *Reasons and Persons* that self-identity is not what ultimately 'matters', using this as the basis for a utilitarian account of the basis for ethical judgements in ch. 15. However, to accept that identity should not matter to us so much as it does is not the same as saying that it does not matter at all: unless one puts the requirements of a neat philosophical analysis above making sense of our actual lives. (On Parfit's behalf it might be said that at the core of his vision lies a confused perception – distorted inevitably by his rigorous adherence to nonegocentrism – of the illusion underlying the belief in the continuity of my subjective world.)

An alternative that does not involve rejecting identity would be to rule that the two duplicates are to be regarded retrospectively as always having been two individuals, who, before the matter-duplication, shared the same body. It would then be possible for a single living human body to be regarded retrospectively as having been shared by any number of individual selves. (Wiggins, in *Sameness and Substance* pp. 167-169, objects to this on the grounds that it mean constructing persons out of the dubious logical fiction of person-moments or person-stages. However, no such parallel conception is involved in making sense of our seeing one and the same length of tree branch as the common part of several extended branches; instead, we identify an extended branch counterfactually as what would result if all the other branches were lopped off.) Although it takes some getting used to, that solution does seem to be the one which both satisfies logic and requires the least alteration to our social and legal practices. One should note that it is still far from perfect, however. For example, if a convicted criminal gained access to a matter-duplicating machine, we might find ourselves faced with the prospect of punishing hundreds of men for what was, originally, a single crime.

There remains a strong sense, however, in which our proposed solution remains a matter of mere convention. For one might well begin to wonder why continuity of an organized bundle of matter should be thought so important for self-identity. Suppose that a man who had committed a vicious murder was kidnapped, and replaced by his doppelganger, as in the first thought experiment. Were we to discover that this had taken place, we should then face the prospect of living with someone who possessed the character and consciousness of a murderer in our midst. Leaving aside the question of the need to protect society from such an individual, which is not a question of justice but only of practicality, how could we look him in the face – a person knowing all that he knows? How can we regard him as a perfectly innocent victim, while he flaunts himself as an unrepentant murderer? It is surely not inconceivable that under such circumstances we might be tempted to relax the requirement of continuity of matter, so that any perfect duplicate of a person, however it was made, or perhaps even a slightly imperfect duplicate, could be regarded as identical with the original.

The point is that, in the face of these thought experiments, the question of self-identity can only be decided by the criterion of what would give maximum coherence to our moral attitudes and legal practices. (The question raised in the last chapter, whether self-identity might differ from personal identity, has to be decided by just such a criterion.) We cannot rule out, therefore, the intrusion of an element of arbitrariness. If we opt for one of two equally acceptable choices at one point, the slack will be taken up elsewhere. The result of our deliberation will be a well-founded convention, which satisfies our conflicting requirements at least as well as any alternative choice might have done.

7. Before turning to the crucial question of how, from my subjective standpoint, I should regard the prospect of my own duplication, let us first consider briefly how a person, according to our objective account of identity, should view that prospect. What ought a person such as myself to believe? What would it be appropriate to feel? It is part of the concept of belief that one aims to believe what is true. Yet in this case, there are two contradictory truths, the truth that Klempner will be set free and the truth that he will be operated upon. The belief that he will be operated upon is thus true and false; while the contradictory belief that he will not be operated upon but set free is correspondingly false and true. The only way to deal with this apparent contradiction is to think of myself as if I were already two persons, one believing that he will be operated upon, and the other believing that he will be set free. One might think of this as holding the two contradictory beliefs in trust for the two persons for whom the beliefs will actually be true. According to the first belief, I ought to prepare myself for the ordeal ahead. According to the second belief, I ought to plan what I am going to do once I am outside the laboratory and how I am going to persuade people to believe my story. What it would be like to hold such contradictory beliefs, on the other hand, is a question to which one cannot give a useful answer. If matter-duplication became a common occurrence, we should simply get used after a while to employing a different concept of belief from the one we use now.

Similar considerations apply to the question of what emotions it would be appropriate to feel when facing the prospect of one's duplication. Under certain circumstances, such as those described in the thought experiment, should I feel fear and relief? Yes, but not in the way in which persons are now able to feel mixed emotions. The case is not exactly like that of belief, for the way the emotions moved us would depend to some extent on how we came to deal practically with the effects of the emotions in various circumstances. Here there is room for a further conventional element: different societies might evolve alternative conceptions of the place of these emotions, different attitudes which it would be conventionally appropriate to express. Under such circumstances, the emotions themselves would feel different also.

8. How do things appear from my subjective standpoint? or, rather, how do things at least seem to appear when I first reflect on the

thought experiment? In the predicament in which I picture myself, these lofty considerations of what a person should believe or feel seem totally irrelevant. Tomorrow morning, I shall be placed in the duplicating chamber. Shortly afterwards, that one person will have become two. It seems that there is no way I can represent this situation to myself in terms of the adventures which will be undergone by my subjective world, except as one in which I either find my absolute I standing on the left, or find my absolute I standing on the right. Here and now, my subjective world spreads out before me. There and then, it seems, my subjective world will again spread out before me. And in between those two times, there is a series of states of a subjective world connecting one with the other, each of them mine. As now, now, now... becomes then, so here, here, here... will become precisely there. In short, at the end of a series of here's and now's lies either a subjective world in which I find myself standing on the left or a subjective world in which I find myself standing on the right.

Despite what my imagination tells me, however, I know that the possible situation in which I, the absolute I could find myself on the left and not on the right, or find myself on the right and not on the left, is a state of affairs which in neither case presents an aspect to the objective standpoint. As far as any mere observer is concerned, there is only one possible situation: there will be two duplicates of Klempner, two relative I's, one on the left and one on the right. The semblance of two possible alternatives must, therefore, according to our rejection of the egocentrist's infallible power of judgement, be sheer illusion. Yet how can I render intelligible to myself the idea that it is only an illusion? How am I to save the appearance, or, rather, the appearance of an appearance of a series of connected states of my subjective world, without conceding that my absolute I must find itself either on the left or on the right?

The swift answer to this question is that the possible situation in which my body is duplicated is not one which I can represent to myself in terms of what will happen to my subjective world, because my subjective world, the absolute I with its incommunicable *this*, is not something to which anything will happen. Just as the Kantian egocentrist rejected the illusion that I can track the continued existence through time of Descartes' mental substance, the ghostly container of ideas presented to my introspection in which my passing mental states are contained, so we reject the egocentrist's illusion that I can track the continued existence through time of my subjective world.

Returning to our familiar example, *this* keyboard, as an object in my subjective world, is indeed none other than the very object identified from the objective standpoint as the keyboard which Klempner is using to type these words. *This* keyboard, like the objective keyboard, is an object which persists through time. Only now, as I write, there is no longer (and never was) 'this' keyboard but only *this* keyboard, that is to say another, or, rather, the very first this-keyboard, and then yet another, again the first, each in turn identical with the objective keyboard. For each this-keyboard, each keyboard that the *this* makes mine, though it cannot as such claim continuity through time, is taken as having a past and future which coincide exactly with the past and future of the objective keyboard. – The very same applies to the individual I call 'my Klempner'.

9. My subjective world as it spreads out before me now is but a moment stolen from the objective world. Only we must remember that in taking objects and making them this or mine, the absolute I does not merely capture them in their momentary state, but grasps and makes its own the world as an articulated whole, the subject matter of all judgements, whether about the past, present or future. Thus it follows that in anticipating the outcome of my duplication from my subjective standpoint, the absolute I, or rather the I-now, necessarily contains two my-Klempners, not one; for that is what the objective standpoint sees. For the Kantian egocentrist, by contrast, while there are two empirical Klempners, only one can be the living body within which the viewpoint of the transcendental ego will be located; so long as I continue to construct a world of my possible experience on the basis of a single path traced through space and time. The statement, 'I shall end up on the left' must turn out, by virtue of the obtaining of the non-empirical condition that singles out one and only path as mine, to be either determinately true or determinately false.

The uncertainty concerning my impending duplication is indeed exactly like the fear we referred to earlier in discussing the different possible reasons for wishing to avoid death: the fear that my subjective world might be taken away from me. The uncertainty, like the fear, has no object and therefore no content. Objectively, there is no uncertainty. One person will become two: the person on the left will find himself on the left, while the person on the right will find himself on the right. If that is the case, however, then the appearance that the thought experiment of matter-duplication presented, of somehow inducing in me greater uncertainty concerning the fate of my subjective world than did the thought experiment of the doppelganger, must also be illusory.

The reader will recall that when we discussed the question of the doppelganger in chapter 7, we spoke as if it were almost a foregone conclusion that my subjective world would be that of the person who was captured, and not that of the doppelganger who replaced him; although we had to allow that I might conceivably discover that I was 'my' own doppelganger. However, the idea that there is a balance of probability which weighs more in one direction than the other is, in the light of the conclusions we have reached, completely nonsensical. There is no greater or lesser chance that my subjective world will be the world of either, just because my subjective world is not something to which anything will happen. All one can say is that my subjective world would have exactly the same character as it has now if I were a doppelganger who had been put in the place of the real Klempner. The only probability that arises in connection with this supposition is the extremely low probability that I objectively attach to there actually having taken place the events described in the thought experiment. Were I do discover that the substitution was about to take place, however, there would be no further question I could intelligibly raise concerning the relative likelihood of my absolute I ending up as the real Klempner or his doppelganger.

10. It is time now to step back a little, so that we may begin to grasp the significance of the strange conclusions to which we have been led by the dialectic of the non-continuity of my subjective world. The fact that once seemed so familiar to me, the fact of my existence as it presents itself to me alone, has assumed a disturbingly alien aspect. We saw that this discovery does have a flip side: the non-continuity of my subjective world means that one motive for fearing death is irrational. Still, the question arises whether my existence has acquired its alien aspect only because I am looking at it in a peculiar way. Normally, when we are not doing metaphysics, we take our existence for granted, we don't look at it at all. Only when we try to contemplate the certainty of our own death, or think about the kinds of improbable thought experiment that philosophers are so fond to describe, do we begin to manifest symptoms of philosophical illusion, symptoms which further philosophical argument is then needed to correct. Might it not be the case that my existence is seen in its truest light, not when I gaze into myself in my solitude, or try vainly to catch hold of or steal a glimpse of the essential thing that makes my life mine, but when I am actually living it? If that is so, how can we describe the process of actually living philosophically, without making

133

the very same mistake again, and finding ourselves back where we started? In other words, how can we look without stopping to look, and thereby disrupting the very process we were trying to describe?

Superficially, our predicament might seem to be very similar to that of the Hume who, as we remarked in chapter 3, was able to reconcile his philosophical conclusions with the commonsense beliefs indispensable for living in the world, only by resorting to irony. That impression is mistaken. Hume's theory that reality is nothing but a succession of sensations and ideas is meant as a vision of how things really are, contrary to what we all believe prior to philosophic enlightenment. As beings who experience themselves as living in a world, engaged in projects which depend for their success on our unquestioning acceptance our basic commonsense beliefs, however, we simply are not free, as Hume recognizes, to repudiate our life as an illusory appearance in favour of a bleak and unrecognizable vision of the true state of affairs. That is not what we are now saying. The non-continuity of the subjective world is false to our experience of living only because it is one-sided: it is a philosophical answer to a philosophical question, a question which we do not normally stop to ask. As our irrational fear of death shows, that question is indeed not so far below the surface as one might suppose. So there is some degree of conflict: commonsense, when it begins to dabble in metaphysics, is led astray. Yet there is still much that metaphysics can learn by reflecting on the nature of our unreflective attitude to our life. In raising a question mark against the world itself and our relation to it, in refusing to take the world for granted, one of the things metaphysics has to investigate is the very attitude of taking the world for granted which seems to preclude metaphysical reflection. The question which remains to be answered is whether it is possible to conduct such an investigation without destroying, in the process of analysis, the very thing one is attempting to analyse.

11. The one-sidedness of the conclusions we have so far reached about the nature of a two-world theory, and in particular the form of the subjective standpoint, resides in the fact that up to now everything has been couched in terms of the concept of experience. Indeed, we have repeatedly used metaphors associated with the faculty of vision. Thus, we have talked of points of view from which one is able to make judgements or apply concepts. We have also asked what it is that I see when I attend to my incommunicable sense of my own existence. The subjective and objective worlds are themselves defined in terms of standpoints, the objects of philosophic contemplation. Some of this talk is unavoidable: after all, metaphysics is a form of theoretical,

134

reflective knowledge. Nevertheless, the vocabulary of our two-world theory has up to now reflected a bias inherited from the positions which it rejects, but in rejecting is obliged to define itself against. This bias is an inevitable consequence of the dialectical method. In repudiating, as we did in chapters 2 and 3, any original starting point of our own, we have no alternative but to borrow the tools of our opponents.

Now that we have worked through the dialectic to the point of having disposed of the opposition, however, we have earned the right to look beyond the range of concepts to which the argument has so far been restricted. What we are looking for is a bridge that will extend the scope of our theory of subjective and objective worlds without weakening its foundations; a concept that will enable us to apply the results of the dialectic to the analysis of life as it is lived. In that way, we might succeed in bringing our newly articulated metaphysical vision, a vision first dimly perceived in the speculations of naive metaphysics, into harmony with the actual reality we have known and lived in all along. If our theory is indeed the only coherent way of dealing with the problem of the subjective and objective standpoints, then such a bridging concept must be available.

There is no mystery about what the bridging concept might be: it is the notion of the standpoint of the agent. The difference between the vision of a two-world metaphysic derived from the purely negative process of refuting nonegocentrism and egocentrism, and my unreflective grasp of my life as I live it, consists in the fact that whereas the former treats my agency in a static way, as something given as a fact that theoretical understanding has to reckon with, my actual awareness of my own agency is dynamic. My actions are not given to me when I act, for I am the one making them happen.

We have already encountered the concepts of an action and of being an agent. We saw in chapter 5 that a subject of consciousness can be identified from the objective standpoint only as a language user and agent; to that extent we share with the nonegocentrist the principle that physical agency is a necessary feature of any world in which subjects are to be found. The egocentrist too, as we remarked in chapter 8, can argue, in a phenomenological vein, that the world of my possible experience necessarily includes my experience of being a language user and agent. Both the nonegocentrist and the egocentrist admit that agency is in some sense necessary. Only both immediately go on to treat agency as something that is simply there as one of the features of the world to be described, and whose differences from other kinds of happening, the events which we ascribe not to human agency but merely to physical causes, we may reflect upon. As far as my life, my subjective world is concerned, however, the performing of actions is not merely something which I discover as a necessary feature of the world, in my coming to recognize the existence of other thinking subjects through their actions; nor is it something which my inner, experiencing self discovers about its outer, active body. For I, the absolute I exist primarily as an agent: my being is not an experiencing but a doing.

The rejection of egocentrism and nonegocentrism thus provides us with an opportunity to make something more of agency: to grasp it in a dynamic rather than a merely static way. How can we ensure that the opportunity is not missed? A first step towards constructing a bridge between the vision of a two-world metaphysic and my life as an agent, would be to find some means to enrich the description of the form of my subjective standpoint, so as to embody the recognition of the incommunicable difference between my actions, the actions which I do, and the actions of others which I merely experience and describe. It will not suffice to say simply that the difference consists in the fact that the actions which are mine are the actions which occur in me, in the person for whom there is *this*; since that once more reduces doing to experiencing. The difference has got to be found in the gap which separates doing from experiencing.

So far, we have established that my subjective standpoint takes objects from the world of the objective standpoint, making them *this* and mine. In doing so, it gives an absolute sense to spatial proximity. This formal schema says nothing about action. What then is the essential difference between my viewing my actions from the objective standpoint, and viewing them from my subjective standpoint? It should be clear by now that this is precisely the wrong question. For we have already admitted that my grasp of my actions from my subjective standpoint is not a viewing but a doing. It is therefore not enough to say that from my subjective standpoint my actions possess a thisness which they do not possess from the objective standpoint. Or, rather, the mistake made in talking of vision rather than action consists in my thinking of my incommunicable *this* as something which has been simply given to me and which, like a magic wand, transforms a world of objects into a world of my objects without touching them in any way. On the contrary, it is I who transform the objective world into a world of objects which are *this* and mine through my actions, through my possessing the standpoint of an agent.

136

11 My standpoint as agent

1. FOR the metaphysician who seeks to discover more in our life as human beings than an object of disinterested contemplation, it is initially disappointing to learn that the two-world theory which emerges from the dialectic of egocentrism and nonegocentrism appears no less false to our experience of the world and our relation to it than the positions it rejects. The reality of my incommunicable sense of my own existence has been saved, it seems, at the cost of denying that what it points to can be identified as the same from one moment to the next. The only way we could explain this failure to fit our common sense notion of self-identity was to say that common sense is itself led astray by a primitive form of metaphysical reflection. Yet that still leaves us with the task of relating the results of the dialectic to a truly unreflective experience that has not been led astray. That is why we raised the question towards the end of the last chapter whether there might not be a bridge which would extend our two-world theory to the analysis of life as it is lived. We then gave a preliminary account of the reasons for taking the bridging concept to be that of the standpoint of the agent.

The question goes deeper, however, than the general problem of the application of a metaphysical theory to our unreflective experience. The standpoint of the agent promises nothing less than a reconciliation of the subjective and objective standpoints. In embracing both, we have taken our stand on the reality of a metaphysical contradiction; yet we are still far from making sense of such a state of affairs. What needs to be shown is that the problem of grasping the contradiction, and ultimately of reconciliation, is the very same as that of applying the two-world theory to the analysis of our actual life. In that case, the bridging concept which applied our metaphysic to our actual life would also serve as a bridge between the two standpoints themselves.

Let us speculate for a moment on how that might come about. On one side, we have the theoretical position of our two-world metaphysic, which says that the subjective and objective standpoints, conceived as ways of viewing the world as such, stand in a relation of conflict or contradiction. On the other side, we have our unreflective forms of life which embody, on the level of practice, a parallel conflict between subjective and objective. This second conflict cannot, by definition, take the form of a metaphysical theory, however primitive, since it exists prior to all reflection. The conflict is not, therefore, a contradiction between different ways of viewing or conceiving the world, since the world as such and our relation to it have not even come up for discussion: it is a practical conflict embodied in the very structure of our life. If, in the light of the bridging concept of agency, we succeed in connecting this second conflict with the theoretical contradiction between the subjective and objective standpoints, then we shall indeed have constructed a bridge between the two standpoints, thereby providing the means to reconcile them.

2. Whether agency can provide the bridge we are seeking depends, in the first place, on whether there is anything novel in the claim that my subjective standpoint is the dynamic standpoint of the agent qua agent, as opposed to the static standpoint of a subject to whom actions are simply given, the agent qua subject of experience. We discovered back in chapter 5 that whether I am a physical agent cannot be a matter of contingent fact: my way of being in the world, and consequently my experience in general, is necessarily that of an agent. For in order to present an aspect as a thinking subject to the objective standpoint, I must be capable of expressing my beliefs both in language and in my actions. How then could there be room for any real distinction between my necessarily experiencing myself an agent in this way and my occupying the subjective standpoint of an agent? The question turns on whether, in providing our account of the dual reality of subjective and objective worlds, agency is to be taken as the primary concept, or whether there exist more fundamental concepts in terms of which agency may be defined. If agency were not primary, then it would be possible to analyse the performing of an action as a combination of several factors which, by coming together in a certain way, produces the phenomenon of action. Proving that agency cannot be so analysed, however, would not by itself establish that agency is primary in the sense that interests us, unless we can find, in addition,

some attribute which belongs to agency when taken as primary, which it lacks when analysed as a combination of other factors.

This is still a rather abstract account of the problem. The argument has four distinct stages. We begin by describing our naive, unreflective notions about agency and what is involved in performing an action. These notions appear inseparable from the very idea of ourselves as agents; yet they cannot, paradoxically, be defended against philosophical attack. As agents, we are not what we necessarily take ourselves to be.

In the second stage of the argument, we shall play devil's advocate and argue for the philosophical theory that seems to follow from the rejection of our unreflective notions about agency. According to this theory, the physical events we call actions are only a certain kind of bodily movement or behaviour. This behavioural theory, it should be noted, is not the same as the behaviourism of experimental psychology, according to which the investigator proceeds as if there were no such things as inner mental states, but only outer dispositions towards physical behaviour; a theory which received a philosophical inflection in Ryle's project, undertaken in *The Concept of Mind,* of defining psychological concepts, including that of the will, in dispositional terms. The behavioural theory that concerns us denies only that there is anything that corresponds to the idea of willing an action, as that notion is understood prior to philosophical reflection. What we call action, says the behavioural theorist, is only a combination of beliefs and desires accompanied by the bodily movements which, as a matter of conceptual necessity, such psychological states causally bring about. (The view that the relation between psychological states and the actions they explain can be at once a priori and causal is defended in Davidson's seminal article 'Actions, Reasons and Causes'.)

The third stage of the argument points out that one vital component of our unreflective notion of agency denied by the behavioural theory can be reformulated in such a way as to resist the criticism directed against the original naive account. This is the thought that the standpoint of the agent, as opposed to the standpoint of a spectator of the agent's behaviour, is a standpoint from which actions must appear as if they had no prior cause other than an act of will; even though no such thing as an act of will is ever observed.

Finally, in the fourth stage, we shall give the reasons why a theory of subjective and objective worlds requires the rejection of the behavioural theory; and indeed provides the only conclusive basis for rejecting it. There is a sense in which our unreflective notions about agency cannot be denied without incoherence. For the metaphysical contradiction between the subjective and objective standpoints becomes intolerable if we are not permitted to take the notion of agency as the primary concept.

3. According the naive picture, the I that is aware of itself performing an action exists, not as an inner observer of a person's thought processes and of the bodily movements resulting from them, but as a will that controls and directs those processes and movements. The contrast between the notion of an inner observer and that of a controlling will may be pictured in terms of the metaphor of a horse and its rider. An observer is carried along by its horse – the body as it presents itself to introspection – wherever the horse, as the result of processes that remain necessarily opaque to the observer, chooses to go. The only function of the observer is to enjoy the passing scenery. It may happen, of course, that wherever the horse goes, the observer wishes to go also. In that case, the observer would be in the happy position of always having its 'decisions' acted upon. Even so, that 'would only be a favour granted by fate' (*Tractatus* 6.374). The observer is not actually controlling the horse; there is only a reliable conjunction between where the observer wants to go and where the horse actually goes without which there would be no application for the concept of riding a horse, of willing a bodily movement.

A controlling will, by contrast, remains in charge of the horse, directing it to turn to the left or to the right, to speed up or slow down. The will moves itself; and the horse, the body, then responds. This picture applies with equal force, whether I deliberate before acting, or simply act without thinking. When I act without thinking, I do not merely find my body moving, I will the action; recognizing my bodily movement not only as one which I wished to take place, but as one which my will brought about. When I deliberate before acting, my will controls the movement of my thoughts, whether I attend to this consideration or that, and then, my course of action having been decided upon, my will chooses the precise moment to put the decision into effect. Now, just because this notion of willing is unreflective, we do not stop to ask how it is that the will can stand above the whole of nature in causing actions to take place without itself being caused to exercise its controlling influence by an agency or processes of which the subject is unaware. The rider is in charge, not the horse; nor is there a second rider on the rider's own shoulders, directing the first rider's movements.

The naive picture of human action disintegrates, however, under pressure of philosophical criticism. In order to perform its controlling function, the will must be thought of as operating outside the network

140

of cause and effect that governs the natural world. That is to say, my actions cannot result merely from processes occurring in my body, processes which could in principle be explained by the laws of physics. If they did result merely from physical processes, then the agreement of my bodily movements with what I willed would be for me just a 'favour granted by fate': there is no room for an extra impulse that only my will can supply. It makes no difference whether or not we believe that from a complete physical description of my body and its surroundings at any one time, it would be possible for a Laplacian super-mind to deduce exactly what movements my body was going to make next. According to the naive picture, when my will operates, when it exercises its causal power, it chooses between one bodily movement and another, supplying the necessary impulse without which that movement would not have occurred. This impulse is its own and is not merely granted to it by the way things turn out in the world; whether those events happen as a matter of predictable, causal necessity, or whether, on the contrary, their occurrence on any single occasion is ultimately a matter of pure chance, as in the indeterminist interpretation of quantum theory. In short, my will possesses a causality which is completely uncaused.

Now the problem with thinking of one's will as an uncaused cause is not that such a belief entails the abandonment of the laws of physics. If there were evidence that our known physical laws did not operate effectively in the realm of human action – say, that the brain was not the causal source of actions but only a relay mechanism tuned in like a radio receiver to a mental ether – then we should initiate the search for the invisible stuff that made up the substance of a person's true mind, the source that generated acts of will. However, this will-stuff would still have to undergo processes and changes according to laws of its own, laws which the will could not overrule; if it were not governed by laws of some kind, if its processes were its own continual creation, then the will could only act randomly. We would then face a dilemma. If the laws governing the mental ether turned out to be deterministic, then the will would once more be reduced to passivity; a mere self-awareness generated by ethereal processes, the observer carried along by the horse. If, on the other hand, the mental ether were governed only by statistical or non-deterministic laws, then to avoid ultimate randomness we should have to search again for the true source of individual acts of will in some further realm beyond the mental ether, where the very same choice would again confront us.

This criticism is confirmed from a different angle when one tries to look inside oneself in order to catch sight of one's will in action. My body shifts its position, say, as the result of some slight discomfort. At

141

what point did my will tell my body to move? All I am aware of is the movement itself and the discomfort that prompted it. Suppose now I am reaching for a book on a high shelf. I stretch my arm and my hand to their fullest extent, willing my fingers to reach just another two inches. What we have described is not the process of willing as such, but only the process of trying. Trying is something one is aware of doing when an action is difficult or hindered in some way. If willing is to be found anywhere, however, it is in the decision, whether or not consciously formulated, to try, not in the trying itself.

What then should one say about the process of coming to a decision? At what point does my will enter? As I deliberate over some course of action, I am aware of this or that consideration occurring to me; I represent different possible outcomes to myself; my attention is perhaps held by a point which requires deeper thought. Finally, I make up my mind, and my body moves. At each stage of my thinking process, either a reason can be found for my thinking a thought or picturing an image in those which preceded it, or the thought or image comes into my head unannounced. In either case, there is no need for an added act of will to call the thought or image to my attention. The reason for my final decision can, in the same way, be found in all the thinking that led up to it. As Dennett has persuasively argued, this procedure of 'generate and test' provides a completely adequate model for the process of deliberation (*Brainstorms* pp. 193ff.); there is no need to posit an uncaused will directing the process from behind the scenes. What then of my final decision to act, when I have made up my mind, and it is only a question of choosing the precise moment to move my body? If nothing in my surroundings prompts that final choice, then nothing happens of which I am aware other than the fact that, at some precise moment, my body does actually move.

4. One may sum up these criticisms of the naive notion of agency and of the will by saying that a will that is truly in charge of one's body must be a rational will, a force mentally aimed in a specific direction. Yet whether we seek out the physical source of our decision making in order to unravel the laws of its operation, or entertain conjectures about some non-physical, ethereal source, there is simply no room left for the operation of any further force or cause, an added power of willing. Nor, when we look into ourselves as we perform an action, do we see any trace of the process of willing, of the power being exercised, but at most only the process of trying. It is thus only a short step to saying that an agent's reasons, the desires and goals that her action is meant to fulfil in the light of her beliefs, are the sole

cause of the action, of the intentional bodily movement that actually takes place.

It would seem to follow from this that in order to comprehend my own actions, I have to consider what I should say about an agent like myself; that is to say, I must conceive of them from the hypothetical standpoint of a spectator of my behaviour, the standpoint from which they are explained as the result of my psychological states. I must at least be able to do that, in order to explain and justify my actions to others. Nor, when I express my beliefs and desires, is any extra information given to me that is not in principle available to others. Yet from the outside, to a spectator explaining or judging what I do, my actions are just bodily movements or behaviour falling under certain psychological descriptions, movements that have been caused in a particular way. There is another question to ask, however, a question not about the nature of psychological explanation as such but rather of pure metaphysics: how am I to account for the way my actions appear to me from the inside, from my own perspective? Having rejected the naive theory of the controlling will, it seems all there is left to say is that I exist for myself essentially as an inner observer of my own thought processes and the behaviour that results from them.

Note that in rejecting the picture of the rider in control of the horse, the behavioural theory does not accept uncritically the alternative picture of the observer carried along wherever the horse chooses to go. For the suggestion that it is only a matter of good fortune that the observer's desires correspond with those of the horse cannot be right. Desires which related only contingently to the horse's movements would amount to extra information available exclusively to the subject, aspects of the subject not presented to the objective standpoint. (It is here that the metaphysical presuppositions of Wittgenstein's remark become apparent.) One might think that in my attitude of detachment, I watch myself just as another might watch me; the only difference between us as regards my own actions is that I am the one who is actually being taken for the ride. What is wrong with that thought is that the other does have desires of his own, which my bodily movements either satisfy or fail to satisfy; whereas the picture of the inner, observing I can only be that of a pure consciousness, aware of Klempner's desires and the actions that follow from them, but with no desires of its own.

5. The behavioural theory does at first seem to draw the only lesson that can reasonably be drawn from the discovery that, when I look into myself, the act of will which I naively supposed to be the uncaused cause of my actions is nowhere to be seen. On second

thoughts, one may begin to suspect that, far from being a conclusion which follows from the incoherence of the naive view, the behavioural theory has all along been the basis of the objection on the grounds of the will's invisibility. For it was simply assumed from the start that the nature of my agency can be discovered if I take up the attitude of an inner observer of my own thoughts and bodily movements.

A supporter of the behavioural theory may well reply that there is no other way in which the operation of my supposed acts of will could be detected. How else can you see something except by looking? And how can you know something that you cannot see or in any way become aware of? – The short answer to this is that the sense that I have of being in control of the bodily movements I call my actions is not based on observation of any kind. To be in charge of one's movements, to be active rather than passive, is just to be in a state where the things that happen when one's limbs move are not events that one merely observes in the way that a spectator of one's actions would observe them. For the willing of an action gives knowledge of that action independently of observing it; nor is the willing itself known by observation.

In this way, the assertion that my actions are those movements of my body which I will may be seen as a negative rather than a positive claim. It is not that I have to believe in the existence of a mysterious entity inside me which I call my power of willing, an agency which causes my actions without itself being caused to act. It is only that I cannot look upon my own mental or bodily actions as something external to an inner, passive, observing I; as mere happenings which occur alongside the other events which I observe either in my own mind or in the world outside my mind.

6. Earlier it was said that the question whether agency is to be taken as the primary concept, and not as a concept to be analysed into a combination of factors, would be interesting only if a primary notion of agency possessed some attribute which an analysed notion of agency lacked. In the light of our negative reinterpretation of the naive view of agency, can we say what this attribute might be? We have seen that the behavioural theory attempts to analyse action in terms which a spectator would use to describe the actions of another person. In applying the theory to myself, I have to make myself an inner observer of my own actions. What is missing from this picture is precisely the difference between my merely observing or describing an action, and my actually doing it.

This difference remains invisible, or at least reduces to a tautology, so long as I think of my standpoint as being that of an inner, observing I for whom the movements of my body, or indeed the thoughts and images in my mind, are no less external than the events that occur in the world outside my body. The actions I do are simply the ones I observe to occur in me. From this imaginary viewpoint, one has every reason to be sceptical of a willing that makes movements of my body my actions. However, we can apply a similar line of criticism to the notion of an inner, observing I as the behavioural theorist used against the notion of an act of will. When I perform an action, I have no immediate knowledge of an observing I whose sole function is to be aware of my performing that action. Indeed, we do many things completely unselfconsciously. Suppose then that I deliberately set out to observe myself as I move my arm. Am I also aware of performing the mental act of observing myself moving my arm? If I am, that can only be because I have performed the second mental act of observing my first mental act. That second mental act must in turn be observed by a third, and so on. However far one goes back, one never finds the pure, passive I which observes the action one is doing, but is not itself the result of an act of observing.

Now there appears to be a way of taking the point about one's relation to one's own actions which serves merely to deflect it, so that it becomes something quite innocuous. The behavioural theorist does not wish to deny that we each have a special relation to our own actions: it is, after all, patently observable that an agent is able to know what she is doing without having to observe the movements of her body. Indeed, this feature of actions is fully apparent in the different kinds of backing we expect someone to give to the questions, 'What is she doing?' and 'What are you doing?', 'Why is she doing X?' and 'Why are you doing X?'. This point is fully taken care of, the behavioural theorist would argue, by the fact that the very applicability of the concept of intending or willing an action depends upon certain conditions, of which the observed difference between the first- and third-person view of actions is one upshot.

That is not what we are saying. The metaphysical vision we are concerned with is from innocuous. To recognize the inner, observing I as my own true self appears nothing less than the annihilation of my separate identity, the invasion of the world into my innermost being: a vision of my I as nothing more than a piece of flotsam carried along by the tide of external events. But why, a philosopher might ask, may I not think of myself in this way? Is not the stubborn refusal to see oneself as an inner, observing I merely a reflection of one's personal psychology? The fact that a metaphysical vision conjures up feelings of distaste or despair is, as we have noted before, no argument against it. Nor should we have anything to say to someone who just as vehemently denied the possibility of conceiving of oneself as ultimately occupying the standpoint of an agent, refusing to submit to the mind-numbing vertigo of being responsible for every moment of one's self-conscious existence.

Nor indeed does the criticism that the behavioural theory leads to an infinite regress of acts of self-observation suffice to refute it. If we have difficulties with locating the observing I, they are no less worrying than the difficulty in identifying acts of pure will. One could say that I am simply aware of willing the actions that I do, so long as I do not stop to observe myself willing; so long as I do not try to catch sight of the act of will that makes my action mine. Equally, one could say that every act which I do can be reduced to movements of my body and thoughts which occur in my mind, except the one act of inner observation that reduces all my other acts to happenings which I observe. It seems almost as if I have a free choice in adopting either the standpoint of an agent or the standpoint of an observer. The question which we still have to answer is which notion comes first: is my standpoint ultimately that of an agent, or ultimately that of an observer? The only point that can be made on the basis of what has been said so far is that, for all that seems to turn on the question, I can declare either standpoint ultimate without incurring any penalty. The behavioural theory cannot be criticized for applying the third-person account of action to my own case; after all, I am one person amongst others, an other to those who are other to me. Equally, the naive view of action, reinterpreted as the negative thesis that the willing or doing of an action cannot be reduced to the object of internal observation has not been refuted. It seems that we have reached a stalemate.

7. If we remain convinced that there is a real question here, then there must be some other consideration not envisaged in the way the dispute was set up which will decide the matter. The problem can only be solved by expanding its terms of reference. Indeed, we have no choice but to do so. For the question is not simply whether the concept of action can or cannot be analysed into a combination of other factors, but rather which concept of action, the fundamental concept belonging to the standpoint of the agent, or the analysed concept belonging to the standpoint of the observer, is required by our metaphysic.

The classic attempt to justify the primacy of the standpoint of the agent is that of Schopenhauer, whose view may be seen as encapsulated in the conjunction of two theses. The first thesis, derived explicitly from Kant, is that there cannot be appearances without

146

'something that appears'. Now 'appearances appear' is, on the face of it, just a tautology. What Kant had in mind, however, in rejecting the vision of a reality constituted exclusively of appearances was that there had to exist something ultimately responsible – although one cannot legitimately speak of causality, a concept limited to the sphere of possible experience, in this connection – for the very fact that there are appearances at all, something which was not itself appearance: the ultimate, unknowable aspect of reality outside the limiting conditions of the world of mere phenomena, the objects of empirical knowledge. It remains the case, however, that all I can represent to myself are appearances. Thus, what Schopenhauer calls the 'world of my representation' cannot, he claims, be all there is to reality; otherwise 'it would inevitably pass by us like an empty dream, or ghostly vision not worth our consideration' (*The World As Will and Representation* Vol. I, p. 99).

Schopenhauer's second thesis is that I know my own actions, not by means of representations, but directly through my willing them; I am conscious of my will 'in an entirely different way' from my consciousness of my body as I represent it to myself (op. cit. p. 103). This we may recognize as a reiteration of the point already noted, that I know my own actions without having to observe my bodily movements.

These two theses fit together in a remarkably simple way. Schopenhauer's view is that this immediate knowledge of my actions, knowledge not mediated by representation, is none other than my knowledge of Kant's unknowable reality. And since, being beyond all representation, nothing can be said, according to Schopenhauer, about the attributes of non-phenomenal reality, even to the extent of representing it in terms of the notion of number and talking in the plural, as Kant did, of things-in-themselves, what I really know in knowing my own actions can only be the one universal Will, the one thing-in-itself that lies behind the world as I or others represent it to ourselves.

Through a further, daring act of generalization, Schopenhauer then draws what he sees as the only conclusion consistent with there being only one Will: that one and the same Will is manifested throughout the world of representation not only in the actions of every human being, but in the impulses that lie behind the strivings of all living things, as well as accounting for the forces governing all non-living processes. In this vision, which bears a strong resemblance to certain strains of Eastern philosophy, there is, ultimately, no reality but Will; and all our battles against adversity, our struggles to succeed in competition with neighbour and foe, are but manifestations of a single force turned against itself; which to the enlightened philosopher appear as futile as a dog chasing its own tail.

Setting aside the aesthetic merits of Schopenhauer's vision, and our view of his ethical conclusions on the value of self-sacrifice, one's initial reaction to the core theory is that it involves a blatant non-sequitur. The reasons why the world of the thing-in-itself and the actions of my will cannot be objects of my representation are, prima facie, quite distinct. It requires nothing short of a leap of pure speculation to identify them, a leap which, on first encountering Schopenhauer's vision, one may have little inclination to follow. However, it is possible to give a more sympathetic reading, in which we can at least see the point of the identification, and perhaps feel some of the force of the vision also. Schopenhauer's theory, as we noted back in chapter 8, is a form of nonegocentrism. For the nonegocentrist, all one can say about the special, unique status that my actions appear to have for me is that each person has a special relation to his own actions, and that I am just one person amongst others. Yet we can also turn this line of thought around. If, despite embracing a nonegocentrist commitment to the exclusive reality of the objective standpoint, I continue to insist that my actions do actually have the special status they appear to possess from my illusory subjective standpoint, then every action must be granted that status. The only way that can be is if the I that I am immediately aware of as the author of my action is the I of all agents: every action is my doing. In effect, the objective standpoint of the Schopenhaurian nonegocentrist is the subjective standpoint of a universal agent of which my own separate consciousness, my own personal subjective standpoint, is only an illusory manifestation.

8. One cannot concur with Schopenhauer's mystical conception of the true nature of my standpoint as an agent. Yet, as we shall see shortly, there is an aspect of his vision that we can and must hold onto. In discussing the question whether or not the concept of action can be analysed into a combination of other factors, we deliberately avoided any reference to my subjective standpoint: a term which acquires its special meaning only within theory of subjective and objective worlds. The standpoint of the agent and the standpoint of the observer, as they appeared in the discussion of the naive view of agency and the behavioural theory, are only different conceptions of every person's mode of access to her own actions. Thus, the question whether we should approach action primarily from the standpoint of the agent or primarily from the standpoint of the observer is a question which the non-Schopenhaurian nonegocentrist is fully able to

comprehend. Such a philosopher could only agree with what has been said so far, that both approaches appear equally valid. Once nonegocentrism is rejected, however, then the issue of the relative priority of the standpoint of the agent and the standpoint of the observer acquires a completely new significance. This was the question which we had reached at the end of the last chapter; and the answer we gave there was that the standpoint of the agent is primary. Yet in the light of our failure to decide the truth or falsity of the behavioural theory, how can this answer be justified?

The appearance here of an obstacle in our path, a question that we are unable to resolve, and yet must resolve if we are to go forward, turns out to be imaginary. The only justification which it would be reasonable to demand is a demonstration that the primacy of the standpoint of the agent is required by the theory of the subjective and objective worlds. If it can be shown that we need to take the standpoint of the agent as ultimate, then no further question arises as to whether the standpoint of the agent really is the way we take it to be. There is no other consideration in virtue of which the belief which our theory requires to be true might turn out, contrary to our requirements, to be false. For we have seen that the question cannot be decided on the basis of the dispute between the naive view of agency and the behavioural theory. And there is no ground for believing that any other issue would be relevant to deciding it, other than a proof that our two-world theory is consistent only with the naive view of agency, re-interpreted as the negative thesis that my actions cannot be reduced the experience of an inner, observing I.

Some of the argument was anticipated in the last chapter. In brief, the proof divides into two parts. We shall argue, first, that viewing my subjective standpoint as the standpoint of an observer rather than that of an agent pushes the contradiction between the subjective and objective standpoints to an extreme that can no longer be tolerated. The reality of the contradiction becomes sheer incoherence. Having established that conclusion, it then remains to be shown that taking my subjective standpoint to be the standpoint of an agent does not lead to a similar result.

9. If my subjective standpoint is the standpoint of an observer, then the two-world metaphysic assumes the form of a double vision that sees a subjective world and also an objective world, but cannot comprehend the relation that obtains between them. For the only significance that the term 'also' can have for me in such a circumstance is the purely negative meaning deriving from the dialectic of nonegocentrism and egocentrism. When I try to form a

vision of the outcome of this dialectic, all my mind can do is oscillate between one standpoint and the other, between seeing the keyboard in front of me as *this* keyboard, in the sense in which it relates to my incommunicable sense of my own existence, and seeing it as the keyboard to which the author of these words is referring. Nothing in the objective world can explain why there is a subjective world to be seen; the objective world remains untouched by its existence or non-existence. Yet we have also discovered that my subjective world has no identity over time, no substance of its own to carry it along. It is therefore totally dependent on the objective world, while at the same time the objective world still refuses to have anything to do with it, and takes no responsibility for its existence.

Now so long as this metaphysical double vision is expressed in words, so long as we think of it only as a pattern of logical relations between different assertions, it does seem possible to hold onto the reality of the contradiction. One simply says the things that it is necessary to say. However, when we try to bring the two visions together in our minds, when we try to end the oscillation between the subjective and objective standpoints and hold onto both visions simultaneously, the result is incoherence. The two worlds simply collide.

In the light of this intolerable situation, we are forced to admit that the reality of the contradiction between the subjective and objective standpoints cannot be conceived on the model of a double vision. My subjective standpoint cannot, therefore, be the standpoint of an observer. How then could taking my subjective standpoint to be that of an agent make any essential difference? Surely the conflict between the subjective and objective standpoints remains exactly as before? It is certainly true that my existence, whether as an observer or as an agent, remains unaccounted for by the objective world on which it depends. However, whereas for an observer, the subjective world must be thought of as something simply given, whose role is simply to exist as the object of an inner vision, for an agent an entirely new set of questions arise, to which the mere observer will always remain blind.

My action cannot take place without the co-operation of both the subjective and objective worlds. What I do now has the unique, essential property of being an actual doing, a property which it can be said, timelessly, to possess only at the very moment while I am doing it. Yet that unique, momentary doing can only appear as such if at the very same time it presents the contradictory aspect of being an event in the objective world which happens alongside other events. Instead of saying, therefore, that my absolute I contemplates the keyboard before me as the object which possesses the incommunicable property of being *this* keyboard, what I should say is that from my standpoint as an agent, the keyboard is... . At that point, instead of merely saying something, or, rather, repeating the inarticulate cry, 'This!', I simply strike a key, and thereby show by my action, my doing, the way in which the keyboard is *this* for me. For spectators of my action, on the other hand, as for my future self when I look back some time later on the effect of my act, the event which was at the time both a doing and a happening appears as a mere happening, a bodily movement to be described in terms of psychological concepts, and explained in the light of my beliefs and desires.

As I act, there is no question for me of choosing whether at that moment to see my subjective world or see the objective world: both are there, simultaneously, the moment I take the risk of changing the way things will be for me, whether I like it or not; for better or for worse. The objective world is no mere belief or conception of which I needs must remind myself from time to time as I sit back and make judgements about the world as I find it: it rushes up to meet me. Now it becomes clear that the non-continuity of my subjective world, far from being a worrying paradox, is exactly what one should hope for and expect: for the time of action is always this very moment. We have thus achieved what we set out to do: the two standpoints are held fast together, and at the same time the two-world theory is brought into line with our actual life as agents. – Yet to get this far is not to put all our philosophical problems behind us. The real contradiction between the subjective and objective standpoints will reveal itself in a conflict that is primarily practical: the dialectic of the agent and the spectator.

151

12 Metaphysical freedom

1. MY subjective standpoint as an agent is primary: it comes before my standpoint as an observer. My subjective world is not something I see or describe but something I do. Yet this second proposition presents us with a logical difficulty which will not be solved by refusing to speak and resorting to action instead. It makes no sense to say, 'I do my subjective world,' or, 'I do my absolute I,' in the way it at least seemed to make sense to say, 'I see my subjective world,' or, 'I see my absolute I.' Yet surely reflection must have something to say on the matter. There ought to be some way of expressing in words my recognition that ultimately what there is for my subjective standpoint is not something to be described or pointed to but rather, '...'. Finding the right words may not add anything of philosophical substance; all one can do is express one's recognition of something that has already been proved. Unless the right words are found, however, we shall end up babbling.

In order to put together the proposition we are seeking, we first have to alter our notion of the predicate: whatever there is for my subjective standpoint is not an object to be seen. Nor, in consequence, can it be described as an action, conceived as something done and finished with. It is rather something that exists only for an agent at the moment of acting. A word that comes to mind here is 'issue'. What there is for my subjective standpoint is an issue; a situation that involves me in some way, to which my being present makes a practical difference. However, if that is the right predicate to use, then the subject of our proposition also needs to be changed. I do not do an issue; rather, what I do, I do in the face of an issue, in the face of something which prompts my decision to act. Then let us say: my subjective world is not an object which my absolute I contemplates but rather an issue which my absolute I faces. The sense I have of the incommunicable uniqueness of my existence is the fact that my subjective world is an issue for me, and for me alone. Nor can there be anything in my subjective world that is not an issue for me but only a mere object. The most distant galaxy, insofar as my absolute I takes it from the objective world and makes it mine, is an issue for me, no less than the computer screen flickering in front of me; even though I cannot now foresee my ever being in a position to do anything with it or in the face of it.

Just as there cannot, as a matter of logic, be anything in my subjective world which is not an issue for me, so there can never be a time when things cease being an issue for me. At no time am I given a holiday from the task of existing, of deciding what to make of my present situation, a period during which I might step back for a while and simply observe myself being carried along by my own momentum or by the train of external events. For observing is itself an action, a stance towards the world for which I am responsible and from which practical consequences follow. Inaction is no less my doing than the most extreme physical or mental exertion. To be an agent is not an obligation I am under; as if I could be more of an agent at any given time, or at some times rather than others. The only possibility for me – and this is itself ultimately a matter of my choice and not simply an experience that happens to me – is to be more or less aware or convinced of the fact of my agency. At one extreme lies the metaphysical illusion that my true I is an inner, passive observer of the states and doings of my active body; an illusion fostered by the behavioural theory. At the other extreme is the existentialist's vertigo of responsibility: the dizzying realization that every action that is physically possible for me is one I choose either to perform or not to perform (an insight that, thankfully, strikes most persons only when they are doing philosophy).

There are some apparent choices that I cannot make. In chapter 10 we disagreed with Heidegger's view that I have the choice of whether or not to undertake a life of 'authentic' action, as he understands it. There is no intelligible contrast, we argued, between the mundane reasons I can give for my actions which others can understand and criticize, reasons that would justify a person like me in my situation doing what I have chosen to do, and reasons that necessarily apply only to myself. It would be no less an error to regard my freedom to act as a state to which I might attain to a greater or lesser degree, a state which I strive for and either succeed or fail to realize. As far as metaphysics is concerned, I am, within the world of my subjective standpoint, simply and absolutely free.

2. This is by no means an easy claim to admit or even to understand. In the last chapter we saw how the naive conception of the will, the idea of a controlling force which directs the movements of my body without itself being caused to exercise its power, does not stand up to philosophical criticism. A will that is not merely random in its effects must act according to reasons. These reasons do not stand outside the causal order that governs the universe, but are merely a description, cast in the psychological mode, of some state of the agent's brain, or if one likes the agent's non-physical soul, which causes her bodily movements to occur, and is itself caused by other states of the agent together with input from the outside world. If we say that those bodily movements are my actions are those that I will, then we must also acknowledge that my will is not the uncaused cause of my actions. For if it is indeed the case that the physical movement of my body follows with causal necessity from previous states of my brain, or my soul, in such a way that it cannot deviate from what is determined by prior conditions, then there is no place where an uncaused act of will could interrupt or intervene in that causal train of events. Nor, on the other hand, if there are any events that are not determined to occur by prior conditions, can my will with any right claim them as events which it is in any way responsible for bringing about.

It is true that we did not reject the naive view completely. We saw that the naive conception of the will could be reformulated as the negative claim that I cannot look upon my own actions as mere happenings external to my inner, passive, observing I; as the behavioural theory in its insistence on viewing my actions as they would appear to a spectator requires me to do. This claim received its confirmation in our discovery that the only coherent formulation of the two-world theory is one that interprets my subjective standpoint as primarily that of an agent and not that of an inner observer of my own thoughts and bodily movements. Yet far from resolving the question, this sets what seems on the face of it an insoluble problem. To be truly an agent, to be faced at every moment of one's existence with real choices, implies that one is free to make those choices. The question is what such freedom can possibly amount to.

Before proceeding further, it would be well to remind ourselves that, as with the other questions which have arisen in the course of this investigation, our interest in the problem of freedom of the will is determined solely by the commitment we have undertaken to follow the dialectic of the subjective and objective standpoints wherever it may lead. What we hope, although this cannot be guaranteed in advance, is that it will lead finally to their reconciliation. No other result would establish the basis which our two-world theory needs in order to defend itself against attack. If it proved impossible to provide such a basis, then, in the light of our rejection of the alternatives of egocentrism and nonegocentrism, one could only draw the conclusion that metaphysics itself is an impossible enterprise. It would therefore be quite wrong to depart from the main path in order to explore the consequences that would follow if the two-world theory were established on a firm basis, if those issues are not essential to the dialectic. In the ensuing confusion, we might persuade ourselves that our results had provided us with sufficient grounds for validating our theory, when they had in fact done no such thing.

The reason why the problem of free will must be tackled at this point is that uncertainty about the nature of freedom stands in the way of understanding the nature of the subjective standpoint as the standpoint of an agent. We said in the last chapter that the standpoint of the agent is the standpoint from which actions 'must appear as if they had no prior cause other than an act of will; even though no such thing as an act of will is ever observed'. Since the rejection of the original naive view of agency entails that every action must be assumed to have a prior cause in the agent's previous states, the status of this 'as if' is very unclear. What does it mean to say that I possess a necessary sense of freedom, a sense corresponds to my incommunicable awareness of my own existence, if I am not, in reality, free?

3. In order to answer the question, we need to fix the relation of this metaphysical notion of freedom to the forensic distinction we are accustomed to draw between acts that are, and acts that are not done through the exercise of the agent's own choice. In the strict forensic sense, a free action is one that results from the agent's own selection, whether or not consciously formulated, between alternative courses of action; however high the cost that external circumstances - to take an extreme example, a gun pointed at one's head - might raise any action other than the one that the agent chooses to perform. That a blameworthy action is done under duress is certainly a mitigating circumstance; though for any given degree of duress it is not mitigating in every circumstance (for example, pressing the button to start World War Three) so long as the agent still has the power to put an alternative choice into effect. That an action is not done as the result of the agent's own choice, on the other hand, completely absolves the agent from blame as far as that action is concerned;

although there may indeed be other blameworthy actions on the part of the agent which resulted in the agent's being in a position of not having a choice to make, or of being ignorant of the other choices that were available.

We continue to apply the forensic notion of freedom even though, as the result of exposure to science or philosophy, we acknowledge that every bodily movement may for all we know be the causal upshot, on a physical level, of the agent's prior states taken together with impacts from the external world. That admittedly needs some explaining. The way the forensic notion of freedom is able to accommodate determination by prior causes will serve to throw into sharp relief the very different attitude taken up by my sense of metaphysical freedom, when it acts as if the law of cause and effect had been abrogated for my benefit alone.

The most worrying aspect of the contrast between forensic and metaphysical freedom is the apparent refusal of my sense of metaphysical freedom to grant the same power of abrogating the law of cause and effect to other persons as I claim for myself. While forensic freedom applies symmetrically to myself and others, my sense of metaphysical freedom appears radically asymmetric. The reader may recall that we referred briefly to this problem back in chapter 2, calling it an intolerable result. We are in fact dealing here with the central question for a metaphysic that aims to reconcile the subjective and objective standpoints: the problem of the relation between the self and the other. I am related to my own actions as the agent, and to the actions of another person as a mere spectator. At the same time, that person is related to her actions as the agent and to my actions as spectator. Of course that does not go any way to establish symmetry: for it is an essential attribute of my subjective standpoint that it cannot be generalized, without giving up its incommunicable attribute of being mine. By the end of this chapter, we shall still not have resolved the problem of the asymmetry between self and other, but at least we shall be clear what the problem is.

4. The justification for our forensic notion of freedom consists in showing what role the distinction between free and unfree acts performs – the meaning we attribute to it and the purposes it accomplishes – within the lives of persons who explain and criticize one another's actions; that is to say, every human society. While it is indeed possible for our moral practices to be criticized when viewed from the more elevated vantage point of a more fully developed morality, or simply from the perspective of a different moral code,

there is a sense in which all moralities share the belief in the reality of the distinction between acts that are performed as the result of the agent's own choice and those that are not; between acts for which the agent is to be held to some degree responsible, whatever the mitigating circumstances, and acts for which the agent is not responsible. A similar notion of responsibility underlies criticism on prudential grounds. It is appropriate to praise or blame someone only for those actions for which he may be held responsible; that is a principle that holds good whatever standards we may have for actions deserving of praise or blame, and whatever specific beliefs we may hold about human psychology or the extent of human powers. Our confidence in applying this principle undoubtedly receives a knock when we first encounter the philosophical problem of the apparent incompatibility of freedom and determinism; it is, however, a blow from which the forensic notion of freedom soon recovers.

According to the thesis of determinism as we shall understand it, given total knowledge of the state of a person's body, or soul, at any one time, together with knowledge of every impact subsequently received from her environment, it would in principle be possible for a Laplacian super-mind capable of directly intuiting the state of every particle in the universe to predict every movement which her body made from that time onwards. Modern physics has, as we have already indicated, given some grounds for doubting this deterministic principle, but we shall for the sake of argument assume that it is valid. It would indeed be a consolation to know that we lived in a universe where, as the libertarian hopes, we all have a sporting chance to escape the dread hand of necessity, a universe where it is a genuinely open possibility how my biography will develop (cf. David Wiggins 'Towards a Reasonable Libertarianism'). However, that is a possibility to which the forensic notion of freedom remains indifferent. (Indeed it appears, independently of that argument, that a libertarian ought to be equally happy whether the indeterminacy is located within the agent's brain or in the external circumstances that prompt the agent's actions, or indeed in the consequences that follow from it. Whether or not one grants such liberty to the agent is immaterial.)

Now our common sense grasp of morality tells us that it would be wrong to blame an individual for an action if she could not have chosen to do otherwise. Yet the admission of the possible truth of determinism means that we must acknowledge that the very activity of choosing between different courses of action may, from an external point of view, be a consequence of processes that go their own way without any possibility of deviation. It follows that the agent could not, in one very important sense, have done otherwise than she in fact did.

Does that mean that no action is deserving of praise or blame? Few would embrace this paradoxical and morally repugnant conclusion, even if we are not sure exactly why we are justified in resisting it. Instead, our awareness that every action springs from an agent's character and past history makes us far more cautious in making final moral judgements, realizing that the moral choice may have presented a very different aspect to the agent than it does now to us. On the other hand, there are cases where our knowledge of the person concerned appears to rule out any such mitigating factors, such as when a close friend betrays us, when we do not hesitate to display a justified sense of anger and resentment. Intuitively, we are able to grasp that there is another important sense in which a morally responsible agent could have done otherwise. If only my friend had thought more deeply about the meaning of our friendship, she would not have done as she did. How can this intuition be explained?

The philosophical basis for the intuition has been fiercely debated. It is generally agreed, however, that the key lies in the fact that a will that is truly in control of the agent's actions must, as we argued in the last chapter, necessarily be a rational will. We may, therefore, give a second definition of the forensic notion of freedom as the power to be determined to act by one's own reasons. This power is in no way undermined by the fact that what we call reasoning or having reasons is merely a description, cast in the psychological mode, of physical processes which, for all we know, follow strictly deterministic laws. The possibility of reasoning and the possibility of choice go together: it is characteristic of practical reasoning that one represents different courses of action to oneself, and their possible consequences, and then chooses between them. (In the rare circumstance when, strictly, only one course of action is physically possible the agent's action is already effectively determined, and reasoning has no essential part to play.)

When we assert that a person who has done something wrong could actually have chosen to do otherwise, and not merely have done otherwise if he had chosen, what we implicitly have in mind may be something like the following. We suppose ourselves being present when that person was deliberating over his action, or perhaps when he was just about to act, having declined to give the action the proper thought that it warranted. If only we had been able to reason with the agent, we think, he might have done otherwise than he in fact did. The agent lacked nothing that was required for making that alternative choice, other than the fact that we were not actually there to prod his conscience, or point out things that he had overlooked. Belatedly, we show that we regard the wrongdoer as responsible for his past action by rehearsing the reasons that ought to have dissuaded him from doing it, even though the action cannot now be taken back. (Similarly, in self-criticism, I imagine arguing with my own past self, bringing to bear the wisdom I now possess but then lacked. There is also a cognate story to tell about praise: in this case, we imagine defending the agent against those who might have sought to persuade the agent to have done otherwise.)

Blame, and the anger and resentment which go with it, is in a sense irrational in that it necessarily comes too late. One cannot change the past. Indeed, when we are dealing not with everyday wrongdoing but with radical evil, we know for certain that all our arguments would have fallen on deaf ears. Yet recognition of these stark facts does not prevent us from continuing to indulge in our fantasy. That is simply the way human beings are; it is not clear that we ought to change, as some philosophers have urged, nor even that we can. This is not to ignore the fact that taking persons to task for their misdeeds also serves a useful purpose – though one that would not on its own justify our present attitudes – in that the activity of moral criticism develops our sensitivity to moral questions, while blame and punishment increase the likelihood that those on the receiving end will do better next time. (The practical point is one that has been urged by so-called 'compatibilists' to the exclusion of the element of fantasy. The view closest to the one described here is Strawson's in 'Freedom and Resentment'. He makes the error, in our view, of seeking ultimately to justify feelings of anger and resentment in terms of their effects within the social fabric; their role within inter-personal relationships. That is something which the person in the grip of those emotions cannot do without insincerity.)

5. As far as my sense of metaphysical freedom is concerned, things appear very different. The comparative ease with which the apparent incompatibility between forensic freedom and determinism is overcome, stands in contrast with the absolute refusal of my will to entertain the possibility that its operation is only the result of causal processes that allow no scope for deviation. My will says: what I will, will be; and had I willed differently, things would have been different. Determinism says: what is determined will be; and given the prior conditions, no other course of events is possible. What we call freedom when we engage in the practice of moral or prudential criticism is by no means what my will intends when it assumes its own absolute freedom of action.

When, for the sake of philosophical example, I demonstrate my freedom to myself by choosing to move my arm, there is only one sense in which I could have done otherwise that interests me. When I consider that I might not have chosen to move my arm, but might have decided to move my leg instead, I do not imagine that the prior conditions that led up to my arm moving might have been different, or wish they had been so. On the contrary, it seems to me, as I mentally transport myself back in time, that irrespective of prior conditions my will would still have retained the power to aim at one thing or another, to turn its force in this direction or that. The paradox is that, while I am describing the way things necessarily appear to me when I perform an action, I no longer naively believe that my will actually possesses the power to choose an action in defiance of the conditions that causally determine the movements of my body. So what necessarily seems to be the case is also necessarily not the case. How can we make sense of this contradictory attitude?

The question we have to ask is, what is it about the thought that my bodily movements might be fully determined by prior conditions that my will finds so objectionable? Up till now, we have relied on the metaphor of a track from which no deviations are allowed. According to determinism, causal processes determine one single track, one and only one possible course of events. My will, meanwhile, does not consider itself to be on any track; it is free to go to the right or to the left, whenever it chooses. Yet for all I know, the route that my will actually chooses to take, the track which it seems to beat through virgin forest unhindered by any constraint other than the natural obstacles which it encounters, is the very same track that causal determinism has laid down in advance, indeed long before I was born.

The critical element here is the thought that what my will seems to decide has in some sense already been decided. My will cannot regard its own decisions as a mere illusion, without ceasing to be a will and becoming instead an inner, passive observer of my own thoughts and bodily movements. It is essential to its notion of deciding that, at the time of making the decision, the future is open and undecided. Yet, according to determinism, the future is closed, a foregone conclusion, not open. Whatever decision was made, was made at the beginning of time. Consequently, the actual process that appears to my will as its deciding on a course of action is in reality completely different from what my will necessarily takes it to be. The decisions made by my will are an illusion; but they cannot appear to my will as an illusion without my will ceasing to be a will and becoming instead a passive observer. Now we have already established that as far as the theory of subjective and objective worlds is concerned, my subjective standpoint must be that of an agent and cannot, on pain of the ultimate incoherence of a metaphysical double vision, be taken to be that of an observer of my own actions. The illusion is therefore a necessary illusion.

What, then, if determinism is not true? We pointed out above that gaps in the causal order due to an element of indeterminism, such as those random events which according to quantum theory take place at the sub-atomic level, can only produce random effects; and the will can no more be what it takes itself to be if it is uncaused in this sense than if determinism is true. However, let us set that argument aside for one moment, and assume, along with Wiggins, that all the will demands is that the future should not be completely determined. The will knows immediately through the sheer fact of willing that the different possible futures which open up before it are all equally capable of being realized until the moment it makes its decision. Now it might have been the case that the universe was deterministic up until yesterday, when a development neither anticipated nor recognized by current scientific knowledge led to the breakdown of determinism. My illusion that my will was metaphysically free would cease, according to this more modest proposal, to be a false belief and become a true belief. However, it would not thereby become knowledge, for knowledge of the truth of a proposition cannot result from a merely accidental relation to what makes the proposition true. My sense of freedom would remain illusory as the supposed insight into the nature of reality which it takes itself to be, in the same way as would a visual illusion that accidentally led to a true belief. My sense of metaphysical freedom, however construed, remains an illusion whether or not determinism is true.

6. It is easy to fall into the temptation to dilute our paradoxical result, by mistakenly comparing the necessary illusion that my will is, or knows itself to be undetermined by prior conditions with other things that we call a necessary illusion. What we normally mean by an illusion or false belief that is necessary is only one that is either unavoidable, given the circumstances in which the subject finds himself, or else necessary for some purpose. For example, the experience of falling in love may, as some suppose, involve the necessary illusion that one's beloved has attributes of character or beauty that no-one else in the world could ever possess. Or, to take a different example, the bravery of a soldier in battle may be due in part to the soldier's necessary illusion that he alone, of all his foes and comrades, is invulnerable. The necessity of my illusion of metaphysical freedom has a different status altogether. An illusion that is unavoidable, or necessary for some purpose, is necessary relative to a given factor that might not have been present. By

contrast, the necessity of my illusion of freedom is a consequence of the reality of my subjective standpoint, which we have established cannot be other than the standpoint of an agent. Now a necessity that is relative to a fact that is itself necessary, is not relative but absolute. The necessity of my illusion of freedom is nothing less than a metaphysical fact, a state of affairs which the course of our argument has shown cannot be otherwise.

How can a mere illusion be necessary in this sense? The answer has to be that, for all that the notion of the primacy of the standpoint of an agent serves, as we argued at the end of the last chapter, to yoke the subjective and objective worlds together, the two worlds remain radically separate. It is the absolute I of my subjective world – the I that exists only at this moment – that possesses a necessary sense of freedom, while the relative I of the objective world remains just another individual whose movements follow the natural course of events. From my subjective standpoint, the world does not merely revolve around me, it flows from me; from the objective standpoint, I am just another satellite making its erratic way around the universe, pushed this way and that. When I compare my absolute I with my relative I, as I am inevitably led to do, I am forced to conclude that my subjective sense of freedom is, when considered objectively, a mere illusion. Yet the reality of my situation is no more purely objective than it is purely subjective. My freedom is necessarily real and unreal. For what we are dealing with is none other than the metaphysical contradiction between the subjective and objective standpoints themselves.

7. While one may be tempted to reduce the necessity of my sense of metaphysical freedom to a purely relative necessity, there is, on the opposite side, a temptation to inflate its significance, by arguing that if the necessity is absolute then it cannot be illusory. Thus, one may try to prove that the necessity of my sense of freedom, the impossibility of my abandoning my standpoint as an agent, can yield knowledge concerning the objective world. The argument is this. (The idea comes from L.W. Beck *The Actor and the Spectator* pp. 128ff., though it is given here a dogmatic slant that Beck does not intend). Let us suppose that a spectator of my actions sets out to predict my future behaviour. It is possible that these predictions should be true. Indeed, if the movements of my body do result from strictly deterministic processes, then there seems in principle no limit to the amount of knowledge of my future behaviour that a spectator could come to possess. Here we seem to have the clearest possible case where my belief that I am able to decide what actions I shall do is illusory. The

spectator already knows, my actions have already been decided. However, one might argue, that overlooks one vital point. The only reason the spectator's predictions are able to be successful is that I remain ignorant of them. If someone says to me, 'You are now going to move your arm', the very fact that I have been told the prediction gives me a reason, which I did not have before, for not following it. No prediction of my behaviour can be certain, so long as there remains the possibility that, on hearing the prediction, I shall set out deliberately to falsify it. The conclusion of the argument is that my subjective sense of freedom gives me the objective knowledge that I can always falsify any prediction that a spectator makes concerning my future behaviour, if I so choose.

If this argument were valid, there would be no need to invoke a two-world theory in order to explain how my subjective sense of freedom can exist side by side with the objective possibility that all my actions are decided in advance by deterministic laws. For what the argument purports to show is that my actions can never finally be decided in advance by any mere spectator; I, the agent, always have the last word on the matter. There is nothing in the world that a spectator might learn that could be used to predict my behaviour that I could not simply decide to refute, were I to hear about it. If that claim were true, then my freedom would after all be a fact about the objective world and not an illusion.

On closer examination, however, the argument collapses. It is undoubtedly the case, and it is this which gives superficial credence to the argument, that no means of predicting human behaviour has yet been devised that can resist a subject's determined attempt to falsify the predictions that are made. However, that is only a reflection of our present physical limitations. If my bodily processes do follow deterministic laws, then it would be possible in principle for an all-seeing spectator, a Laplacian super-mind to predict my future physical movements on the basis of detailed knowledge of those processes (even if, in the light of the irreducibility of psychological to physical descriptions, the spectator remained necessarily ignorant about the psychological descriptions under which my future movements appeared as actions).

Of course if I am to be told of the prediction in advance, then one of the things that must be taken into account in the calculation of the trajectories of my physical parts is the fact that I will be told of the prediction, or, rather, that my senses will receive a certain barrage of physical stimulation. Let us then suppose that a voice comes out of nowhere and whispers, 'Klempner, your left arm will move in five seconds time!'. Resolved to falsify this prediction, I grip my desk tightly, keeping my arms pressed into my sides. Suddenly, I feel a stab of pain in my left knee and instinctively reach down, forgetting my resolution. Or perhaps a wasp lands near my hand, and I decide that proving a philosophical point is not worth the pain of getting stung. Or perhaps again, despite my strenuous mental effort to block out all thought other than that of my resolution, I suddenly remember a phone call I had to make and move to get up. Or perhaps finally I simply succumb to an inexplicable, irresistible desire to move my arm. It might take several incidents such as this to convince me, but eventually I should have to concede that I was indeed powerless to falsify the voice's predictions.

8. One notable feature of this thought experiment is the way in which, in each of the examples given, a reason appears why I fail to falsify the spectator's prediction: a stab of pain, the fear of a wasp sting, remembering the phone call, a sudden irresistible desire. Now what might happen sometimes clearly could not happen all the time: an account of how, one after another, reasons just came up why I failed to falsify a continuous series of predictions would become increasingly improbable, and in the end would simply not make sense. Nor can the gap be filled by saying that on hearing the prediction I find my body moving outside my control. That is not because that is something that could not happen; it could, and it is a frightening prospect. Yet once again, what happened sometimes could not happen always. As we noted in the last chapter, in criticizing the Tractarian account of my willed actions occurring only as a 'favour granted by fate', the reality of the objective standpoint, the necessity that my subjective states present an aspect to the objective standpoint in my words and actions rules out the possibility that I could exist as a subject of experience whose desires did not correspond with the movements of its body. The all-seeing spectator's scope for telling me of its predictions is therefore limited to cases where some special circumstance may be relied upon to overrule my desire to falsify the prediction. The spectator could only escape those limits by destroying me as a self-conscious subject and making my body into a puppet. However, that concession cannot be taken to show, as the original argument intended, that my sense of freedom is not after all illusory. If the logic of the situation prevents the spectator from providing me with a continual advance commentary on my bodily movements, that in no way shows a limitation in the spectator's predictive powers. The spectator does know, and can prove to me by numerous examples, every move I am going to make.

164

There is, however, something else the all-seeing spectator can do which we have not yet considered. Suppose that the spectator decides against communicating with me directly, but instead causes to have written down its version of the complete story of my life, from my birth to my death. Most of the ingredients that conventionally go to make the story of a life would, admittedly, be missed out; it would hardly work as a biography. What the story did contain, however, would leave no scope for any physical action on my part that did not correspond with the bodily movements which it predicted.

One day, let us imagine, I notice an unfamiliar volume lying on my desk. The cover bears my name and today's date. Opening the book near the middle I am astonished to read the following: '12.33.29 GK's hands grasp book. 12.33.37 GK opens book at p. 141. 12.33.38 GK's eyes turn towards page...'. Skipping back, I find everywhere I turn my day's movements described in boring, meticulous detail. Having read enough to convince myself, I close the book, and remain motionless in my chair for several minutes, not knowing what to do. If my worst fears are confirmed, if every move I shall make today is written down for me to read, then it seems that I really could become a passive observer of my own bodily movements. Suppose I yield to temptation, and read the remainder of the book. How could I bring myself to get up from my seat knowing in advance every move I was going to make and not being able to do anything about it? Then I think: it is logically impossible that I should know this about myself. I cannot cease to be an agent without ceasing to be, and the author of the book knows this. Yet the book is right here in my hands. I check my watch and find the entry for the present time. Sure enough, I read, '12.43.46 GK opens book at p. 143. 12.43.47 GK's eyes turn towards page...'. I have barely reached the bottom of the page when I notice that the paper is turning dark yellow. The book is crumbling in my hands like rotten wood. Seconds later, all that remains of the volume is a pile of dust.

9. The sense of freedom that characterizes my subjective standpoint as an agent is a rather fragile thing. For my bodily movements are, for all I know, completely determined; in that case, all that saves me is the logical necessity that I remain ignorant of the causal antecedents of those bodily movements. Now one question we have so far ignored is how I am to conceive of another person's freedom. For we can change the thought experiment, and imagine instead that the volume I discover relates not to me but to someone I know, say, the old woman who lives next door. Once again, I consider the consequences of my reading the book from cover to cover. Without straining my credulity, it does now seem perfectly possible that I could

165

know every movement that my neighbour is going to make. The metaphysical freedom I necessarily attribute to myself is not something I feel compelled to attribute to her also. From the objective standpoint, it is of course true that my neighbour must have the same sense of freedom as I have. As far as I am concerned, however, the necessity which she feels is, to revert to a distinction we used earlier, relative, not absolute. Whereas the freedom I sense is something I must take to be real, an essential attribute of my subjective world, the freedom she senses is just something she believes. Turning the pages, I know with complete certainty that her belief is false. As I imagine her, going through a day which for her is new and unmade, but in reality encountering every little incident, making every move precisely at its appointed time, I feel a mixture of awe and pity: pity for the futility of all human endeavours; and awe at the absolute divide that separates my own subjective standpoint from the world of others.

If that is the first word on the question of self and other, however, it is certainly not the last. My relation to another person is not, after all, a relation to an object whose movements I seek to predict in order to serve my own purposes; one of the moving obstacles that make up the furniture of my world. I do not merely observe and record the behaviour of individuals with whom I share a common living space, as if they were only repositories of knowledge with whom I communicate in order to exchange information, or machines whose labours serve my interests. The other calls me and I respond; for the other's sake and not my own. In this simple transaction lies a depth that cannot be fathomed, either in terms of the absolute equality of the objective world, or by measuring the other person by means of the yardstick of my own subjective world. The greatest challenge for metaphysics is to comprehend that depth: to comprehend how, to use Kantian terminology, persons can be ends in themselves and not merely means to serve my ends. For now, we shall undertake the more modest task of describing how the problem of self and other is transformed when we reject the notion of my subjective standpoint as the standpoint of an observer, in favour of the primacy of my standpoint as an agent. In terms of the standpoint of an observer, it will be argued, the problem is simply insoluble. The only hope for a solution, therefore, lies in the possibility of interpreting the problem of self and other in terms of a further refinement of the dialectic of agent and spectator.

The subjective standpoint of the inner observer is related to the objects that make up its subjective world simply by virtue of calling them *this* or mine. If the observer inside me were ever to raise the

166

question of the reality of other subjects of experience, then the only form that question can take is whether or not there exists something by virtue of which objects are *this* but not mine. The reality of the objective standpoint will not give me what I want, for that establishes the absolute equality of self and other at the cost of ignoring the reality of my subjective standpoint. Yet how can anything be *this* without being mine? When I try to represent to my self a *this* which belongs to the other, I find that I have merely reverted to the fruitless attempt to comprehend the subjective and objective standpoints within a single domain, undertaken by the refined cartesian dualist or the identity theorist. If everyone has a *this*, then, as we argued in chapter 6, so must my perfect replica. The whole point, however, of referring to the *this* was to distinguish me from a perfect copy who was not me. If I give up the uniquely identifying role of a *this* that necessarily makes objects mine and no-one else's, then I have once more reverted to the objective standpoint.

That is as far as one gets with the problem of self and other when the only thing that makes my subjective standpoint real is the existence of *this*. To get any further, it is first necessary to acknowledge that my subjective standpoint is the standpoint of an agent and not that of a mere observer. Now, we see that the terms of the problem alter dramatically. What the other demands of me is not that I should recognize that the other too has *this*, a proposition I simply cannot comprehend. What the other demands is that I should recognize the other's metaphysical freedom as I recognize my own, with a necessity that is absolute. The forensic freedom presupposed by our practice of moral criticism will not suffice. Nor is it enough to establish the relative necessity of a sense of freedom that I, the spectator, attribute to the other only as a belief; a belief, moreover, that I from my superior position already know to be false. Then how can the demand ever be satisfied? Could it be that when the other calls me and I respond, the other becomes superior – to me?

13 Self and other

1. 'WHAT are others to me?' – To raise this question, revives memories of an insecurity concerning our very existence which predates the activity of philosophy, both in each person's own life and in the history of human culture; a primitive fear which lies so close to each one of us that it gives the lie to any claim on the part of the philosopher who approaches the problem of self and other to maintain the attitude of a disinterested seeker after truth. We are not prepared to accept the truth at any price; we demand reassurance. Intellectual curiosity, philosophical wonder are revealed as superficial poses which conceal our terror of being abandoned in the midst of an alien universe.

Psychologists trace the fear of abandonment to the earliest experiences of childhood. Novelists have described the many disturbing forms in which it manifests itself. Yet still its proper analysis remains the concern of metaphysics, not psychology. The basic form of human existence, underlying all its psychological variations, is to live under the threat of a self-imposed solitude, that despairs of ever making contact with the reality of other persons in their otherness. Mere thinking cannot, it is true, alone counter this threat: what one is ultimately called upon to do is simply respond to the appeal of the other, an appeal far more immediate than any argument. We are not lost, so long as we can sense the response within us; even if, through moral weakness, we may on occasion fail to act on that response, or even if it should so happen that we ourselves are abandoned and cast aside, and find that the other refuses to respond to us. What reflective thought can and must do, however, is counter the specious philosophical arguments, the illusory visions that cover up this basic form of existence, and which, far from dispelling the threat of solitude as they promise to do, render us all the more vulnerable to it.

What is the problem of self and other? Let us put the question concretely. What is it that I seek, and fear that I might not find, when I contemplate the face of the other? The other has the characteristic features of someone of my kind. Objectively, we are both blood, sinews, flesh and bone constructed according to a universal pattern: the human species. Perhaps there is also something else, a non-physical soul; that is just as much a matter of speculation or doubt in my own case as it is with respect to the other. What is not a matter of doubt is that I exist for myself in a way in which no-one else exists for me. The existence of my subjective world is an additional fact, over and above facts about the objective world, facts which include the common nature which I must assume I share with others, whatever that nature might ultimately turn out to be.

The philosophical question is not whether the latter assumption is correct. (If a malevolent demon has placed me alone in a world of zombies or automata, whose physical states are all under the demon's direct control, that is something that logic can never disprove.) Our question can only concern the status of the other within a metaphysic of subjective and objective worlds. In terms of that theory, the one thing I cannot meaningfully seek in questioning the reality of the other is a second non-objective fact, parallel or symmetrical to the existence of my subjective world. For the notion that I and the other stand in parallel takes one back immediately to the one-world metaphysic of nonegocentrism, the denial of the reality of my subjective standpoint, the refusal to recognize any facts other than objective facts. From the objective standpoint, I and the other appear as two of the same, two 'I's and equally two 'you's, neither of whom possesses any attribute, whether physical or non-physical, that marks that individual out as being the person I refer to by means of the pronoun 'I'. The question of the reality of the other thus arises only in the context of recognizing the radical asymmetry that my subjective standpoint imposes on the structure of reality, and consequently on the form of my relation with the other.

2. What I seek with regard to the other is not to overcome the asymmetry between us. For nothing, no metaphysical vision, could bring me so far out of myself that I ceased to identify with one of the persons in the relation. On the contrary, the other is forever located at a distance from me that I could never be placed from my own self. Now, in one sense this appears self-evident: I am here while the other

169

is there, facing me. We are not, however, talking merely of spatial distance. For the distance between myself and the other is fundamentally different from the distance that separates me from the tools, the obstacles, the means of sustenance or background scenery that together form the material out of which my familiar environment is constructed. The distance of a mere object is one which always depends in principle on me, and which I am free to dissolve. The hammer in my hand is no longer separated from me, and becomes an extension of my body. The obstacle in my path may be pushed aside or destroyed. The food I eat literally becomes a part of me. And nothing is so far in the background that I could not imagine how it might be reached, and made into a tool, or food. What is it then, in the face of the other person, that resists any attempt I might make to dissolve the distance between us? What prevents me from treating the other as a mere tool, or food, or an obstacle to be overcome? No physical resistance prevents me. What I see in the other's look, is something that tells me that the distance between us is simply not to be dissolved, either by me or by the other.

The question then is what is it about the other that tells me this. It cannot be a matter of mere physical resemblance; the sign that we are both of the same kind or nature. For there is no reason why our being of the same nature should hinder me in any way, if that is all that hinders me. It is surely not like this: that were I a hammer, I should be free to use any object as a tool, but never a hammer; were I made of gingerbread, I should be free to eat any food except gingerbread! Even granting a distinction between mere outward form, or physical substance, and my essential nature, it is still not clear what counts as something's being of my nature. All the members of the animal kingdom share my nature to a greater or lesser extent; what justifies my drawing the line between humans and other animals? On the other hand, if intelligent aliens of grotesque countenance were to appear amongst us, with bodies so unlike ours that we could not even identify corresponding parts, such beings would surely not, just because they had evolved on a different planet with a different nature, be precluded from being granted the same indissoluble distance that one grants to human beings.

Then let it be said that what human beings and intelligent aliens have in common which distinguishes them from all lower animals is self-consciousness; and that this attribute has a unique value. By virtue of possessing this value, the other must never be used by me as a mere means to satisfy my own desires. The question still arises what it is about the attribute of self-consciousness that renders its

170

bearer so pre-eminently valuable, and indeed why that value is damaged when the bearer is used as a mere means.

3. It is clear that our question lies at the basis of ethics, and that what we are seeking is a philosophical justification for moral conduct. My recognition of the reality of the other person consists in my granting to the other a value over and above any instrumental value that she might happen to possess in relation to my needs and interests. Now it may appear to the reader that we have identified two things that ought to be kept logically separate. One question is whether the other person is real, whether there is, in addition to all that empirical investigation could ever reveal, something belonging to, or 'inside' the individual who claims my respect or calls out for my help which is the same as I possess, or have inside me. The second question is whether as a consequence of this I am obliged to act ethically towards her.

The idea that the first question is separate from the second question, however, is an illusion. Whatever form, substance, nature or kind I may share with the other, I still exist for myself in a way that no-one else, as a matter of logic, could ever exist for me. That asymmetry is sufficient to put the reality of the other into question. We are not, and never could be, two of the same. For one has put aside once and for all the strategy of nonegocentrism, a strategy which, in its insistence that the relation between self and other be comprehended from the objective standpoint, would make my own subjective standpoint unreal. Thus, the doubt that the other may not be real for me, that I may in some metaphysical sense be alone in the universe, can only be laid to rest by my coming to recognize the logical basis for the unique status of the other amongst all the objects I may encounter, which forbids me to treat the other as an object. The force of this argument is of a sheer process of elimination: if one starts from the position of the ultimate asymmetry of self and other, then there is nothing other than the rational demand upon my conduct in which the reality of the other could consist. The question of the reality of the other and the question of justifying my moral conduct towards the other are therefore one and the same.

Still, it might be objected that we are seeking a reason for moral conduct where none is to be found. Granted that my regarding the other as real, my sense that I am not alone in the universe, consists in my responding ethically to the other's appeal, in my taking the other's interests into account when I decide what I am to do; is it not absurd to ask what it is about the other person's being a self-conscious individual that rationally justifies my performing acts which I should do anyway without hesitation? One may admit that it is, taken as a straightforward request for information, an absurd question for someone to ask. A typical characteristic of philosophical questions is to seek answers which we must in some sense know already. The trouble is that we lose confidence in our knowing. Not only do we find ourselves faced with questions concerning the conflicting claims of oneself and others which have a range of possible answers, and which our unreflective moral intuitions are not equipped to decide with any degree of certainty. That problem of moral philosophy is difficult enough. Rather, in certain moods we are led to question the very basis of morality itself. How we fall prey to these moods is a matter of individual psychology; it is certainly not always as a result of doing philosophy. Yet it is to philosophy that we look in order to resolve our doubts.

4. I glance at a man's face, let us say a stranger hurrying past in the street, and what I see, as the other person returns my look, is a self-consciousness like myself. The other is aware of me as I am of him. Just as I am, he is also aware of being aware of me, and of my awareness of him, and of his awareness of my awareness, and so on. The complexities of this momentary transaction could be analysed endlessly, but what actually takes place has the appearance of absolute simplicity: the original and universal event of mutual recognition that lies at the basis of human social existence. When doubts arise concerning the reality of the other, neither the simple appearance nor the complex underlying structure of the experience of mutual recognition is called into question. What is called into question is rather our conception of its significance.

We may imagine an individual who engages in the practice of mutual recognition but interprets it in a completely different way from us. For reasons that will soon become apparent, we shall call such an individual the practical solipsist. When the practical solipsist converses with us, when he discusses or criticizes our actions, or allows us to discuss or criticise his actions, the practical solipsist's one and only interest is to get us to do what he wants. When he asks, in an apparently concerned tone of voice, how we are feeling, it is only to obtain information that will be useful in predicting our behaviour. The practical solipsist is not really troubled, except insofar as our actions threaten to frustrate his own plans. Indeed, he has no conception of what another person's suffering pain means, for example, other than that it is a physical state caused by some illness or injury that causes the sufferer to behave in certain predictable ways. Pain is only real only when he is the one suffering it. The interest of such a hypothesis

172

for metaphysics is this. However unpleasant it may be to imagine what it would be like to encounter, or indeed to be an individual such as we have described, the very notion that such a subject might exist raises two questions: Is practical solipsism a coherent possibility? and, if so, what possible reasons might one give for not being a practical solipsist?

The unpalatable truth is that our description of the behaviour of the practical solipsist is perfectly coherent. We referred in chapter 3 to the more familiar, though for present purposes less accurate term psychopath. Nor indeed, if one were to encounter such an individual, is there any ground for hoping that one could ever affect his conduct by mere reasoning. There is nothing one can point to, which the practical solipsist has not seen but could be made to see, which would make any difference to the his ruthless reinterpretation of all practical questions in terms of the exclusive reality of the his own needs and desires. You cannot cure blindness by turning up the lights.

Now we have called such a solipsism practical in order to contrast it with the position we ought to be attacking, which is theoretical solipsism. It is in fact a gross error to think that the philosophical justification for moral conduct depends upon our being able to convert the practical solipsist by logical reasoning. The solipsist laughs at our reasons; but we for our part need not take any notice. For our doubts concerning the reality of the other, doubts which philosophical argument is called upon to allay, are only indirectly practical. We do not doubt that we shall continue to act morally, lapses apart. What we do doubt is whether our finding ourselves motivated to act morally, our exhibiting moral attitudes, has any real foundation, whether as we walk the moral tightrope there is anything holding us up, other than a deeply ingrained convention based ultimately on self-interest, or else an irrational natural sympathy for the wants and needs of others. For in either case, the reality of the other would then be a complete illusion; albeit one that we were constitutionally incapable of casting aside.

5. Given the reality of my subjective standpoint, as an appearance whose reality as appearance cannot be explained away, the relation between myself and the other necessarily contains a permanent, built-in asymmetry. I can never ascend to the point of view from which we appear as merely two of the same. If the other is real, that cannot be on the basis of any account that treats myself and the other in the same way. My reality entails the reality of my subjective standpoint; the reality of the other can consist only in the other's having a unique status apart from the objects I encounter, which

prevents me from treating the other as a mere means to my end. This status depends upon the structure of a metaphysic, in a way yet to be decided. That is the basic framework we have to work with. One need make no apology for the repetition; if one loses sight of this framework, the point of the discussion of practical and theoretical solipsism will have been completely missed. For it follows from what has been said that an explanation of moral conduct on any basis which disclaims the possibility of rational, logical justification, whether that explanation be couched in terms of ingrained convention, or in terms of natural sympathy, entails theoretical solipsism: the other is, in a metaphysical sense, unreal.

That is far from being an obvious conclusion. On the contrary, when one reflects on the basis of morality, one may at first feel little resistance to embracing the sceptical alternatives of either nature or convention, or perhaps a vague mixture of the two. On behalf of the sceptical view, it may be conceded that the explanations offered go very smoothly, and are far from appearing the affront to common sense that, say, scepticism concerning an external world appears to be. As we have already remarked, in certain moods one is prey to doubts which attack the very foundations of one's moral beliefs. If one is not prone to philosophical reflection, these doubts may pass as quickly as the mood which prompted them. If, on the other hand, one turns to metaphysics in order to quell the doubts, then the conclusion is inescapable: if you believe that morality is based only on an ingrained convention, that is to say, on an unspoken pact that prevents all-out warfare between totally self-interested individuals; or, alternatively, if you believe that it is based only on an irrational sympathy biologically imprinted on human nature; in short, if for either reason you believe that morality has no logical foundation, then you must also believe that you are alone in the universe.

What saves many a moral sceptic is that one holds inconsistent beliefs. One continues to think and act as if moral conduct had a logical foundation, as if the other were real. Moral philosophers who side with scepticism would naturally disagree with that claim; and indeed have expended much time and energy trying to prove that, when everything is taken into consideration, it is always in one's best interests to be moral rather than amoral: the moral sceptic does not need to be saved. In terms of our framework, that is equivalent to saying that although the reality of the other is, ultimately, only an illusion, it is an one we should be irrational to cast aside. According to these philosophers, if one wishes to act consistently with the belief that the only basis for morality is either nature or convention, then one will not abandon morality. On the contrary, when we contemplate

174

the mean, brutish life of the practical solipsist, or amoral psychopath, the moral life will always appear more attractive. There is every reason to embrace the illusion with open arms, and to pray that it never disappears.

That seems a very precarious position to hold. What if I wake up one morning to find that the illusion has disappeared? The bleak prospect facing the individual who sees morality for what it truly is, far from being banished by such arguments, would surely appear all the worse. In vain would one strive to act out the moral life: such a performance might well be to others' benefit but not one's own. Let us allow, however, that the illusion is too deeply ingrained, at least in most of us, ever to disappear of its own accord. It is easy enough for most people, in their day-to-day existence, to concede to the demands of morality; no great effort is required. And even when circumstances arise that make it hard to do the right thing rather than act for narrowly selfish reasons, the consequences of making a consistent practice of narrow selfishness are far worse than the effort and pain involved in developing the habit of resisting one's selfish impulses. Yet there may yet arise an unprecedented occasion when one's very commitment to morality is put to the test. It may happen only once in one's lifetime. Say, that the advantages to be gained from this one evil act, the fearful consequences of holding back, are so great that all one's previous calculations are overturned. The rational thing to do now is choose evil over good. – Most persons would, on reflection, reject this conclusion: evil necessarily arises out of a failure to perceive the good, or else to act on one's knowledge; it can never be rationally justified.

6. We shall now investigate two strategies for establishing a logical foundation for moral conduct. Each seeks in its own way to interpret the reality of the other in terms of the special, pre-eminent status granted to the other within a theory that acknowledges the reality of the subjective standpoint. In both cases, the question being asked is not, Why should there be such a thing as moral conduct?, or, Why are persons moral?, but rather, Why should I be moral? We are seeking a reason for being moral, not in the sense of an account of why people in general are motivated to act morally, nor even why it is a good thing that they should be so motivated, but rather in the sense of considerations which, as a matter of logical necessity, have bearing on my conduct. (One may note that even the strategy we have summarily rejected, that based on the nonegocentrism, recognizes that the question, Why be moral? must be understood as addressed primarily to the first person. The non-egocentrist's strategy is one of

self-effacement: an attack on the illusion that I have a unique place in the world. I am just one person amongst others, a person whose wants and needs, for all that I may be in the best position to satisfy them, have no greater importance than any other person's wants and needs.)

One strategy for establishing a logical basis for moral conduct derives its credentials, ironically, from the theory of egocentrism. At first sight, it may indeed seem a hopeless task to seek an account of the reality of the other on the basis of a theory according to which only my subjective standpoint is real. However, the egocentrist has an ingenious argument, one that at least deserves a hearing. It is only after we have identified the fatal shortcomings of the egocentrist's strategy – problems that arise independently of the criticisms that have already been levelled against that theory – that we shall be able fully to appreciate the alternative offered by the two-world theory.

The supporter of egocentrism certainly faces a difficult problem. If all that is real is the world of my subjective standpoint, then other persons can exist only as characters in the story of my world, the world of my possible experience. Consider, for example, what it would mean to acknowledge that one of these characters suffers pain. When I try to conceive of the actual, raw painfulness of the other's pain, the thing which moves me to act when I feel pain, I find that the supposed object of my thought either reduces to the empty tautology 'pain is pain', or else appears as something for which there is no place in the world of my possible experience. In my world, all there can be to the other's pain is the illness or injury which caused it, the physical state of the affected bodily part, and the behaviour to which that state gives rise. Thus, I find myself saying the very same thing as a practical solipsist would say: others may suffer so-called 'pain', but only I suffer real pain.

However, the egocentrist now points to a surprising loophole in this line of reasoning. By calling pains, and in general all feelings 'real' only when I have them, I have reduced the statement that only I have real pains, or real feelings, to a mere tautology. One might just as well say that only real pains are real pains, or only real feelings are real feelings, since being real makes the pain or the feeling mine by definition. The very notion that I am the logical subject to whom these mental states belong becomes redundant. In that case, there must be something more to my being the self-conscious subject that I take myself to be, than simply the fact that there is such a thing as 'my world'. To know myself as a self-conscious individual, to have experiences which do not simply colour the world but rather belong to the I, the subject, entails my having a concept of what it is to be a

176

subject; and that means knowing what it would be like to encounter subjects like myself. Yet other subjects can be like me in this logical sense only if they are so constituted as to be able to have the same kinds of feelings as I have: if I can have real pains, then, as a matter of logic, so can they. It follows that I can no longer say that when pain threatens me, its raw painfulness is the reason for my preventing it, but that when it threatens someone else I have no such prima facie reason. Pain is pain, real pain, whether I happen to be the one feeling it or not. (If the other person has been brought up to believe that to admit that one is in pain involves social disgrace, or even that to suffer pain is good for one's soul, then I shall of course have to modify my behaviour accordingly.)

7. The argument we have just outlined, were it valid, would constitute a logical foundation for moral conduct. The judgement, for example, that one ought not to disregard the physical pain one might cause others in the pursuit of one's own ends, does not depend for its validity on my just happening to feel sympathy for the feelings of others, nor on the existence of a convention whereby I respect the interests of other persons, on the understanding that they respect mine. The judgement follows simply from my recognition that I am a subject amongst other subjects, that the concept of a self-conscious individual applies to myself and to others in precisely the same sense. For in that case, were my actions to cause any person other than myself to suffer pain, the fact that the pain would not be actually hurting me, that the inexpressible something I call its raw painfulness would not exist in my world, is no less a reason for me to avoid that action. If the term 'I' has any meaning, as a means of distinguishing me from others, then all pain is real pain.

What is wrong with that argument? The notion of a logical foundation for moral conduct was meant to imply a form of rational compulsion: I have to recognize, not just theoretically but in my actions, the validity of moral considerations; there is no rational alternative. Now it is not a conclusive objection that, for the egocentrist, the moral constraint upon my actions ultimately reduces the necessary experience of an inner, passive, observing I for whom there is no 'ought' but only 'is'. If one accepts the egocentrist's starting point, then one must also accept the egocentrist's reinterpretation of the nature of my agency. The real objection is rather that starting from the unquestioned basis of egocentrism, the necessity which the egocentrist's argument yields is still only hypothetical: if the notion of my being a subject is a concept that I, as an egocentrist, use in describing the world of my possible experience, if, as the egocentrist says, I 'take myself to be' a self-conscious individual, then I cannot deny that the feelings of other individuals are as real, in a logical sense, as my own. Yet what is there to prevent me from giving up this concept of a subject, from converting to the practical solipsist's way of seeing things? I might still find it convenient to retain a word in my vocabulary for the outwardly similar beings whom I encountered and used; but I should cease to identify myself as one of them. There is no necessity that I should identify myself as anything, other than the world itself, or perhaps God.

This objection is effective against any attempt to bootstrap a genuine, non-solipsistic recognition of the reality of other selves from the starting point of an egocentrist metaphysic. However, the egocentrist's account of the conditions for selfhood might still be criticized, from a different direction, for failing to provide the best possible case: it is too thin, to transparent a deception for the purpose to which the egocentrist would put it. (The argument we have attributed to the egocentrist is derived from chapter 3 of Strawson's *Individuals*: it is doubtful, however, whether Strawson would care to be identified as an egocentrist; nor does he argue for a link between the necessary recognition of the reality of other selves and moral conduct.) If one thinks about all that is involved in the possession of self-consciousness, something more seems to be implied than the mere act of self-reference, of using the term 'I' non-redundantly. When one sees what that something more is, one will find that it is not a feature that can be simply given up in the way we have suggested. My recognition of the reality of other subjects is not just a logical condition for the use of a certain term, a term that I might equally well decide not to use, but rather an essential moment in the process of self-realization.

The egocentrist may have in mind here Hegel's famous dialectic of master and slave (*Phenomenology of Spirit* pp. 104ff). We are concerned, as above, with the use to which the argument, originally conceived from the position of a strict nonegocentrism, might be put by an egocentrist; in this case, as a piece of phenomenology in the sense in which that term was used in chapter 8 (bracketing Hegel's controversial starting point that consciousness entails self-consciousness, ibid. p. 101). It might be argued that when one unravels all that is packed into the notion of my recognition of myself as one subject of consciousness amongst others, the story of someone who deliberately gave up the notion of being a subject no longer appears intelligible. In one way, however, this argument misses the point; while in another respect it makes the egocentrist's position even less tenable. I have undoubtedly travelled a long road to become the self-conscious individual that I take myself to be; and what I have acquired in the process of attaining this level of consciousness is not so much baggage that I can just throw off. For all that, as an egocentrist I cannot close my eyes to the logical possibility that I shall, for no reason at all, come to see things differently. Nor, as it now becomes clear, even supposing that my moral vision never wavers, can I really be satisfied with a grounding for my moral conduct on a metaphysic in which other persons exist as ends for me only insofar as they serve ultimately as mere means for my own self-realization.

8. If, starting from the reality of my subjective standpoint, there exists a logical foundation for my moral conduct, that can only be on the basis of a theory that denies that the world of my subjective standpoint is the only reality. Whatever prevents the egocentrist, for whom the world appears as a story whose characters are treated merely as if they were real subjects, from converting to the practical solipsist's way of seeing things, can only be interpreted either in terms of the entrenchment of the concept of the self, or – as best as an egocentrist can interpret such facts – in terms of either self-interest or an irrational, natural sympathy. It cannot be the perception of a rational necessity. Thus, the only theory that remains to be considered is the two-world theory of subjective and objective standpoints. We must now examine its claim to provide a logical foundation for moral conduct.

Let us remind ourselves what exactly it is we have to prove. Earlier, we spoke of a distance between myself and others which, unlike my distance from objects available for me to use, cannot be dissolved. The reality of the other consists in his possessing a value which prevents me from using him as a mere means to satisfy my own desires. Obviously, in the light of the failure of egocentrism to provide the needed proof, my recognition of the reality of the objective standpoint has got to make the vital difference, but how? It will not do to say simply that, from the objective standpoint, I and the other appear as two of the same. That is the nonegocentrist's argument which we have dismissed, since it fails to acknowledge the way in which the question of the reality of the other can only be raised properly from my subjective standpoint: self-effacement gives a reality to the other, but at the cost of denying reality to my subjective world. Merely to add to what the nonegocentrist says, as it were as an afterthought, that my subjective world is also real, would be a futile move; for that would entail the admission that I and the other are not, after all, 'the same'. The argument, if there is one, must depend essentially on the reality of both the objective and subjective

179

standpoints. Its starting point will be my recognition of the lack of self-sufficiency of my subjective standpoint. What it has to show is that my recognition of the reality of the objective standpoint entails, without any further conditions, the reality of the other.

At the end of the last chapter, we reached the conclusion that what the other demands of me is that I recognize the other's metaphysical freedom, to the same extent as I recognize my own, as something whose necessary appearance is not merely relative but absolute. All that my recognition of the reality of the other can amount to, we argued, is my satisfying that demand; and it was suggested that this could be done only in my actions, in my behaviour towards the other. What now has to be shown is, first, that there is something that I recognize when I recognize the other's metaphysical freedom, that what I seem to see is not merely my invention but corresponds to something real; and, secondly, that the reality of the other's metaphysical freedom does indeed provide a logical foundation for my moral conduct.

9. Before we can tackle those two questions, however, we need to be clear about the distinction between metaphysical freedom and the notion we called forensic freedom; and in particular about the role of forensic freedom in relation to morality. Many philosophers would approach such a distinction with considerable scepticism. Such scepticism can only increase when one learns that there are in fact two distinct notions of metaphysical freedom; that the metaphysical freedom I attribute to myself is essentially different from the metaphysical freedom I attribute to the other. In the end, the only way to meet such criticism is to let the arguments speak for themselves. We ought at least to remind ourselves, however, why such scepticism should arise. So-called compatibilists, those who argue that recognition of the truth of determinism has no consequences for our attributions of moral responsibility, would claim that there is only one concept of freedom, that of forensic freedom or some similar notion, and that metaphysical freedom is just a chimera. So-called incompatibilists, on the other hand, reject what they consider to be the ersatz conception of moral responsibility embraced by the compatibilists, and claim that a metaphysical freedom incompatible with determinism is the only notion of freedom worth the name. We are not saying that either of these positions is simply wrong; nor are we arguing for a third position in-between the two. Rather, it seems that the dialectic of subjective and objective standpoints has taken us altogether outside this dispute. What is true is that both forensic freedom and metaphysical freedom are in different ways presupposed

by our ordinary moral beliefs and attitudes; but not in the ways that the compatibilist or incompatibilist respectively take them to be.

The notion of forensic freedom as we find it rests upon the existence of the practice, universal in human society, of praise and blame; a practice accompanied by feelings which, according to the analysis suggested in the last chapter, can only be made sense of as the irrational acting out of a fantasy that one could, by one's words, change the past. We claimed that it did not follow that we ought to discard such attitudes, once we had perceived them for what they truly are. Nevertheless, it might happen that these attitudes should one day be discarded (one might think of a society set up by philosophers on the model of Spinoza's *Ethics*). One would still recognize the validity of moral considerations – even employing praise and blame strictly as tools of moral education – retaining terms that corresponded exactly to our notions of moral evaluation, only stripped of the reactive connotations such terms have for us. ('You should not have done that,' would then be understood simply as a contribution to moral theory: one ought not to do such a thing.) Forensic freedom, in short, is not necessary for the institution of morality.

Nor is it sufficient. Just as we blame someone for doing an action we consider morally wrong, so we may scold someone for imprudence, feeling this time not anger but rather contempt for her failure to act in her own best interests. Now it is possible that there might have existed a society where the validity of moral considerations was not recognized, a society where Hobbes' mythical state of nature was actually realized. In such a society, individuals might be admired or scolded for their prudence or imprudence, but never praised or blamed. There would be forensic freedom, but no morality. However, if there is a logical foundation for moral conduct, then any society such as this which failed to recognize the validity of moral considerations would be in the wrong: members of that society would stand convicted of irrationality. By contrast, a society which recognized moral considerations but in which the notion of forensic freedom, in our sense, had no legitimate place would claim a kind of emancipation from irrationality to which we are not compelled by reason to aspire. – If the metaphysical freedom of the other does provide the logical foundation for moral conduct, then it seems we must allow a place for both metaphysical and forensic freedom.

10. The first question we had to answer in seeking the rational basis of moral conduct was whether the metaphysical freedom of the other does in fact correspond to something real. We shall now argue that it does. The key notion here is the authority of the other to correct my

judgements. We have seen that the reality of the objective standpoint depends upon the logical impossibility that my subjective standpoint should become self-sufficient: I can never be the final authority on the reliability of my powers of judgement. As we argued in chapter 5, the authority which I recognize in others to correct my judgements cannot logically be reduced to a subject matter for my judgement. If I were to try to attain a position from which I might judge on every occasion, as I do on some occasions, whether or not others are right in correcting my judgements, then I should be engaged in a necessarily self-defeating project. What I can do sometimes, I cannot, in principle, do always. How are we to picture this? The paradox of the heap seems to threaten here: if I can judge whether or not other persons are right in correcting my judgements, say, fifty per cent of the time, then surely there is no reason why I should not, through an increase in my powers of perception or reasoning, get into a position to judge whether or not other persons are right in correcting my judgements fifty-one percent of the time, and so on. If I can become more self-reliant in the judgements that I make, then, for any given degree of self-reliance there is a yet greater degree; inevitably, one might think, a point could be reached where I did not need to defer to the authority of others at all.

The fallacy in this argument consists in its misinterpretation of the nature of the generality involved in talk of 'all others'. It is logically possible that my perceptual and mental powers should so increase that none of the individuals I actually encountered had the authority to correct any of my judgements. Yet even so I should remain confined within my own system of representation: my own physical senses or forms of perception, as well as the beliefs and assumptions which guided my investigations and which interpreted all incoming data. Whether that system as a whole was reliably putting me in touch with reality is a matter which could in principle be judged authoritatively only from a vantage point outside that system, from the point of view of another possible subject, even if no actual subject was in a position to make such a judgement. That is what was meant by saying that the authority I grant to the other is no mere empirical fact about the world but rather a necessary condition for my making judgements at all. In actual fact, of course, things are very different from what we have imagined. Every person I meet, however limited his or her mental or perceptual powers, is in a position to correct at least some of my judgements, if only about what that person is thinking and feeling; and I recognize that person's authority to do so. The source of objectivity, the normativity of meaning and judgement, lies in this recognition that I am prepared to grant to persons whom I

182

encounter, an acknowledgement which is not my judgement but the condition for the possibility of my judgement.

However, a recognition I am prepared to grant I may still withhold; it is not logically necessary that I should recognize any particular person as an authority. If I do withhold my recognition, how must I then think of such an individual? The subject without authority remains a source of information for me to use, a source whose reliability is a matter entirely for me to judge. Such an individual would then have the same role for me as, say, a remote-control television camera, or a computer. What makes the source of information reliable is that its performance is in principle totally predictable; what makes it useful is that I am not in a position to predict the information it will give me. If the camera has given sufficiently accurate pictures in the past, if the computer appears from its past performance to be correctly programmed, then I do not even need to know how the device works; although I do need to believe that it is not by sheer luck or magic. The same applies to the individual whom I treat as a mere source of information. I must assume that it would be possible in principle for me to predict the subject's behaviour on the basis of detailed knowledge of the subject's bodily workings, even if I know that with my human limitations I could never get into a position to make such a prediction. On the basis of this judgement of reliability, I can use the individual to correct my judgements, just as I might use a camera or a computer.

The very opposite is the case, however, if I do not simply use the individual whom I encounter as a means of correcting my judgements but recognize that subject's authority to do so. For I know that if I ever were to find myself in the position of being able to predict that subject's judgements, those judgements would cease to have authority for me. It would be up to me to judge whether or not those judgements were true, or whether or not I could rely on their being true. Now we saw in the last chapter that my metaphysical freedom consists in the real appearance, necessary for my existence as an agent, that my bodily movements result from real decisions I make now, and are not decided for me by processes whose outcome could have been predicted in advance; and that I cannot exist except as an agent. In a cognate way, the metaphysical freedom which I grant to the other consists in my acknowledgement, bound up with my recognition of the other's authority to correct my judgements, that I cannot be in a position to predict the judgements that the other will make; and that I must be prepared to grant this recognition.

It follows immediately that my metaphysical freedom and the metaphysical freedom that I grant to other persons cannot be simply equivalent. On the contrary, each form of freedom appears to possess, in a different respect, a more elevated status than the other. First, the necessity that attaches to the metaphysical freedom of the other cannot be merely illusory, as my own necessary sense of metaphysical freedom must ultimately be taken to be; yet, second, the scope of this non-illusory necessity, when seen from the point of view of the other, turns out to be restricted in a way in which my own necessary illusion of metaphysical freedom is not.

There is, first, no illusion about the necessity of the other's metaphysical freedom, because, if I could not recognize the authority of other persons to correct my judgements then my judgement would have to judge itself; something we have proved in the dialectic of egocentrism to be a logical impossibility. By contrast, the double vision of subjective and objective worlds which would result from the denial of the primacy of my standpoint as an agent, appears as an intolerable oscillation, but not a logical impossibility. The second point, however, is that the non-illusory necessity that the judgements of the person to whom I grant authority should never be predicted, is a necessity only in relation to what I, and I alone, could ever come to know about the other; it remains open to me to believe that a third party could be in a position to make such a prediction. By contrast, my necessary thought of my own metaphysical freedom relates to what any person could come to know about me, and not only those persons who acknowledge my authority to correct their judgements. The lack of equivalence between my metaphysical freedom and the metaphysical freedom of the other may be seen as a reflection of the asymmetry of self and other within a theory of subjective and objective worlds. There is no avoiding, however, the paradox entailed in the denial that the metaphysical freedom I grant to the other is the truth of the belief in his own metaphysical freedom that the other possesses qua self-conscious subject. As we saw in the last chapter, the other's sense of metaphysical freedom is as far as I am concerned a mere belief; an illusion which, unlike my own absolutely necessary sense of metaphysical freedom, is only relatively necessary.

11. Why, then, should I be moral? What is it that I see, when I recognize the metaphysical freedom of another person, that prevents me from seeking to make that individual a mere means to my end? In order to demonstrate a logical foundation for moral conduct it would suffice to show that such an intention, in the face of my recognition of the other's metaphysical freedom, either cannot be consistently formulated or else is necessarily self-frustrating. In either case, it follows that my attempting to act in such a way that the other

became a mere means to my end would necessarily show my failure to grasp a certain logical truth: that no project I might possibly undertake could ever be consistent with the maxim of my action. In other words, it is logically impossible for me to do wrong knowingly. Once aware of this philosophical principle, all that remains for me to do is seek out all aspects of the situation in which I find myself, and act consistently with that knowledge; neither allowing a self-deceiving will to ignorance to draw a veil over what is really going on, nor giving in to weakness of resolve in putting my decisions into effect.

The proof of our principle is a one-line argument. In order to make some particular person a means to my end, I must act on the maxim that other persons are in general a resource available to me to use as I will; but that is something I cannot do consistently with my recognition of the authority of other persons to correct my judgements.

Perhaps I am in a hurry to catch a train, and an old man blocks my path. A firm shove would give my project of making my appointment on time considerably greater chance of success than waiting politely for him to move. Of course, it would be inconvenient if I hurt my victim and he cried out; he might succeed in calling someone else's attention to my misdemeanour, and then I might be stopped and possibly even held against my will. But then I think, that cry has a meaning: 'You've hurt me, you shouldn't have done that!'. A judgement has been made with which I must either agree or disagree. Let us say I agree. I know I shouldn't have hurt the old man, but my not being late for my appointment was more important. However, that makes no sense. If I really ought not to have hurt him then my not being late was not more important.

Then I must disagree with the judgement. Again, two possibilities face me. I might allow that my victim's feelings were to be taken into consideration, but deny that on balance they outweighed the importance of my not being late for my appointment. Alternatively, I might deny that his feelings counted at all. The first case could conceivably be a matter of debate, if my meeting was sufficiently urgent and if there was absolutely no way to avoid harming him. By admitting as much, I ought to be prepared, in principle, to debate the question with the old man or anyone who challenged me; and not regard my own judgement as having sole authority to decide the matter. If I were to lose the argument, I should have to admit that I was wrong after all.

The only way I could ensure that I did not lose the argument would be by refusing to allow that the old man's feelings counted in any way. Whatever he says he feels is henceforth not admissible as evidence, of no interest to me or to anyone with whom I am prepared to discuss such matters. Now, if the old man is an authority about anything, he is an authority on whether, say, the bruise in his shoulder hurts, not to speak of his pride, and that both these things very definitely ought to count in any person's deliberations. In that case, if I am to act consistently with my resolution, I cannot allow that the old man has the authority to correct my judgements: henceforth all he believes and knows is only information for me to use. Only now I think: that individual whom I have reduced to the status of a mere object neither lacks nor possesses any attribute that explains why he alone should not be an authority for me. Consistency demands that I refuse to recognize the authority of any other person to correct my judgements. And now I see that this is a project that I cannot, as a matter of logic, undertake. For if all self-conscious subjects other than myself are to be reduced to the status of mere objects, if no-one in principle has any longer the authority to correct my judgements, then the very light by means of which there exists an objective world for me would have been extinguished.

14 Reality of now

1. THE asymmetry between self and other finds its analogue in the relation of the present time to future times. Just as the other possesses an authority with regard to the evaluation of my judgements which I can never claim, so the judgement of the future retains its absolute authority with regard to our predictions, however much knowledge we may gather about the present or the past. Even if determinism is true, that cannot be a logical truth; as we saw in chapter 12, when we considered the possibility that the universe should cease at some time to follow deterministic laws. It is always logically possible that the predictions of a Laplacian super-mind should be falsified by the actual course of events. The laws governing causal interactions could simply change, for no reason at all, so far as any being confined (as all must be) to gathering data from the past or present could ever perceive or know.

It is significant that philosophers who have taken note of the connection between the reality of other selves and the reality of other times have concentrated on the past (cf. McDowell 'On "The Reality of the Past"'). The problem is seen as one of overcoming what first appears, through a psychologistic illusion, as an unbridgeable epistemological gap. The characteristic movements and expressions of the other, as in a similar way the images or representations of the past as they appear in memory, far from being more or less dubious evidence for states of affairs whose existence I can never conclusively verify – the very conception of which is thereby thrown into doubt – serve rather to bring the other's state of mind, or things that happened in the past, in some manner directly to my awareness. What begins, however, as a critique of bad epistemology is all too easily misinterpreted as a denial of transcendence in the cause of a nonegocentrist metaphysic: what is there for me in my own consciousness is just what I find in the face and characteristic expressions of the other.

By contrast, when one treats the problem of other times in the context of the reality of the future, it becomes apparent that the critical insight at the heart of the two-world theory, that no expansion of my knowledge can take me outside my own system of representation to attain the vantage point that some other person might occupy in judging the reliability of my powers of judgement, is mirrored precisely in the way human knowledge pushes outwards against a temporal limit that always recedes but is never reached or transcended. Moreover, just as the nonegocentrist seeks to reduce self and other to two of the same, so in contemplating the nature of time one is tempted to deny the nowness of now, the absolute otherness of the future in relation to this present, with the result that now becomes just another time, the same as any other past or future time. However, as we shall soon find out, it is not so easy as it seems even to express the nowness of now, let alone justify granting now pre-eminent status. We have to use language in order to defeat language, to undermine the claim of the statement to comprehend all the facts that go to make up a world.

2. Philosophizing about the nature of time appears to suffer from the fatal drawback that, in order to elevate ourselves to a standpoint from which we may reflect upon the phenomenon of time, it is necessary to effect an attitude of mental detachment from that lived experience of temporality we wish to investigate; as a result of which we end up talking about something completely different. Just because the truth about time is true equally of all times, it has no special connection with the time that is now. Even as we discuss theories of time, however, we remain aware that our detachment is only a pretence. We do not cease to live through time even as we argue about its essential nature; even if the rules according to which the game of philosophical reflection is played seem to preclude the making of any such admission. For example, I show myself to be immersed in temporality in the very act of typing these words. Every stroke of the keys is a new now, dividing what I have written from what I have yet to write. When for a short while I stop my typing, I continue to be aware of other temporal processes: the flux of my thoughts, the progress of a fly on the window pane, the sound of the traffic outside, my breathing. The flow of time never stops.

Yet, paradoxically, no sooner do such observations acquire the status of a philosophical example, then they cease to express their intended meaning. Since I am no longer typing those words, the words I was typing while I was in the process of giving the example, all it now conveys to me is the general truth that while human beings can choose to stop what they are doing in order to reflect, they cannot detach themselves from their involvement in temporal processes to the extent of ceasing to be immersed in time. In asserting that detachment is only a pretence, however, I intend something which goes beyond the mundane truth that every standpoint is a temporal standpoint; I mean to give due recognition to the nowness of now, *this* very moment. Yet the nowness of now is equally the nowness of all nows, and only by virtue of that is it the nowness of *this* now. What I seem to recognize but cannot express is that *this* now alone is actually happening now, while all other nows are not now, but only have been or will be called 'now'. However, in saying that I have not yet said what I meant to say and indeed cannot say it.

Our inability to find adequate words to convey the thought that when we say 'now' we mean *this* now, and not just any now, is not a problem in the sense of something to which one might hope to find an solution if only one thought hard enough. For we encounter here an absolute barrier to thought, a metaphysical wall. In ignorance, one approaches the wall as one would any obstacle, looking for some way to get past. A wall made of bricks and mortar can be climbed over, or tunnelled under, or if all else fails knocked down. A metaphysical wall is different. Thought grasps repeatedly at the wall only to find itself each time facing in the opposite direction. Thus, someone who is moved to make such a metaphysical assertion as, 'The presence of the present moment is an objectively real attribute of the world', is trying to get across what the vehement emphasis of the word 'now' was intended to express. However, any such attempt is futile. We know in advance that such an assertion can never succeed in its intention, but merely substitutes other, no less empty forms of emphasis, such as the emotively charged terms 'objective' and 'real'. It is therefore a waste of time to argue for or against such a thesis, as if the use of terminology could in some magical way succeed where the vehement assertion of 'now' failed.

For the same reason, it would serve no purpose to emphasize the openness of the future in relation to all that we could ever know about the present or the past, that which gives the judgement of time its authority. If the future is open, then one may define now as the cutting edge of existence, the moving boundary that divides a world fully formed or made from a world that has yet to be made. However,

189

we are still talking here of any now. The statements, 'that which is open is open' or 'that which is closed is closed' convey no more than the statement, 'now is now'.

In this chapter, we shall try a different approach. While there exists no way to state what the nowness of now consists in, it might still be possible to exhibit the content of our vehement assertion dialectically. If the attitude of mental detachment is no mere pretence but can be shown to entail an illusory conception of our relation to the world, then in finding an adequate expression for that illusion we should after all have found a means to convey indirectly that essential feature of time which eludes all forms of direct statement. In other words, what the dialectical approach seeks to do is not to sneak past the barrier at which all thought turns – something that can never be done – but rather to catch thought at the moment of its turning.

3. A metaphor one may be tempted to use in order to characterize our experience of temporality is that of a window of consciousness which passes along the series of events ordered by the relation of before-and-after. The events we call present are those that can be seen from the window; past events are remembered as having already 'gone past' the window, while future events have yet to appear in the frame. Now it would be unfair to criticize the metaphor on the grounds that any attempt to define time in terms of movement or passage is circular. We are not seeking a definition of time, whatever that might mean, but only a way of expressing the content of the vehement assertion, 'now is now'. So let us imagine that we are looking out through the window of a moving train. Every point along the line is a 'here', but only one point is here, the place we have actually reached in our journey. Thus, one might exclaim to a fellow passenger, 'look here!', intending to call attention to some passing scenery of particular interest. To note that here is here is to note a fact that might have been otherwise, had the train been behind or ahead of schedule. There is of course no question of providing a parallel explanation of the putative fact that now is now, for the reason we have already given: one cannot take literally the notion of time as movement or passage. To say that now might have been an hour ago had time run more slowly, or had time begun an hour later than it in fact began, presupposes a second time in which the passage of the first time is measured. The nowness of now is not a fact about the position of the window of consciousness with respect to the before-and-after series of events in the way that the hereness of here is, for a passenger on the train, a fact about the location of that train.

190

What other kind of fact could it then be? The very fact that we find the metaphor compelling, it might be argued, despite our recognition of the impossibility of understanding time in terms of movement or passage, shows that we remain under the illusion that the nowness of now is a fact about our position in time. This, therefore, would be the true meaning and point of the metaphor: as a characterization of the way we seem to experience time, even though we know, from our detached philosophical standpoint, that things are in reality otherwise. There is, after all, a fact associated with the nowness of now, namely the fact that we cannot help but succumb to the illusion that 'now is now' expresses a fact about the position of the window of consciousness with respect to the before-and-after series of events.

It takes only a moment's reflection, however, to realize that the status of this so-called illusion is untenable. What the philosopher who adopts the standpoint of mental detachment from temporal processes appears to be saying is that the experience of temporality, our seeming awareness that now is now, is on the one hand not nothing; on the other hand, there is nothing for the experience of temporality to be an experience of, since it is only an illusory appearance. Now if it is a fact that we have this illusory experience, if the appearance actually exists, if only as appearance, then that is something which characterizes or determines reality in some way; that is just what a fact is. In that case, far from being illusory, our experience of temporality is exactly what it purports to be: a reflection of the temporal aspect of reality.

4. Still, it might be held that the self-contradictory assertion that temporality is both nothing and not nothing results from interpreting the notion of an illusion in the wrong way. What the image of the window of consciousness is meant to convey is not that of something that distorts or falsifies our perception of reality, but rather a restriction which narrows our vision, so preventing us from taking in the whole truth. If perception is distorted, then what one seems to see is not really there, or at least not really as it appears to be: that is something that cannot be true of our perception of temporality, since the seeming perception of temporality cannot be conceived as other than temporal. If, on the contrary, our failure to stand in the ideal form of contact with reality presupposed by our theory of time is conceived on the model of a restriction of our vision, then our illusion is merely a failure to take in the whole view.

This difference emerges more clearly when one considers two contrasting pictures of what it would be to experience reality as it really is, from the supra-temporal standpoint of a deity. On the first picture, the ordering of events by the relation of before-and-after has a purely logical significance: to God's undistorted vision it appears as no more a temporal ordering than the ordering of words in a book or the grooves in a gramophone record. In reality, time simply does not exist as time. On the second picture, however, we are invited to imagine what it would be like if the window were progressively widened. There might well exist beings whose specious present, the span of time within which events are counted as happening now, is far wider than our own. Extending this by analogy, a deity who experienced reality as it really is would take in the whole of time in a single specious present, a single now.

However, the incoherence in treating our perception of temporality as an illusion is only disguised by such a manoeuvre. For either God is or is not capable of perceiving which time within his own single specious present counts as now for us: if he is, then as before our experience of temporality is a genuine reflection of the temporal aspect of reality; if not, then there can be no such thing in reality as a given time now seeming to count as now for us. Wherever the illusion concerning temporality is located, it cannot it seems be in our experience of temporality. In the absence of any third alternative, it must therefore be in the philosophical attitude of mental detachment that leads us to dismiss our experience of temporality as an illusion.

5. At this stage, we are still in relatively shallow water. Exhibiting the self-contradictory consequences of a false metaphysical model does not require any real insight into the subject matter under discussion. Moreover, so long as the model is found to be compelling, our opponent will find ample means of resisting such attempts at reductio. If all else fails, one can always fall back on the plea that the model has been taken too literally: the theorist of mental detachment might simply deny that such a view implies anything about the supra-temporal standpoint of a deity.

Thus, in a similar vein, we could have remarked that talk of the window of 'our' consciousness is question-begging, implying as it does that the window of each individual's consciousness is located at the same point in the before-and-after series of events. This opens up a novel version of the problem of the reality of other selves. Perhaps the consciousness of the person I am now talking to is an hour ahead or behind my own consciousness, so that like imperfect Leibnizian monads of a less than omnipotent deity, each of our two consciousnesses confronts the outer appearance of a subject disconnected by a time lapse of one hour from that subject's inner reality. All that could save us from such a scepticism would indeed be faith in pre-established harmony. An observation such as this has only limited utility, since it does not enable one to uncover the illusion ultimately responsible for the false model of time from which these absurd consequences follow, but merely provides further opportunity for the illusion to manifest itself.

An adequate expression of the illusion must accomplish something more. We need to know why we seem to find the model compelling; and we need to loosen the hold it has over us. The strategy which we shall pursue will seek to locate the window-of-consciousness model of time within the context of a wider metaphysical vision. Once a certain type of metaphysic is adopted, the model follows as an inevitable corollary. The aim of our investigation is ultimately to uncover and give adequate expression to the illusion of detachment. This turns out to be the most general characterization of our tendency to succumb to false metaphysical visions.

6. When one thinks of the window-of-consciousness model of time in relation to the unrestricted view of temporal reality accorded to a deity, the theory of nonegocentrism would seem to provide the indispensable background. However, that is far from being the case. The very same model arises, and indeed in its most vivid form, within egocentrism, or, rather, Kantian egocentrism. The pure, non-Kantian egocentrist who accepts that absolutely nothing can be said about my subjective world other than that it is *this* has no model of time, or of consciousness; for the *this* does not recognize a past or a future, nor any distinction between one moment and another. To call *this* either 'I' or 'now' would be equally meaningless: there is simply nothing in that inexpressible vision in which the concepts of self or time could get a grip. The Kantian egocentrist, by contrast, has a seemingly less austere view, in which the familiar notions of time and self form essential components. We saw how Kant's proof of the existence of an external world consisted in demonstrating that the hypothesis that a conscious subject might make judgements about a purely subjective, non-spatial world is incoherent. The data given to me in sensation can only be meaningfully interpreted as my perception of external objects. The question we have to decide is the status of time within such a conception of the task of the egocentrist's judging I.

Time is not a datum: it is not given to me as an identifiable element among the materials which go to make up my experience. Nor is time something about which one might be prompted to raise the question whether it really exists, in the way in which the existence of an external world comes into question. Time appears equally real, whether it is the time within which a purely imaginary, subjective experience such as a dream appears to unfold, or the time within which events in the external world are perceived to occur. Time functions rather as the ordering principle of the data.

If my seeming experience is not a dream, however, I must recognize a second aspect to time: in addition to the ordering of the data there is the order in which events in the world actually take place. How am I to conceive of this objective aspect of time? It cannot be regarded as merely an unknown something outside my possible experience. In that case, all that remains of my conception of objective time is the logical form of the before-and-after series in which all events are ordered. We have then all the materials required to construct the window-of-consciousness model. No description of the objective facts, even including facts concerning the occurrence of one's own perceptions, can determine where the window of my consciousness is now located; it merely says where my body is to be found at different times and the experiences I have at those times. What one would like to say is that what shows where my window of consciousness is now located is the description of the objective facts I am in a position to give on the basis of my perceptual experience up to *this* point in time. However, there is no room in the model for any such distinction between objective, statable facts, and other kinds of fact that cannot be stated. What I am now in a position to perceive can only be understood as an objective fact concerning relations between events.

If only one could resolve to venture forth into the world of objective facts without once looking back, one might avoid the fatal contradiction of an illusion of temporality that cannot be said to exist even as an illusion. Yet that is the one thing we cannot do while remaining within the egocentrist metaphysic. The data with which we began, and the task set by the existence of the data of founding or constructing an objective world remains as a stubborn, irreducible fact. This fact does not belong to the objective world; nor can the fact in its particularity be so much as stated as the obtaining of the transcendental condition for the existence of an objective world; nor indeed is there anywhere outside the objective world where the fact might be said to exist. The immediate, indescribable *this* of each datum, and the nowness of now, the moment when the datum is given, are everywhere and nowhere: no sooner do I try to point to them than the objective world squeezes them out.

In this way, the window-of-consciousness model of time is maintained as a perpetual oscillation between the mundane representation of an objective world, and the inexpressible metaphysical vision of the data upon which the representation is ultimately based. There is only one conclusion to be drawn when one encounters such an oscillation in metaphysics. Since each extreme immediately gives way to the other, and since both cannot simultaneously be held in place, both must be categorically rejected. Time is neither the inexpressible, subjective awareness of the temporality of what is indescribably given, nor the order in which events occur in an objective world founded or constructed on the basis of that given. We have already encountered, in chapter 4, a less roundabout way of refuting the theory that gives rise to this fatal oscillation, but that does not concern us now. It would indeed serve no purpose to know that a certain model of time may be derived from a false metaphysical theory; that same model might still be derivable from some other source which we have not yet examined. We are now able to see that such is not the case with the egocentrist's window-of-consciousness model of time. For the discovery of the fatal shortcomings of that model and the destructive criticism of the theory that gives rise to it are one and the same.

It might appear that there is one way for the egocentrist to avoid this conclusion: to refuse to say anything about the *this*, the mode in which the objective world is made present to me, or indeed about the task of founding or constructing an objective world, implying as it does that there is something out of which the objective world is constructed, something it is founded upon. In that case, there would be no oscillation between different conceptions of time: time is simply and exclusively objective time, the before-and-after series of events. Of course, as we have seen, it is possible for an egocentrist to refuse to say anything at all about anything, and then there is no problem of what to say about time. Yet through a subtle shift, that extreme metaphysical position reveals a flip side. One indulges in everyday talk – why not? – one makes judgements about an objective, temporal world, knowing all the while that something one sees, as if out of the corner of one's eye, renders all this talk ultimately meaningless. In other words, one embraces Kant's 'empirically real' objective world, while refusing to say anything about one's underlying egocentrist vision, knowing that such talk would reveal itself in the course of philosophical examination as nonsensical.

Now if we encountered such a covert egocentrist, we could never tell from outward appearances; nor is there any factual or philosophical question which we could put to someone which would reveal that person's identity as an egocentrist. (It seems that this is the position Wittgenstein must have been thinking of when he declared in the *Tractatus* that 'solipsism, when its implications are followed out strictly, coincides with pure realism', 5.64.) Only now we can say to anyone who thinks this is a consistent position, and may be tempted to adopt it, How could you ever be sure whether or not you had become an egocentrist, or at what point you became one? How would you know that you had the appropriate metaphysical vision, rather than some other, non-egocentrist vision? Or perhaps no vision at all?

7. Let us follow the letter, if not the spirit of Wittgenstein's remark, and allow egocentrism to transform into nonegocentrism: the *this* flickers for a moment, and then is gone, and all that remains is a reality in which I find myself as just one subject amongst others. The vision that there is something that everything in the world refers back to as if to a point of origin, having given up the language of Kantian egocentrism in which it seemed the vision could alone find expression, disappears without a trace. What happens to one's conception of time? There are in fact two versions of nonegocentrism to consider. We shall have more to say in a moment about the theory according to which time, as for the Tractarian egocentrist or 'solipsist', is simply and exclusively objective time. Returning to the traditional view, such as that of Kant's predecessor Leibniz, we find the objective standpoint identified with the point of view of an omniscient deity, who comprehends all that happens in the world sub specie aeternitatis. (We saw in chapter 4 that Kant himself, in his theory of things in themselves, embraced a position close to this traditional view.)

For someone who holds explicitly to the standpoint of the egocentrist's transcendental ego, and identifies the world as such with the world of my possible experience, the notion of how a deity might experience the order of events serves only as a heuristic device, not to be taken literally: if there really is nothing more to objective time, the subject matter of my temporal judgements, than the logical form of the before-and-after series of events, then that is all the deity I myself might become would perceive of time. What we are now considering, however, is the complete repudiation of the reality of the subjective standpoint which forms the basis for the Kantian egocentrist's account, in favour of the objective standpoint of a supra-temporal deity. The heuristic device now transforms into the centrepiece of the theory. Our question is what substantial difference this makes to the Kantian egocentrist's account of time, with its fatal oscillation between the subjective temporality of the immediate given, and the objective order of events.

The answer is that, so long as the objective standpoint is conceived as that which would be occupied either by a deity who exists altogether outside of time, or else by a deity for whom the world exists in a single specious present, we have merely projected the structure of the egocentrist's window-of-consciousness model of time onto the world of the nonegocentrist. One still necessarily has some story to tell about how the illusion of temporality appears in us, as finite subjects of experience; and that story will parallel exactly the Kantian egocentrist's account of the inexpressible temporality of the immediate given, so that both conceptions come to share the same dubious ontological status. The window of consciousness can be said to be neither real nor unreal, but remains suspended half-way between existence and non-existence.

8. The nonegocentrist, faced with the same fatal oscillation that defeated the Kantian egocentrist, is quick to perceive that the traditional account of a supra-temporal deity, having served its purpose as the most graphic expression for the reality of the objective standpoint, may be altogether dispensed with. While all the Kantian egocentrist could do to avoid the oscillation was retreat to a covert, minimal egocentrism, refusing to stay silent yet refusing equally to engage in any philosophical discussion of the metaphysical basis for the world of our ordinary empirical judgements, the nonegocentrist finds a far more attractive course of action. For it becomes clear that all one requires is the more moderate conception of an objective standpoint that a time-bound deity might occupy, an infinite, ubiquitous intelligence that takes in nothing more than what any actual or possible finite subject of experience is able to perceive. This standpoint is conceived, in effect, as none other than that of language itself. All that there is to the objective world is presented in the totality of its aspects; and exists, in principle, to be described by means of a common language shared by all finite subjects to whom those aspects are, at different times, presented.

The objective world is no longer something founded or constructed on the basis of a subjective, indescribable given; nor does each finite subject, as Leibniz believed, inhabit its own private temporal world, cut off from the worlds of other subjects of experience, all under the eye of a supra-temporal deity. There is only one world, that which is the subject matter of all our questions and judgements; the mundane world that language describes. The window of consciousness remains firmly shut. The whole truth about time is incorporated in the range of temporal facts and generalizations about temporal facts expressible in language. Since amongst the latter generalizations are those concerning the role of time in perception and action which fully account for the practical necessity of using the temporal demonstrative 'now' or some equivalent form of expression, our awareness of temporality as a predicament from which we cannot escape is squared with our metaphysical belief in the exclusive reality of the objective world. (One philosopher who has argued trenchantly for this linguistic view is D.H. Mellor. See, for example, his book *Real Time*.)

It might seem an obvious truism that to account for the meaning or truth-conditions of statements containing temporal demonstratives is to say everything there is to say about the difference between an event's happening now and its happening in the past or the future. On second thoughts, when one recalls what the account omits, it seems so inseparable from our notion of time that one wonders how one could ever get over its loss. My awareness of temporality, the conception of myself as immersed in time whose validity the nonegocentrist is apparently so quick to concede, is nothing less than the sense that the nowness of now – not any now but *this* now – is itself a fact. In addition to all that could be said about now as a particular, describable event in relation to other particular, describable events, in addition to all the general observations that apply to now as one now amongst others, there is one particular fact that shines out with a light that could not be extinguished without reducing all to darkness: the fact that now is *now*. There would be nothing at all if there were not something now. For a philosopher to say that our awareness of the flow of time is fully accounted for by the practical necessity of using temporal demonstratives is to maintain that this pre-eminent sense of the nowness of now is nothing but sheer illusion, whether one explicitly calls it that or not. Even the deity of the traditional nonegocentrist, looking down on our mundane world sub specie aeternitatis, would acknowledge, in its own non-temporal language, the practical necessity of our talking of events as happening now, thus explaining their significance for us by contrast with events that have happened or have yet to happen. The moderate nonegocentrist's standpoint of language acknowledges no more than this.

Our antagonist will no doubt have nothing to say in reply to such an outburst; but one would be a fool to take that silence as submission. For we have now merely returned to the point where this discussion began. The metaphysical belief in the exclusive reality of the objective standpoint of language can never be undermined by the bare assertion that it fails to acknowledge the so-called 'fact' that now is now. For against that assertion there are two obvious replies. First, one simply stands by the claim that in explaining the practical necessity for using temporal demonstratives, for using such a word as 'now', one has fully acknowledged that fact. That this same form of

198

explanation might be available from the standpoint of the traditional nonegocentrist's supra-temporal deity is irrelevant to its truth: in the latter case the explanation is distorted and thus rendered false. Second, and even more tellingly, the bare assertion of a tautology can never refute any metaphysical thesis. If only one could put what one was trying to say in other terms, one might make headway. Yet we have already admitted that vehement assertion is the only way of actually stating our position.

9. There remains only the alternative course of showing that the moderate nonegocentrist's view of time, like that of both the Kantian egocentrist and the traditional nonegocentrist, is an expression of a metaphysical illusion: the illusion of detachment. In attempting to prove that claim, however, we have to work under a serious handicap. For in this case we are not given a model of time whose incoherence may be directly demonstrated, in the way that we demonstrated the different applications of the window of consciousness: our claim that this same model – only with the window shut – lies behind the moderate nonegocentrist's conception of temporal reality would be flatly rejected. We are indeed not given anything other than the bare idea of the standpoint of language. Such a position might seem utterly impregnable: if everything one is able to say is said in language, then attacking the standpoint of language robs us of the only weapon that is of any use in philosophy! However, that impression is only superficial. For the standpoint of language is not the simple, commonsense position of faith in the power of words but a sophisticated metaphysical theory; one, moreover, which we have in chapter 7 already found reason to reject.

According to the moderate nonegocentrist, the totality of facts constitutes, in effect, the knowledge that would be possessed by a hypothetical ubiquitous intelligence; a subject that acquires over time information about the world as it presents itself to every possible point of view. Equivalently, every fact is capable of being stated in language and thus becoming common knowledge amongst subjects each of whom occupies a different point of view. Now it might seem at first that the intelligence's very ubiquity robs it of the knowledge of at least one vital fact: in knowing all that I know, in perceiving all that I perceive and feeling all that I feel, it still does not know what it is like to be me. For one of the things that characterizes what it is like to be me is the respect in which I necessarily lack knowledge of what others know, perceive and feel. What the ubiquitous intelligence knows is that I lack this knowledge; what it does not and could not know is what it is like to lack this knowledge, since it has never lacked that knowledge. It could only make up for this deficiency by ceasing to be what it is and becoming me.

This objection, though initially plausible, falls down when one realizes that a parallel argument would establish that I cannot know now what it was like to have been sitting at my desk an hour ago; on the grounds that, for example, I did not know then what sentence I would now be writing. On the contrary, I remember perfectly well what it was like. In just the same way that in thinking myself back in time to what it was like to be sitting here an hour ago I compensate for the knowledge which I now possess but then lacked, so the ubiquitous intelligence compensates for its total knowledge of all that finite subjects know, perceive and feel when it considers what it is like to be me. In the sense, then, in which what one might call the 'I-ness of I' is understood merely as what it is like to be me, this is an uncontroversial fact which, though in its richness it might never be fully captured by any finite description, contains no elements that are in principle incapable of being communicated in language and thus becoming common knowledge. Exactly the same, of course, applies to the you-ness of you, the she-ness of she etc. Yet, as we now know, the I-ness of I contains an additional element over and above the other examples. I may consider what it is like to be myself or any other person indifferently; but my sense of actually being the person I am, of the meaning that the proposition 'I exist' has for me, is unique and incommunicable: an appearance whose reality as appearance I cannot coherently deny.

Now, while it may be obvious that, as far as the ubiquitous intelligence is concerned, there can be no such fact concerning my existence over and above the fact that one of the things that it is like to be any self-conscious subject is to have a sense of one's own unique existence, it is not so immediately clear why the ubiquitous intelligence cannot take in the fact that now is now, since, by hypothesis, it perceives objects in time as we all do. This is the question which we must now investigate in more detail.

The fact that there exists an objective difference between its now being the case that a certain experience happened to me eight hours ago, and my situation eight hours ago when the experience was actually happening, which I described then as 'happening now', may be stated in terms which do not use any temporal demonstratives. Indeed, we have in effect just done so, for in using the phrases 'its now being the case' and 'eight hours ago', there was no intention to refer to any actual times. The example works because one is able to read it twice: first, as referring to a particular time, say, 8.30 this morning when the sun momentarily shone through the trees, and secondly as a general example applicable to the relation between any experience and the subsequent memory of that experience. Yet the presence of an experience now seems to be a fact that cannot be comprehended in any such relative terms. How is this appearance to be explained?

As far as the Kantian egocentrist's metaphysical subject was concerned, we saw that the presence of an experience now, while not admissible as an objective temporal fact, does still have a shadowy reality as an inexpressible datum concerning the position of the window of consciousness in relation to the before-and-after series of events. From the standpoint of the traditional nonegocentrist's supratemporal deity, by contrast, all times appeared equally now. The finite subject's immersion in time is something the deity cannot ever perceive as the finite subject perceives it, but only as an illusion of temporality whose ultimate nature only the deity is able to comprehend. Let us now look at the matter from the point of view of the moderate nonegocentrist's ubiquitous intelligence. Far from being omniscient, the ubiquitous intelligence, even with its far greater capacity for making predictions, still like all of us has to wait for events to unfold. It may never yet have been proved wrong, but there is always a first time: as we argued earlier, determinism might, for no reason at all, break down. As time passes, therefore, its knowledge grows. That is to say, the difference between two given times may be described, not only in terms of the difference between positions in the before-and-after series of events, but also in terms of the differing extent of the ubiquitous intelligence's knowledge at those times. Surely, one might think, in knowing the extent of its knowledge at different times, it must also know the actual extent of its knowledge, that is to say, what it knows now. However, that contradicts the assumption that all the ubiquitous intelligence knows are facts about the mundane world which we are able to describe in our common language. There are no additional facts concerning its own existence as a subject of experience which we have allowed the ubiquitous intelligence to know. For the ubiquitous intelligence as we have defined it, there are indeed, as there are for us, statements employing the temporal demonstrative 'now' which it takes to be true; but there is no such time as now.

Still, it seems that can soon be remedied by altering the original hypothesis. Instead of defining the ubiquitous intelligence as nothing more than a tabula rasa on which is inscribed all that could be known and expressed in language, as a pure capacity for knowledge based on what can be perceived by any finite subject, let us first enrich the definition by allowing that the ubiquitous intelligence is given

201

something, an actual input of data, which it then interprets as its perception of an objective world. It is clear that we should then have simply multiplied or expanded the point of view of the Kantian egocentrist's metaphysical subject, once more opening up the window of consciousness. To start with, it seems that this might be done by replacing the nonegocentrist's world of the objective standpoint once more by the egocentrist's world of my subjective standpoint; but the limit of this expansion, where every possible point of view served as an actual input for the expanded subject's data, would indeed be a form of nonegocentrism.

Now let us now imagine, by contrast, a ubiquitous intelligence reduced to the stature of just another mundane being, a self-conscious subject that finds itself in a world. An example of this would be the science fiction possibility that the brains of all the creatures in the universe have been wired up with transmitters, which convey all the perceptual information which their senses are able to register to a super-intelligent 'Master of the Universe'. This super-intelligent being, however, now becomes an I like the rest of us: in order to form a conception of the metaphysical standpoint of an objective world in which every I is equally a you, the Master of the Universe must resort to the conception of a truly ubiquitous intelligence with which we began.

10. What is it then about viewing the world from my own subjective standpoint, in the context of our two-world theory, that could possibly render visible temporal facts that remain invisible from the objective standpoint of an ubiquitous intelligence? How could my knowing less result in my knowing more? There is no question here of any such trivial point as the objection considered earlier, that the ubiquitous intelligence's universal knowledge deprives it of the knowledge of what it is like to remain ignorant. Rather, the question concerns our conception of a fact. A fact can be something that is the case; what every true statement states. It can also be understood in a wider, or less specific sense as something whose being, rather than not being (to use the least descriptive ontological terms) makes a difference to reality: take away the fact or change it and reality itself is altered. The problem of the meanings of 'now' and 'I' which we have been wrestling with turns on whether, in addition to the obtaining of facts, the existence of objects or the occurrence of events, all of which may be understood in terms of the truth of propositions, there can be facts of some essentially different kind.

According to both the nonegocentrist and the egocentrist there cannot. On the one hand, both admit that the practical necessity of including the terms 'now' and 'I' or their equivalents within the expressive powers of any language is a fact. On the other hand, it makes no difference to the world of statable facts, whether that be conceived as the world of the nonegocentrist's exclusive objective standpoint or the so-called 'objective world' founded on the egocentrist's exclusive subjective standpoint, that I am Klempner or that it is now 10.50 am on the 17th May 1994, in the way that it does make a difference that the person who types this sentence is Klempner or that it is typed at 10.50 am on the 17th May 1994.

Let us then suppose that I have planned to go out later this morning to buy a paper from the corner newsagent. If I leave it too late the shop will be closed for lunch. It is therefore an issue for me what time it is now. The world that presents itself to me here and now is not the world of two minutes ago or the world that will exist in two minutes time, nor the world of two hours ago or the world that will exist in two hours time, but the world of now; a world that does not suffer itself to be replaced by more recent worlds, nor stand in line patiently waiting for me to come up and meet it, for it never was nor will be but only is.

For the ubiquitous intelligence, surveying the objective world from every point of view, as for the detached metaphysical subject passively observing the world from my subjective point of view, the fact that what time it is now is an issue for me consists wholly in the truth of certain propositions. That is indeed the only way I can view what is happening now, when I look back from a historical perspective. Yet that is something I cannot now do. Depending upon what time it actually is, I shall make certain decisions and act upon them when I judge the time is right. There being an issue for me is thus constitutive of what it means to comprehend reality from the standpoint of the agent that I necessarily take myself to be. The issue that the time is now, no less than facts that obtain, objects that exist and events that occur, belongs to all that metaphysics, on pain of failure to cohere with the facts, must seek to comprehend.

11. From the standpoint of my existence as an agent, nonegocentrism, like egocentrism, appears as a manifestation of the illusion of detachment: the illusion that represents my agency as ultimately nothing more than an object of thought. We have seen that detachment can follow two directions. I can seek to escape in thought to a point of view outside my own self, outside my actual existence as an agent, and look down on my actions as if they were mere events that occurred alongside other events. I can also seek to withdraw into myself, denying my essential identity with the agent within whose

body my point of view finds itself located. In either case the nowness of now, my sense as an agent that what time it is now is an issue for me, is destroyed, or at best can only enjoy a shadowy reality. Then, having seemingly accomplished the mental feat of detaching oneself from one's existence as an agent, one inevitably seeks, as philosophers are accustomed to do, to make a virtue out of necessity. The unmasking of the so-called 'illusion' of temporality, the rejection of the naive conviction that there is something more to time than the before-and-after series of events is represented as an achievement, indeed the very epitome of the philosophical attitude.

What we have tried to show in this chapter is that there is no way of giving expression to the sense of temporality that we mean when we assert vehemently that now is now, other than by providing an adequate expression for the illusion of detachment: one which not only shows that detachment is wrong but why it is wrong; and indeed why as philosophers we find the illusion so compelling. One has to recognize, however, that since there is no limit to the ways in which a metaphysical illusion can manifest itself, nor consequently to its possible dialectical expressions, the adequacy of any attempt to express the illusion can in the end only be a relative matter. The more sides from which we view the claim that detachment is a metaphysical illusion, and indeed the ultimate metaphysical illusion, the stronger will be our grip on the idea that the one and only valid metaphysic is the one founded upon the standpoint of the unique agent that I must necessarily take myself to be.

15 Existence of matter

1. THERE is one question that anyone engaged in metaphysical inquiry must, it seems, at some point face up to: Amongst the assorted things that go to make up reality, what is the primary real? what is the ultimate? The answer that emerges from these pages is that the ultimate is simply my unique subjective standpoint as agent. That is the answer as far as I am concerned, the person asking the question. I cannot put the question on any other person's behalf. By comparison with the ever-present issue of my existence, comprising as it does my sense of metaphysical freedom and of the singular fact that the time is now, the traditional ultimates of substance, experience or God all appear more or less dependent: each no doubt important in its own way, but only in relation to my subjective world.

All that is true; yet it is only half the story. For my subjective world is not self-sufficient. If I did not recognize the authority of other persons to correct my judgements there would be no objective world for me, no stage on which to exercise my agency. Reflecting on all that means, one is almost inclined to say that the other in general, as the very source of truth and objectivity, is more real than my own insecure, naked self. Or perhaps these reflections only show how pointless it is to play that old philosophical game. Once we have recognized the dual reality of subjective and objective worlds, once we have seen how the objective world, without which there can be no subjective world, is sustained by the reality of the other, and how even so the two worlds are brought together only through the medium of my own physical agency, then one has taken in all the relevant metaphysical facts. Whenever one thinks about what is really real, one must think twice; and that is the final answer.

Up until now we have not, admittedly, given these two realities equal attention. From chapter 8 onwards, the argument has come under the heading of 'deductions from the form of the subjective standpoint'. We must now turn our attention away from the subjective to the objective standpoint, from myself to the world. That is not so much a change of subject, however, as a shift of emphasis. For just as, when raising questions about the form and attributes of the subjective standpoint, it was necessary to bear in mind that my subjective world is not self-sufficient, that since I can never be the final authority on the reliability of my powers of judgement I must never cease to think of myself as just one of many subjects to be found in an objective world, so in raising questions about the form and attributes of the objective standpoint, one must never forget that the person who is asking these questions is none other than the unique subject that each and every one of us calls myself, an individual for whom there can only ever be one subjective world.

By virtue of the reality of the objective world, I exist beyond myself. There is more to my existing as a self-conscious subject than I could ever determine for myself. The other, as the source of the objective standpoint, is in a position to make judgements about me, and upon those matters on which I myself have formed judgements, whose authority I cannot in general deny; though I may legitimately question such judgements in particular cases, and even persuade the other that in a certain instance I am right and she is wrong. I am, after all, an other to the other, and have in that respect as much authority over the other as the other has over me. It remains the case that there exists a side of myself that must always remain invisible to me: my reality in the eyes of the other. Only the other is in a position to compare my faculty of judgement, my system of representation as a whole with the world about which I form my judgements, and so judge its reliability as a means of putting me in touch with the way the world is; while I can only compare one judgement, or set of judgements with another.

It follows from my recognition of this superiority, possessed in principle even by other subjects to whose judgements I might never once actually defer, that what the objective world is for me, the subject matter of all our agreements or disagreements, is something I cannot ever conceive of in terms of my subjective standpoint, except as an absolute beyond which limits it. Nor can this limiting be pictured by analogy, say, with one colour on a surface limiting another, such as a patch of red surrounded by blue. For the subjective and objective standpoints each stake a claim for the whole of reality, and not just a

206

part of it; their metaphysical contradiction derives from the fact that each claim is, in its own way, equally justified.

The limiting might more accurately be pictured as the stability that results from an opposition of forces, neither of which can make any permanent headway. My subjective standpoint will never overcome the opposition of the objective, nor, so long as I exist, will it ever yield. Yet even this analogy is misleading in its suggestion that the two opposed standpoints could ever reach a state of equilibrium. Each, as it surveys the ground that it has temporarily won from its opponent, is more like an advancing army which, at the moment of its triumph, is forced to concede humiliating defeat. This, in every metaphysical question that we discuss, is the basic reality with which we have to deal. The contest will never be won or lost, the contradiction will never be resolved; the best one can hope to do is to reconcile the two parties to their perpetual conflict, or ourselves to the vision of the contradiction, or the vision to itself, and learn to see that this is the way things have to be.

2. The first thing to say about the form of the objective standpoint is exactly the same as we said, at the end of chapter 8 and the beginning of chapter 9, about the form of the subjective standpoint: the objective standpoint is a world, which stands in a relation of metaphysical contradiction with my subjective world. Beyond that nominal correspondence, however, their formal properties are quite different. The objective world is, in the first place, self-sufficient in a way that my subjective world necessarily is not: the judgements we make concerning our common world do not presuppose any external authority capable of judging their reliability, in the way that my own judgements presuppose the authority of the other. (The nearest thing in a nonegocentrist metaphysic to what we called in chapter 13 the 'normativity' of meaning and judgement is belief in the existence of a higher world of Platonic forms; and even that would not suffice, in the absence of an extra-mundane judge who, in the light of those timeless standards, could make the comparison between the way we employed our common system of representation and the true natures or divisions of things, and correct our judgements on the basis of that knowledge.)

On the other hand, we have seen that the questions of metaphysics can only be approached from the point of view of my subjective world: the fact of my unique existence for myself, invisible to mundane inquiry, is the foundation of metaphysics; its one starting point and constant. (That remains true in a way even if one seeks to deny the pre-eminent role of the proposition, 'I exist' and embarks on the nonegocentrist project of self-effacement, of explaining away the so-called illusion of a subjective standpoint.) No-one can answer a metaphysical question on my behalf, nor I on behalf of another; even though what I actually say when I describe the dual reality of subjective and objective worlds will correspond exactly to the words of any other person who agrees with me. In that sense, my subjective standpoint does indeed possess an ultimacy which the objective standpoint lacks.

Now this idea, or rather these two ideas, that the self-sufficient is not ultimate, while the ultimate is not self-sufficient, go against the whole weight of philosophical tradition. Since ancient times, metaphysics has sought the ultimate stuff of the world, the ens realissimum, that which underlies or explains in a logical sense all its qualities or appearances, the permanent behind the impermanent. To anyone engaged in such a project, the idea that this ultimate is not also self-sufficient, but dependent on the existence of some other non-ultimate which is self-sufficient, would seem the ultimate absurdity. It is this traditional view, which we attributed in chapter 6 to Aristotle, that is shared by both egocentrist and nonegocentrist, in their insistence on the exclusive reality of a single metaphysical standpoint. Only by our coming to recognize the insuperable obstacles to the construction of a one-world metaphysic, have we been forced to admit that this traditional view is false, in the face of the undeniable difficulty that such an admission entails.

3. A naive thought concerning the objective world is that it is not associated with a standpoint at all. The way we normally understand the notion of a standpoint is as something which organizes a given collection of things into a particular perspective, the way they appear or present themselves to that standpoint. The very same things can be organized into different perspectives, can be grasped from different standpoints. Thus, when we first introduced the objective standpoint back in chapter 1, we described it simply as that of the world itself. The simple idea is that what the objective standpoint grasps is the very things themselves, rather than a way of grasping them. A closely associated thought is that there is a way that things are in themselves, rather than merely for the subject that grasps them. One may well have sympathy with these thoughts. As they stand, however, they do not point in any direction. It would not avail me to know that every judgement that I make either corresponds or fails to correspond with things as they are in themselves, if whether or not any of my judgements did so correspond could never make any difference to me.

Let us give full flight to the imagination and suppose that the world as it is in itself is a conscious subject, fully aware of when my thoughts about the world correspond or fail to correspond with the way it knows itself to be. In addition to my own judgement about a particular matter of fact, there is the judgement that the world itself makes, which either accepts or repudiates my judgement. Yet what is the point of the world's judgement if I never get to hear it? If my false beliefs lead me to undertake a course of action which results in disastrous failure, then one might remark loosely that I had 'received the judgement of the world'. I thought my straw hut would survive the rainstorm but the world proved me wrong. Then again it might be said that the straw hut being washed away and all my possessions along with it is in the end only my experience, my belief. I might decide that it is all just a bad dream and that I shall soon wake up warm and snug in my bed. As long as it necessarily remains up to me to judge the world's judgement then the only world that exists for me is my subjective world. The whole point of introducing the objective standpoint is that it is meant to be something whose reality I acknowledge in accepting that I am not the final authority on the reliability of my powers of judgement. Something more must be included in that thought than simply the truistic observation that the world is the way it is, whatever I happen to think about it. Some provision must be made for the judgements of other subjects, judgements which I do indeed expect to hear about.

4. In chapter 5, the objective standpoint was defined as that by virtue of which there exists a point of view on the world other than my own. It was a deliberately cautious definition. What we wanted to express was the absolute minimum that follows from the rejection of the egocentrist's claim that only my subjective world is real. We went on to assume without argument that if there could be one other point of view then there could be an indefinite number; and then qualified that statement by arguing that a point of view can exist even if it is not actually occupied by a conscious subject. Now these two claims go together. If the actual occupation of a point of view were a necessary condition for its existence, then it would seem that the number of points of view other than my own would become a contingent matter, depending on the number of subjects who happened to exist. Why then could there not be just one other point of view, or perhaps just three or four? In order for that to be the case we should have to think of reality as such as made up of a number of hermetically sealed bubbles of conscious experience floating as it were in a vacuum, each one of which contains a picture or representation of the same external

world, only seen from a different point of view. In reality, there is no such world, except perhaps in the mind of God, who makes sure that all the bubbles of experience remain in harmony with one another, picturing the same world.

That is essentially the view of Leibniz, which we came across in the last chapter in connection with the question of how different conscious subjects are able to share the same now. Leibniz would only have added that God, in deciding which was the best of all possible worlds, would never have chosen to create only a few conscious subjects, when he could have created a bubble of experience or monad corresponding to every existing subject or object, animate or inanimate. (In a moment we shall see why.) However, that claim does not appear necessary to the monad theory. For it might have occurred to a more parsimonious follower of Leibniz that the ideal number of monads was just five. Having defected so far, such a philosopher might decide that the Leibnizian deity, the Creator, was also dispensable. Even if it required a divine agency to set up the monads in harmony with one another, the deity has no further role to play in the story: once the clocks are set to the same time and wound up, they go by themselves. So let us imagine the more austere monad theory is correct. I, my wife, and perhaps three of our friends are mere bubbles of experience, five monads, who together make up the whole of reality; there is nothing else. Under such circumstances, would the conditions be met for the existence of an objective world?

However much one might wish to question the explanatory fruitfulness of such a theory, it does seem that the conditions for the existence of an objective world, that is to say, a reality by virtue of which my powers of judgement could be judged reliable or unreliable, would in one sense be met. There are just four real subjects of experience, my fellow monads, whose authority to correct my judgements I recognize: those special individuals singled out from the multitude whose outer appearance I believe – let us not now question on what grounds – to correspond in each case with an inner bubble of experience in which I myself occur as an outer appearance. It is as if we are all dreaming the same dream, each one of us appearing in the dreams of each of the others. (The moral view corresponding to this metaphysical belief would be that only our feelings and interests count; all other individuals are mere objects for us to use. This would mean repudiating the argument in chapter 13 that consistency demands that either all others are mere objects or none are.)

Despite our best efforts, however, the accounts which we all give of our shared world will sometimes deviate and come into conflict with one another. When that happens, logic dictates that some of our beliefs will be true, and others false. Now when a person's judgement errs, he can sometimes be made to see the mistake for himself. So it may happen that I form a belief, which conflicts with the beliefs of my fellow monads, which they then persuade me to revise. Yet suppose in this case I refuse to listen to their arguments: who is to say that they are definitely right and I am definitely wrong? Clearly, there is nothing for the falsity of my belief to consist in other than the fact that the majority of the monads decree that it is so. Provided that there always exists an odd number of monads, so that the vote is never split fifty-fifty, such a set up does formally meet the requirement that there should be a standard for truth and falsity beyond my own judgements in the light of which my judgements may be evaluated.

On closer inspection, it becomes clear that this idea goes completely against the spirit of the requirement. In the first place, there are many cases in our everyday lives when the majority are wrong. According to the austere monad theory, the majority must always be right. The only reply to this objection would be to say that in cases where the majority are wrong, that is only established when sufficiently many are persuaded to change their minds, so that the wrong view ends up being held only by the minority. But that reply is not good enough. The question is not how the falsity of a judgement is established, that is to say, agreed upon, but rather our conception of what its falsity actually consists in. What do we think of as making it false? If one says that it is false if the majority are fated eventually to agree on its falsehood, even if they now think that it is true, then one has made one of two assumptions neither of which can be justified in the context of the austere monad theory without resort to the ad hoc move of divine provision or intervention: either, first, that there could be such a fact about the future as that the monads are fated to agree that the judgement is false, even though there is by hypothesis no real world outside their collective experiences in virtue of which this fact could have any foundation; or, secondly, that with the passage of time the original erroneous agreement would at least show a natural tendency to correct itself, and would not become ever more firmly entrenched.

5. My belief is false, not when I judge that it is false, but when it fails to match up with the objective world in the way that all beliefs aim to do: that is to say, when the world is different from the way my belief says it is. The world itself, meanwhile, has no authority to correct my judgements; only other subjects can do that. Yet as we have just seen, the bare minimum that would seem to be required for the existence of

other subjects does not provide sufficient materials for a genuine distinction between truth and falsity. The world cannot simply be the collective representation of an arbitrary number of bubbles of experience, one of whom happens to be myself. There is more to matching or failing to match up with a world than merely agreeing or not agreeing with what the majority of monads believe. Leibniz would have said that this just shows up the inadequacy of the austere monad theory, in not allowing a separate bubble of experience for every distinguishable subject and object. Five, fifty or five hundred monads all dreaming the same dream from different points of view does not constitute a real world. Adding up all that we collectively experience still leaves gaps of sheer nothingness which only our beliefs can fill, beliefs to whose truth or falsity nothing in reality corresponds other than agreement or disagreement with other beliefs.

Leibniz reasoned, quite logically, that order to fill the gaps in this picture it is necessary to grant that not only every person or animal, but every existing thing, every cloud, every star, every speck of dust has its own experience of the world. Some experiences, like ours, are relatively clear (though far from transparent); others are much more confused. Everything that happens is represented by, or at least causes, some impression, however faint, in every bubble of experience. This follows directly from the fact that there is nothing to things besides experience, together with the fact that every thing is related by its spatio-temporal position in the external world – or, rather, the collective representation of an external world – to every other thing.

Now we have a genuinely objective world, but at what a price! Within its own terms, Leibniz's theory is perfectly consistent in following up the requirement that there should be no gaps in reality, that belief should always have something real to match up with; but the result is sheer metaphysical extravagance. I glance at my thumbnail, and wonder what experience it is having at the moment. Perhaps it can feel itself growing, sensing the steady pulse in my thumb, the tension in my hand, even hearing the faint murmur of my words as I read these lines aloud to myself, like waves crashing on some distant shore. What could this be but a poetic fancy? But no, this is the way things have to be, there is a logical argument to prove it. – Inevitably, the question one finds oneself asking is, What is it that Leibniz was reacting against, that led him to formulate such a bizarre theory?

6. Leibniz's theory of monads is far from being the only attempt that has been made to construct an objective world purely out of the

materials of experience. There is at least one alternative method of filling in the gaps, which is in some ways much simpler. Let us allow that there is, as common sense assumes, a sharp distinction between subjects who have conscious experience, and mere objects of perception that do not themselves have experience. Consider an event that occurs when no-one is there to witness it, say, a leaf falling in a forest. No finite conscious subject, we may suppose, no bird or insect is present to witness the leaf fall; but God sees it. The event is permanently registered as a perception in God's mind, along with every other event that occurs in the universe. We ourselves, as subjects of experience, are nothing but immaterial spirits, who are privileged to share a portion of God's perceptions.

That, in essence, is Berkeley's theory. Its main virtue, as he saw it, was the instant proof it delivered of the existence of God: every object that exists, my own physical body included, is, literally, part of God's mind. Others might see that as its main defect. For while Leibniz had to invoke God's creative power in order to guarantee harmony between the experienced worlds of all the monads that make up reality, his theory does at least stand up on its own without external support. Arguably, an atheist, or someone who believed that a Grand Architect created the universe but then departed from the scene, could still subscribe to the theory of monads, whereas such a person would find Berkeley's theory unacceptable.

Setting aside objections to the indispensable presence of a deity, however, Berkeley's theory turns out to be no less strange than Leibniz's. Even if this very body, and every move that it makes, are only perceptions in God's mind, there must still be some distance between the creator and his creation: I am not God. What then am I? If I am not my physical body, if that is as far as I am concerned just another object in the world of God's perceptions, then it would seem that I, the essential I, can be nothing more than the sum total of my conscious experience. Yet there is no experience in me that is not also in God. The trouble is that any boundary that one draws around experiences in God's mind such as would correspond with those I call mine appears purely nominal, a logical distinction based on no discernible ontological difference in a world constituted exclusively of God's perceptions. Whatever exists on one side of the boundary is of the same ultimate nature as whatever exists on the other.

It must be said on Berkeley's behalf that, realizing this difficulty, he strove to distinguish between the 'archetypes' of objects in God's mind and the representations or copies of those objects in the minds of finite spirits. As it stands, however, that move secures the distance between the Creator and His creation by mere fiat, leaving their ultimate distinction and connection obscure. In order to justify that distinction one needs, as Berkeley himself was well aware, the notion of a spirit not just as a passive subject of experience but as an agent, capable of acknowledging or resisting the will of God. We are not merely a captive audience at a picture show, but in some sense contribute through our own mental efforts to what comes up on the giant screen. It is not at all clear, however, how the notion of human agency can survive the transportation from a material to a purely mental world. Clearly it must do so in some form if finite spirits are to be saved from total absorption into the mind of their Creator.

7. The basic inspiration for theories such as those of Leibniz and Berkeley is horror at the very idea of matter: the unknown something that remains behind when all sentience and perception are taken away. Near the beginning of this chapter we described the objective standpoint as an absolute beyond, something I cannot conceive of in terms of my subjective world. It is this very intimation of beyondness that horrifies. One way of seeming to reduce it, of making it appear less beyond, would be to insist that whatever exists outside my subjective world can only be, in some sense, more of the same. Now it might be claimed that the very substance of my subjective world is experience, and nothing but experience; the vision of a subjective world is, after all, the common ground shared by our two-world metaphysic and the egocentrist's belief in the exclusive reality of the world of my possible experience. It would seem to follow that the only thing I can conceive of as existing outside my subjective world, if I can conceive of any such existence, must in some sense be experience also. Berkeley was content to reduce the objective world to God's experience. Leibniz thought that this kind of theory makes things too insubstantial: to exist, even in the mind of God, only as a perception, only as something experienced, is a way of being ultimately unreal. Only if things are allowed to exist for themselves, in their own right as subjects of their own experience, can they be said to constitute real objects of the perception of other subjects, or of God. At least, that is how one must approach the question if one rules out totally any meaning to the notion of existing other than experiencing or being experienced.

What then should we say? The scruple that lies behind the edict banishing matter is clear enough. The question is whether the scruple is well founded. The beyondness of the objective world, that which limits my subjective world, is, to repeat, absolute. Turning everything into experience and refusing to acknowledge the existence of matter cannot make the objective world any less of a beyond. On the contrary, to think of myself and another subject of experience as merely two of the same is, as we have seen, something I am permitted to do only after I have mentally shifted from the subjective to the objective standpoint; it in no way renders that shift more intelligible. So it seems that the horror of the beyond can in no way be lessened merely by rejecting matter. The only consistent course for someone who feels that way is to embrace wholeheartedly the metaphysic of egocentrism, and refuse to acknowledge the reality of the objective standpoint.

It is one thing to question the motivation for a theory, however, and quite another to pass judgement on its truth or falsehood. Nor does the objection that one finds a metaphysical theory strange or bizarre have any logical force. On the contrary, we should approach these questions positively expecting our naive beliefs to be challenged; nothing is obvious. Even if the rejection of matter turns everything upside down so that the objective world becomes something completely unrecognizable, it still falls to us to examine logically the question whether a non-material interpretation of our metaphysic of subjective and objective worlds can be justified. Could it be that the objective world is nothing other than, say, perceptions in the mind of God, as Berkeley believed, or else windowless bubbles of experience as Leibniz held?

8. Someone might say in reply to these speculations, 'Of course, all these things are possible, but we shall never know for certain what the world is really made of, whether of matter or experience.' That is to say, even though the metaphysician must adopt the working hypothesis that every question one might come across is capable, in principle, of being decided, it may sometimes happen that one encounters two rival theories, neither of which can ever be disproved by any logical argument. We are left with two perpetually open possibilities, with no basis other than personal preference for choosing between them. Though that seems a plausible thing to say, it is totally wrong. As we shall argue in the next chapter in an analogous case, one can only conclude in such an event that both theories are false.

Let us not debate that contentious point now. For the moment, we shall merely note that an irresolvable conflict does indeed arise when one approaches the question of a world of experience versus a world of matter from the position of a nonegocentrist metaphysic. We saw, in chapter 6, how the misconceived attempt to interpret the incommunicable *this* of my subjective standpoint in terms of a special class of subjective constituents of objective reality leads to the futile dispute between a refined cartesian dualism of subjective and objective

215

aspects and an opposed identity theory. The same elision of subjective and objective standpoints is responsible for the dispute between nonegocentrists who seek to defend pure matter and anti-materialists. Anti-materialism, one might say, simply takes the dualist's rejection of a world constituted exclusively of matter to its logical conclusion. For a genuine nonegocentrist, there is no scope for half-measures: either everything has the pure, irreducible thisness characteristic of experience or else nothing has it, appearances notwithstanding. (Or, at a stretch, everything that exists belongs to a category located in-between pure experience and pure matter: the 'pan-psychism' embraced by Whitehead, and revived in a different form by Nagel.) Unfortunately, that is as far as the dispute goes. Only in the two-world metaphysic, it turns out, can the question be resolved – in favour of the existence of both the *this* and of matter. It is indeed answered in a way that the nonegocentrist would never have anticipated. For if the objective world is material, that can only be because my subjective world is material also.

9. What is matter? The first thing one thinks about when one tries to form a concept of matter is something like this: it is that which our perceptual experience is of, that of which our own bodies are made, and the bodies of the things we perceive. The problem with that simple thought is that all we know of matter is through our experience: picture matter and you picture some kind of experience. If matter is essentially different from experience, then it must as a matter of logic possess at least one property that experience does not; but how could it? I try to picture in my mind the matter of the desk in front of me. It is not the oblong shape that I see, nor its hardness to the touch, both of which exist in my experience. Is it then the invisible atoms which physicists tell me is the ultimate substance of the desk? There again, my only conception of an atom is of something very small, with a certain shape, which fits into arrangements and compounds with other atoms; in short, something I imagine I could experience, if only my senses were sufficiently acute. (Cf. Locke *Essay Concerning Human Understanding* Bk. IV, ch. iii, sec. 25: our idea of the invisible constitution of objects which gives rise to their secondary qualities is of what a being with the senses of an angel would be able to perceive.)

It is clear that this line of thought will never get us anywhere. We have been trying to think of the matter of an object as one of its properties; but no mere property of an object is so remote from us that we cannot grasp it in terms of experience or possible experience. If matter is to be found anywhere, it must be at a different logical

216

level from the properties of objects. Far from being merely added on to its other properties, the matter of an object is that object: every property of a material object is a material property.

What then is a material object? Objects as such exist only because there is an objective world, something by virtue of which there exists a point of view other than my own. We have seen that the anti-materialist understands this definition to mean that there exist other points of view which are actually occupied, either by monads or by God, or both. Our version of materialism, or, to be more accurate, our anti-anti-materialism, is simply the claim made in chapter 5, that points of view other than my own can exist even if none of them happen to be occupied; for example, if all conscious beings other than myself were to perish. It was argued that since the possibility of a thing's happening must always be grounded in what is actually the case, there must be something to make the possibility of a subject's occupying another point of view in relation to the objects of my perception possible. Since other points of view can exist in the absence of any conscious experience other than my own, whatever it is that actually exists to make the possibility of a subject's occupying another viewpoint possible cannot itself be an experience; neither an experience in the mind of a Berkeleian God, nor a Leibnizian monad, an object of perception with its own inner experience. That which actually exists in this negative sense is rather to be thought of as simply an aspect of the world which presents itself to a point of view. The essential property of a material object is to possess indefinitely many aspects.

The dialectical point of defining matter negatively, in terms of an anti-anti-materialism, is to shift the onus of proof squarely onto the anti-materialist. The idea is that, instead of allowing ourselves to be put on the defensive, and trying to explain, as the anti-materialist would have us do, what possible difference the existence of matter, or that which is not experience, could make to our experience or to our thoughts about the things we experience, we force our opponent to justify his position. What is wrong, we ask, with saying that matter simply is that which possesses aspects, that which makes possibilities of experience possible? Even if one cannot think of matter except by reference to one's experience, that does not make matter equivalent to experience.

10. To find out the answer to our question, it is necessary to go back to the anti-materialist's starting point. How, asks the anti-materialist, starting from my own experience, could I so much as form the conception of anything which is not experience, but which possesses

the power to bring about experiences? Our immediate objection to this argument a short while ago was that the anti-materialist's scruple ought to apply with equal force to my ability to form a conception of anything which is not my experience. Horror of matter ought to manifest itself equally as a horror of the very idea of an objective world; for the beyondness of matter and the beyondness of the objective world are, as far as my subjective standpoint is concerned, equally inconceivable. However, that point remains ad hominem. The anti-materialist can reply, 'I agree that it is difficult to conceive of an objective world beyond my possible experience, but I find it still more difficult, in fact impossible, to conceive of what you call "matter"!' But let us look again at the seemingly innocent phrase, 'starting from my own experience'. What does it mean? I am trying to comprehend the objective world starting from my own subjective standpoint. However, starting from my subjective standpoint would be starting from my own experience only if, as the anti-materialist claims, the very substance of my subjective world is experience. Is that claim correct?

The idea that my subjective standpoint is the world of my possible experience, an on-going spectacle revolving around me and put on for my benefit alone, was the notion of a subjective standpoint with which we began our metaphysical inquiry. For we first had to attack both egocentrism and nonegocentrism, both the belief in the exclusive reality of the subjective standpoint and the belief in the exclusive reality of the objective standpoint, and so inevitably found ourselves taking over the egocentrist's and the nonegocentrist's own notions of what the subjective and objective worlds are. Then we discovered, in Chapters 10 and 11, that the egocentrist's notion of the subjective world was seriously distorted. If my subjective world is nothing other than a world of possible experience, then I must exist ultimately as a passive observer, a being whose sole function is to have experiences, for whom existing is experiencing. My life as an agent, as a source of changes in the world around me, becomes a mere illusion: when I seem to act, all that actually happens is that my inner, observing I witnesses changes in the outer world that correspond in certain ways with events in my mind and movements of my body. In that case, we argued, the two-world theory of subjective and objective standpoints, the only remaining possibility after egocentrism and nonegocentrism have been disposed of, reduces to an intolerable oscillation, a metaphysical double vision. We asserted that there must, on the contrary, be a bridge between the subjective and objective worlds, and that the necessary bridge can only consist in the recognition of the primacy of my standpoint as an agent.

In the light of this result, we therefore have no alternative but to reject the premiss of the anti-materialist's argument. It is not the case that I have to form a conception of the objective world starting from my own experience, in the anti-materialist's sense. What I have to start from is the subjective world of my existence as an agent. Whatever the substance of that world may be, it is not experience.

11. When we first came to investigate the form of my subjective standpoint in chapter 8, we arrived at an important result; a result which now plays a decisive role in the argument. We discovered that the subjective and objective worlds are not, as one might first be led to think, populated by two sets of objects, subjective objects and objective objects. Since all language presupposes the objective standpoint, there is nothing I could say about a parallel domain of putative subjective objects other than that they are what they are in relation to *this*; or, rather, I could not even say that 'they' are anything, but only that there is *this*. Far from depopulating my subjective world, however, what that shows is that the very same objects must be found in both the subjective and objective worlds. My subjective keyboard, to return to our familiar example, is simply the objective keyboard conceived or grasped in relation to *this*, my inexpressible sense of my own unique existence. The contradiction between the subjective and objective worlds arises from the ordering that my subjective standpoint imposes on objects, an ordering that places them in a frame of reference with my own absolute I at its axis. For example, objects distant from me are absolutely distant; objects near to me are absolutely near. It is this ordering which remains invisible from the objective standpoint; for what is absolute for me is only relative as far as others are concerned. As a result of this ordering, every object is endowed with contradictory properties: every object belongs, and also does not belong, to my unique frame of reference.

Now the question raised by anti-materialism is the question whether the objects that make up the objective world are material objects, or whether they are on the contrary only experiential objects, that is to say, either subjects or objects of some actual experience other than my own. If the objects that make up the subjective and objective worlds are the very same objects, however, if the only change brought about by my subjective standpoint is an ordering of objects in relation to my unique frame of reference, then we can assert that objects as such will be material provided that the objects in my subjective world are material, and, on the contrary, that they will be experiential if the objects in my subjective world are experiential. Yet we have already seen that the objects in my subjective world cannot be merely experiential. It only remains to clarify in what sense the objects in my subjective world may be said to be material.

Suppose someone were to ask, naively, What happens to objects when I am not perceiving them? If I am perceiving a chair, and then turn away for a few moments, what happens to the chair meanwhile? The Kantian egocentrist would say that the object I describe by means of the concept 'chair' must be thought of as ultimately existing only as a possibility of my experience: a theoretical construct posited by the metaphysical subject occupying my point of view in order to flesh out the framework of a unified spatial world of which I necessarily possess only limited perceptual access at any given time. Chairs cannot be allowed simply to go out of existence from one moment to the next without wrecking the project of describing my experience as the perception of a world of persisting objects in causal relations; which is in turn a condition for the very possibility of my having any experience at all.

If one presses the question what this possibility of my having different experiences of the chair is in itself, or, rather, what actually exists in virtue of which this possibility is possible, then the only answer forthcoming, if one sticks within the limits of a metaphysic based on the exclusive reality of the subjective standpoint (as we have seen Kant did not), is that this possibility of experience must be taken as a sheer fact, not grounded in anything else. Ultimately, all there is consists in the *this* together with an inexplicable power of judgement which discerns objects and thereby constructs a world. By contrast, for anyone who, in the manner of Leibniz or Berkeley, insists on the reality of the objective standpoint and repudiates egocentrism, the objects which I do not now perceive, the objects of my possible experience, remain the subjects or objects of some actual experience. (Belief in Kantian things in themselves or 'noumena', the unknowable ultimate reality in virtue of which possibilities of experience are possible, remains an option for the more sophisticated anti-materialist who rejects as meaningless any attempt to extend the concept of experience beyond the world of my possible experience.) If, repudiating these views, one maintains that the objects that make up both the subjective and objective worlds are neither experiential, nor noumenal, but material, then some other explanation must be found; that is to say, one in which the necessity of the chair's continued existence is made apparent in terms which neither build the chair out of actual experience, nor assert continuity while denying the possibility of any knowledge of its ultimate ground .

By definition, a material object can exist, that is to say, present aspects to points of view, even if none of those points of view are occupied. We have already seen that it is because of the primacy of my subjective standpoint as an agent that the objects in my subjective world cannot be thought of as purely experiential, that they cannot exist for me as mere possibilities of my experience. In what sense does it follow that they are material? The answer is not that they exist as something more, over and above possibilities of my experience but rather, in a sense, that they can only exist as something less. If my agency is ultimate, then the objects in my subjective world necessarily extend beyond the range of what I could ever experience, no matter how far my perceptual and intellectual powers were to be extended. For every action, however deliberate, however self-consciously performed, necessarily depends upon conditions of which I am not aware, which I do not in any sense experience, and which, were I to become aware of them, would reduce that action to movements of my body which I passively observed. Whatever I may come to know about the world, I must at least remain opaque to myself. That is simply another way of describing the absolute necessity of my sense of metaphysical freedom.

Now it would of course be open to the anti-materialist to continue to insist that objects which I do not now perceive might still remain the subjects or objects of some actual experience other than my own, in a world viewed from the objective standpoint. However, the grounds for insisting that they must do so no longer hold. For if my being an agent is the fundamental attribute of my subjective world, then what guarantees the continued existence of those objects which I do not now perceive are conditions already realized within my subjective world, and not, as the anti-materialist believes, conditions whose realization can only be conceived from the objective standpoint. One might say, the world of my subjective standpoint is not a show put on for my benefit but the stage on which I am the principal actor: the stage is not there for me simply so I can experience it, it is there to support me. – And if the anti-materialist replies, 'That is just like Dr. Johnson kicking the stone,' we may retort in good conscience that it is, indeed, just like that.

12. The essential connection between agency and the concept of matter will be familiar to students of Schopenhauer. We have already passed summary judgement on Schopenhauer's position in chapter 11. If I wish to embrace nonegocentrism, yet cannot give up the conviction that my actions possess the dynamic status that could be granted to them only by the primacy of my subjective standpoint as an agent, then I must believe that 'I' am in reality all agents. Every action that occurs in the world – whether Klempner appears as the

agent, or equally some other person whom I appear merely to observe, or indeed the activities of an animal or machine or even the brute force exerted by one lump of matter on another – is in reality my absolute doing. We can now say that if that were the case, then one might indeed regard matter itself as that which 'appears as the mere visibility of the will, so that ultimately it too can be regarded in a certain sense as identical with the will' (*The World As Will and Representation* Vol. II, p. 45). When I kick the stone, the will of all agents manifesting itself in Klempner's movement meets a resistance which is itself a manifestation of that same will. The Kantian thing in itself is thus revealed as nothing but will. Action in general is related to matter as an 'essence' which coincides with 'existence' (ibid.), for apart from the particular perceptible qualities of material objects, all there is to materiality is action.

Clearly, a two-world metaphysic of subjective and objective standpoints must resist this identification of will with matter. If one thinks in terms of the Newtonian law that to every action there corresponds an equal and opposite reaction, then one can see the point of Schopenhauer's thought that what resists my will is itself will. What from the point of view of Klempner appears as a striving to overcome the resisting force of the stone, appears from the point of view of the stone as a striving to overcome the moving force of Klempner's boot. The reason we cannot make this equation in our metaphysic is that the standpoint of agency is locked in to just one point of view: my own as a particular subject in the world. When I kick, that is an absolute doing; when a stone, or a person, resists me that is one more thing that happens.

It follows that matter cannot be in any sense equivalent to will, or to its manifestation. Rather, matter and will are co-ordinate notions. What my kicking the stone proves, as my absolute doing, is indeed not just that there is matter in the stone, the object that actually resists me; on the contrary, as we have seen, matter is first and foremost my own material body, which must necessarily remain opaque to me as an object of possible experience if I am to remain an agent. Yet given that necessary recognition, we have argued, there can be no rational ground for the denial that the object which I act upon, as a constituent of my subjective world, is in its essential being something whose aspects can never be exhausted by my experience; that is to say, matter.

13. It should be clear that our proof of the existence of matter, or, rather, our rejection of anti-materialism, is unavailable to anyone who maintains a steadfastly nonegocentrist (and non-Schopenhaurian)

position, and refuses to acknowledge the reality of the subjective standpoint. Nor does it seem at all likely that any other proof could be found. Since the basis for our resistance to anti-materialism turns out to be the primacy of my subjective standpoint as an agent – the claim that my agency must be regarded as ultimate on pain of an intolerable metaphysical double vision – anyone who denies the reality of the subjective standpoint has simply denied herself the only available means for resolving the issue.

For not a few thinkers who have investigated this question, that will no doubt appear a highly paradoxical result. Many will have toiled under the misapprehension, entrenched in recent philosophy, that the only way to defend the claims of matter is on the basis of a thoroughgoing 'externalism', that is to say, from an exclusively objective standpoint. It is not difficult, however, to explain how the misapprehension came about. Experience is thought of loosely as something essentially inner, matter as something essentially outer. So a theory that established the existence of matter would have to be one that insists on approaching reality from a point of view outside the subject, that is to say, my own self; for only such a theory could be relied on to discount the inner in favour of the outer!

To anyone seduced by such a simplistic view, a few moments reflection on the philosophies of Leibniz or Berkeley ought to cause considerable discomfort. Nothing could be so inner as the contents of a monad's consciousness, or of God's mind. Yet the vision of a world of monads or of God's perceptions is compatible with the most uncompromising nonegocentrism. For anyone who has fought against the vision of a subjective world, and thinks that by so doing one is well on the way to making the world safe for our common sense notion of matter, the hard truth is that the battle against anti-materialism has not even been joined.

16 Truth and verifiability

1. IN seeking to establish the essential attributes of the objective world, we have encountered two theories, those of Leibniz and Berkeley, each of which denies the simple thereness of things. According to either version of the anti-materialist metaphysic, the everyday objects we perceive, which common sense tells us are out there, and remain there when we am not looking at them, are really not there at all. What we take to be objects occupying a common space alongside other objects, capable of coming into relation with one conscious subject or another, but equally able to subsist in the absence of any kind of conscious experience, are in fact built out of the very stuff of consciousness. There are no places for things to occupy, for space itself is ultimately unreal. Having refuted anti-materialism on the grounds of its failure to comprehend the primacy of action, however, we now face a more subtle form of the denial of thereness, one that grants the capacity of material objects to exist apart from conscious experience; a metaphysical position which for that reason proves far more difficult to rebut.

It would seem a truism that our world of material objects contains far more than we can ever come to know. Outside the continually expanding and contracting sphere of facts that remain in some sense close enough to be reached by the exercise of our cognitive faculties, whether through sense perception or inference, there exists a wider sphere of possibilities whose obtaining or not obtaining will never make any detectable difference our world. Some of these possibilities concern the distant past, or places further away than we could ever travel. However, it is not simply a matter of spatial or temporal distance. Our world is full of hidden nooks and crannies, unknowable recesses, which remain unreachable even though they are physically close by us. For example, most of the details of the processes going on inside my body at this very moment no-one will ever know.

It can hardly be a matter of regret that we cannot know everything: that is simply a reflection of our finitude. Yet when one thinks about this situation with the refined suspicions of the metaphysician, committed to the project of determining the strict limits of the real, one may find oneself questioning what it means to say that something is a fact, or that a statement states a fact or is true. Are there, as we naturally assume, facts or truths that none of us can ever come to know? Or does truth depend in some manner on the possibility of knowledge? Suppose that someone asserted that outside the sphere of knowable facts, there is nothing really there, only an open, undetermined range of possibilities: how could one ever prove that assertion false?

One immediate reply is simply to throw the question back: what possible grounds could there be for denying the existence of truths outside the reach of knowledge? The question of the onus of proof seems paramount here, as it was in the case of anti-materialism. That reaction, however, turns out to be ineffective. As we shall soon discover, the opponent of independent facts is happy to admit to having no proof to offer for the claim that facts cannot exist in the absence of the possibility of knowledge, parallel to the anti-materialist's argument that objects cannot exist other than as subjects or objects of perception. Her position is rather that there is simply nothing that one could possibly mean by asserting that unknowable facts exist. We naively picture a fact as just being there in the world, complete in itself, independent of any cognitive relation we may hold towards it. Only on reflection we discover that this picture does not succeed in representing anything. When one tries to compare it with the opposite picture of facts coming into existence as the sphere of knowledge expands, it proves impossible, as hard as one might try, to explain or even articulate the difference between the first picture and the second.

Independently existing facts would not, after all, be like material objects, which occupy space and behave according to physical laws that permit their continued existence independently of their accessibility or proximity to conscious subjects. Nor is knowledge a relation between a subject and the fact that is known, though it does entail cognitive relations to objects in virtue of whose properties and relations the content of the subject's judgement is true. That is just the familiar point that whatever makes a true statement true is not something to which the statement as a whole may be said to correspond in any literal sense. When we raise the question whether a depiction, say, a photograph in a holiday brochure, corresponds with the actual scene it depicts, we are considering the truth of a proposition in which the depiction features as an object. The correctness of representation of the photograph becomes a subject matter for judgement, a pictorial relation which we shall say either obtains or fails to obtain depending on whether certain propositions turn out to be true or false. Truth itself cannot be regarded as a member of the class of relations of correct representation or correspondence without, as Frege argued, leading to a vicious regress (cf. Dummett Frege *Philosophy of Language* pp. 442-4, commenting on Frege's essay 'The Thought'). It is on this point that the argument turns.

2. It was Dummett who, in his article 'Truth', first suggested the possibility of a position, clearly distinguished from Berkeleian anti-materialism, according to which what is true is in some way restricted to the knowably or verifiably true. In his many subsequent writings, Dummett has continued to develop his argument that the correct view of the relation between truth and knowledge can only be established via an account of the form of a theory of meaning for our ordinary discourse; a question he sees as parallel to, and indeed a more general case of the dispute between intuitionist and classical mathematicians over the meaning of mathematical statements. According to the intuitionist, on Dummett's reading, our grasp of the meanings of mathematical statements can only consist in our knowledge of what would count as a canonical proof, rather than in the conditions under which the statement would be true, irrespective of whether it can be proved or not. Since only a truth-conditional account justifies the unrestricted assertion of the law of excluded middle, the adoption of the intuitionist view has far-reaching consequences for mathematical practice. The same, by implication, would be true of our ordinary discourse, were a theory of meaning in terms of verification conditions to be adopted.

In our view, such a claim not only misses the dialectical point of the dispute over the nature of truth (and indeed over the specific problem of infinite generalizations in mathematics, as distinguished from finite generalizations with a very large upper bound, to which Dummett's scruples ought to apply with equal force) but is fundamentally mistaken in its attempt to conflate the tasks of the meaning theorist and the metaphysician; and in practice leads to the prescription of a standard for theories of meaning for human discourse which no theory constructed by mere human beings could ever hope to meet.

226

However, rather than attempt a detailed criticism of Dummett's views on the scope and purpose of theories of meaning – which would take a whole book – we shall simply present an alternative approach; in effect, doing what ought not to be possible if Dummett is right. As we shall represent the dispute, the opponent of facts, or anti-realist to borrow Dummett's term, is fully prepared to grant the validity of the law of excluded middle; but argues that any assertion of the form, 'P or not-P', or of the related principle of bivalence, 'either "P" is true or "P" is false', simply fails to convey what the realist intends it to convey. Nor, says the anti-realist, is there any other form of words that would succeed in getting across what the realist thinks he means.

We shall go on to show, however, that both metaphysical positions are false. It is false to say that there can exist facts that we can never know, and it is equally false to say that there cannot exist facts that we can never know. The argument for this doubly negative claim represents a direct route, reached independently of considerations about meaning, to what will turn out to be a positive and not merely negative metaphysical conclusion; in effect, a third, overlooked alternative. It thus goes against Dummett's precept that the only route to metaphysics can be indirect, via an account of the form of a theory of meaning.

3. Before engaging in the dialectic proper, however, we need to answer three swift objections, in the latter two cases based on our own results, against the very intelligibility of raising a question against the realist notion of truth. The first and most obvious objection is simply that the world is, by its very nature, essentially determinate. (We may put on one side the question of quantum indeterminacy.) The fact that we are prevented by our position in space and time or by the limitations of our faculties from knowing certain facts about an object does not make that object, as it were, go fuzzy. Consider, for example, what one would say if one came to the conclusion that either A or B caused C, though one could never know which. (The objection and the example are both due to Dorothy Edgington.) Whatever made C come about surely could not itself have been indeterminate, even if, owing to the limitations of our knowledge, we are unable to narrow down the range of determinate alternatives beyond A or B. The anti-realist will reply that what is not determinate is not the object that caused C, but rather whether our world is a world in which a determinate A caused C or a world in which a determinate B caused C. To assert that this makes the cause of C into a fuzzy object is to conflate facts and objects. What the objection does serve to bring out, however, is extent of the anti-realist's deviation

from the ordinary notion of what it is to be in a world. We do not stand in any particular determinate world, but rather at the locus of an indeterminate range of determinate worlds.

The second objection is that the argument used to refute anti-materialism, that the primacy of my agency entails the existence of material conditions for my actions that cannot be reduced to the contents of my perceptions, entails the existence of certain facts beyond my cognitive reach, namely, those which describe those material conditions. The anti-realist, however, need not be perturbed. It is certainly the case that the existence of objects which I cannot perceive entails the existence of facts which I cannot know at this moment. Yet there is nothing to prevent me from later coming to know by inference facts which I cannot have known by direct perception; nor indeed is there anything to prevent anyone else from knowing them now. The anti-materialist had to prove that objects which I do not now perceive must be subjects or objects of some actual experience; the anti-realist merely denies that it could mean anything to assert the existence of truths permanently out of any person's cognitive reach.

The third objection, again based on a result we should on no account wish to overturn, is that my recognition of the authority of other persons to correct my judgements entails the existence of facts that I necessarily cannot know; namely facts about the relation between my system of representation as a whole and the world as it appears from a point of view outside my system of representation. The anti-realist, however, can allow that there are facts others can know about me that I cannot ever know about myself. It suffices for their truth that they can be known by those other persons. (We need to bear in mind that these are facts of a very special kind, facts whose significance is destroyed in the very process of telling me, of allowing their statement to be filtered through the very system of representation to which they relate.) What then of the possibility considered back in chapter 5 that all conscious subjects other than myself should perish? Even in that case, the relevant facts about the relation between my system of representation as a whole and the world as it would appear from another point of view would still obtain. For the anti-realist, however, what suffices for the obtaining of such facts is the logical possibility that suitably placed conscious subjects might, at some time, come into existence.

4. Consider then the following method for playing a board game. Instead of throwing dice to determine the moves, the players shake a closed dice-box, the rattle serving as a signal for someone in the next

room to call out a number chosen at random between one and six. No-one ever opens the box to check whether the number on the die corresponds with the number called out; it has no bearing on the correct conduct of the game whether the numbers are the same or not. Even so, while waiting one's turn one may find oneself speculating, as the box is rattled again, whether the number previously called out did in fact correspond with its unseen fall of the die. Such idle speculation about possibilities that can never be verified is a familiar enough phenomenon of human life; it needs no reason or excuse, and almost anything can provide the occasion. Thus, for example, the coincidence of the third call of the third game being a three might prompt one to wonder whether the die in the box fell on three also. Our immediate question is not whether such an activity is rational or irrational, nor even whether its motivation would be intelligible to any rational being. From our human standpoint, we seem to find idle speculation intelligible; and for that reason we ought to be able at least to say what it is that we do when we speculate idly. Yet, as we shall soon see, even this modest aim encounters unexpected difficulties.

Speculation does not in general require any evidence or grounds, nor need it envisage ever being proved wrong or right. It is an activity of the mind at play, which need have no object other than to give some satisfaction or pleasure; though it can also at times become compulsive and morbid. In these respects, it may be compared with fantasy. However, there remains a clear logical distinction between fantasy and speculation. One may fantasize about something one knows not to be the case, a possibility recognized not to be actual; but in doing so one could not be said to speculate that the possibility is actual. Yet speculating implies something more than just fantasizing about an unknown possibility. A fantasy cannot be said to have been in error just because its content turns out to be false. What extra condition then must be added to turn fantasizing about an unknown possibility into speculating that the possibility is actual? One might say that speculation is that species of fantasy which is intended to be true, even though one does not, or possibly cannot know whether it is in fact true. In speculation as opposed to fantasy, the truth, if only in a very minimal sense, matters.

When we come to consider idle speculation, however, a difficulty arises. Whatever pleasure or satisfaction may be associated with the act of fantasizing as such, some additional interest is supposedly involved in conceiving of the possibility one fantasizes about in such a way that it matters whether the possibility is actual or not. The problem lies in finding some aspect of the world or our situation for this additional interest to fasten onto, given that we rule out from the start our ever finding out or being affected in any way by whether or not the speculation is true.

When speculation is not idle, its additional interest is located either in the practical consequences of speculation, or in its relation to a wider cognitive activity of which it forms a functional part and by which it is constrained. Hazarding a guess when one is not at the time in a position to know means, as the term implies, taking a chance on being correct. Action based on a mere guess risks failure if the guess turns out to be wrong. What distinguishes hazarding a guess from fantasizing about an unknown possibility is that one envisages an aim, together with a course of action which would achieve that aim, whose success or failure depends upon the guess being correct. It may not be clear in detail how the various possible courses of action appropriate to the guess would be pursued; there always remain additional variables of which no account has been taken. At the very least, however, some conception of what would be appropriate action is not ruled out from the start.

On the other hand, when the pure theorizing of fundamental physics or cosmology reaches the point of no longer being able to envisage suitable experimental tests, the scope for hazarding guesses is reduced to zero. Where no reasons can be found for favouring one cosmological theory against another, it is meaningless simply to pick one theory as one's own personal guess. The physicist remains constrained by the demands of coherence and comprehensiveness to construct a picture which best fits all that we know from observation and established theory, following the familiar criteria of simplicity and elegance. Where no single theory appears to satisfy these demands better than all its rivals, all one can do, if one aspires to being a rational seeker after truth, is keep one's options open and say nothing. (It is quite consistent with this observation that there should be highly vocal disagreements over which is the best theory.)

The additional interest in idle speculation can neither be theoretical nor practical; but perhaps this classification does not exhaust the possibilities. Consider again the example of speculating whether the die in the box fell on three. Someone might like to think that the number was three for no other reason than because, as one might say, 'three is my lucky number'. The aim of idle speculation is simply this: to fill out one's knowledge of the world with whatever unknowable details satisfy one's sense of symmetry, aesthetics or poetic justice. What makes liking to think different from merely taking pleasure in one's power of imagining is that the satisfactions produced by the two activities are conceived to have different objects. For example, a prisoner fantasizing about eating roast chicken as he chews on his piece of stale bread still recognizes, assuming that he has not lost his grip on reality, that the object which gives him satisfaction is only his mental image of eating roast chicken. By contrast, in liking to think, say, that his associate was on the way to share the loot when tragically gunned down by the police – assuming no-one will ever know for sure – it is a state of affairs there in the world and not just an image in the mind which he intends as his object; the thought that there actually obtains the possibility he imagines. This contrast, however, is itself purely imaginary. The phrases 'in the world' or 'actually obtains' accomplish nothing: the prisoner's mental image of the roast chicken is just as much that of an actual roast chicken in the world for him to eat! (If it were not, he would merely be picturing what it would be like to imagine eating roast chicken.)

These considerations do not of course entail that the scope of liking to think and of imagining or fantasizing must after all coincide. Had one opened the box after the third call and discovered that the die had fallen on four, one would not speak later of liking to think that it fell on three. However, that does not suffice to distinguish between the two putatively different objects of satisfaction, for there is no more to this thought than the point already noted, that the species of fantasy called speculation requires that its content remain an unknown possibility. Yet as we have seen, that gives only a necessary and not a sufficient condition. To turn fantasy into speculation, an additional condition is needed, which in the case of idle speculation is missing: the intention that one's speculation be true. To speculate where one's speculation can only be idle, in other words, is merely to fantasize.

5. Taken out of context, it may seem surprising that considerations such as these should lead to a result of any special value for philosophy. From the point of view of epistemology, the attempt to define the concept of idle speculation appears almost frivolous. Its real interest, however, is for metaphysics. We have discovered that what masquerades as a cognitive attitude (or, rather, a quasi-cognitive attitude, since idle speculation makes no pretence of serving any useful purpose in the process of cognition) cannot be accorded any such status. Idle speculation is not a species of speculation at all, but only a species of fantasy. Only a powerful metaphysical illusion could blind us to that patently obvious fact.

To say that idle speculation masquerades as a cognitive attitude is not to make the familiar Humean point that our affections sometimes lead us to invent aspects of the world, when all the while we suppose ourselves to be describing it. On the contrary, idle speculation is often quite explicitly fanciful. Where our intuitions go wrong is in picturing the content of an idle speculation to be a thought which one is somehow able to direct towards the world; intending by the very act of bringing the thought to mind in a particular way, by as it were not just holding the thought at arms length but really meaning it, to do essentially the same thing as one does when one judges, or hazards a guess, or speculates within the context of a theory. What all these mental acts have in common is that their content is a thought which one aims at reality, however much their antecedents or consequences otherwise differ. Idle speculation too imagines itself to be seeking, however blindly in its case, truth as opposed to falsehood. That it can never know when it has found the truth only means that it can never know when it has succeeded in its intention. It is indeed a remarkable fact about human psychology that we find idle speculation amusing, even compelling; and moreover that what it is that attracts us is not simply imagining the content as such, but rather the thought that such content might, for all we could ever know, be true.

6. Well, can't idle speculations be true? That would be difficult to deny. If one speculates idly that the die fell on three, and if it could not be true that the die fell on three, then the number on the die could not have been three; nor could it, by parallel argument, have been any other number, which is absurd. The content of an idle speculation is something that may be expressed in an assertoric statement; and a statement just is the kind of thing that can be true or false. However, the realization that idle speculation is not what it purports to be, that what it intends is something altogether self-contradictory, should raise the suspicion that we have the wrong conception of what it means to say that a statement can be true.

Let us call a statement which forms the content of an idle speculation, that is to say, a statement whose truth or falsity we rule out once and for all the possibility of any person's ever getting to know, an idle statement. Of course, one can always imagine how we might discover that we had been wrong in our initial judgement, that a statement we thought was idle turned out to be true, however far fetched that might seem to us now. For example, someone might have secretly recorded the result of every rattle of the dice-box using a long distance X-ray machine; or perhaps by means of a mercury switch and tiny radio transmitter inside the die itself. Indeed, since the totality of ways in which knowledge can be gained could never finally be fixed, our vision of what can be known will always remain limited by the present state of scientific knowledge and development of our

232

cognitive faculties. Perhaps the very space around us is a kind of recording medium, whose stored information can be released using a suitable decoding device. None of these thoughts, however, could be used as an argument for denying our right to call a statement about a previous fall of the die definitely idle. On the contrary, we have every reason to believe that the universe is so constructed as to close off certain possibilities of knowledge permanently; and there is no reason – barring global scepticism – why we should not be able to know which these are.

Now, since idle statements, like any other statements, can be true or false, some idle statements, though by definition we cannot know which, are true. This is a statement which we seem to understand perfectly well. What, then, does its truth consist in? If one were sure that some of the statements in this book were true, but did not feel sufficiently confident to assert any one of them unconditionally, then by asserting the logical disjunction of all the statements one could at least be sure that one had said something true. We seem to be in an analogous position with respect to idle statements: we know that some idle statements are true, but not which ones! However, by asserting the disjunction of any idle statement with its proper negation we can be sure that we have made a true statement. For example, either the die fell on three or not. One might well object to this analogy, that to assert the disjunction of a statement with its negation is not to say anything at all, since all the possibilities are covered. This contrasts with the former case, where in asserting the one disjunctive statement one makes a positive commitment by ruling out the possibility that all the statements in the book are false. We should not be surprised, in view of this, to discover a difference between the kinds of explanation one would give of what makes the former and the latter types of disjunctive statement true. In the former case, it is as if we get the chance to try out each of the statements in the book, and all we have to do to make the disjunction true is to hit the target once. Whichever statement or statements turn out to be true will be those in virtue of which the disjunctive statement is true. In the latter case, however, when one asserts that either the die fell on three or not, one has the luxury of knowing that by covering all the possibilities, one has effectively put oneself in a position from which it is impossible to miss the target.

Yet, in that case, are we shooting at the target at all? There appear to be two ways of looking at this question. On the one hand, if a disjunctive statement is made true by the truth of at least one of its disjuncts, then the same applies to the special case of a disjunction of an idle statement with its negation; in that case, the metaphor of shooting at a target appears perfectly apt. On the other hand, we have already seen that it is by virtue of such an empty notion of aiming at the truth that idle speculation wrongly supposes its interest to attach, not to a merely imagined content, but to that actual state of affairs in the world which, for all it could ever know, it has succeeded in describing.

7. Idle speculation considers only individual idle statements; the amusement it takes in them need not depend upon any explicitly formulated metaphysic. However, for the philosopher who has seen through the pretensions of idle speculation, the general statement, 'some idle statements are true' may itself begin to raise deep suspicion. How can this general statement, based simply on the logical rule that allows us to assert the disjunction of any statement with its negation, so much as appear to convey information when, as we have seen, the disjunction of a statement with its negation does not say anything at all? It is as if one is expected to gather from the statement a highly significant metaphysical truth about the nature of truth itself: How wonderful that our world should have the capacity to contain or preserve truths, to enclose them within insurmountable walls, to save them from all change and decay! However, it is one thing to have suspicions, and quite another to identify the object of those suspicions with an explicit metaphysical theory. While attacking the coherence of idle speculation undermines the original, naive version of that theory – the thought that if the unknowable truth really is there in the world, then one can express one's recognition of that amazing fact by aiming idle speculations at it, like arrows shot at an invisible target – that is only the first stage of the dialectic. The philosopher who reflects a little more deeply upon this so-called metaphysical truth soon comes to realize that the inference is patently invalid: even if the unknowable truth is there in the world, idle speculation remains incoherent, a mental act which is in reality pure sham.

How then can the metaphysical truth about truth be expressed? What does it mean to say that the unknowable truth is really there? Consider the idle question associated with any idle statement, formed by prefixing, 'is it the case that'. To assert that an idle question has an answer appears at first to say no more than that the associated idle statement is either true or false. If the statement is true, then the question has an answer; if the statement is false, then the question again has an answer. Either way, it has an answer. Yet this simple deduction now acquires, in the blink of an eye, the appearance of an elementary logical fallacy. That an idle question 'has an answer' need not be taken to mean, or so it now appears, that the world contains or preserves one single answer. On the contrary, the anti-realist refuses to accept that there can be any meaningful talk of the world, except as that which encompasses both answers, both possibilities. That is just another way of saying that idle questions do not have answers. In that case, the realist, the philosopher who believes that the truth is there in the world irrespective of our cognitive relation to it, must deny this: idle questions do have answers.

The conflicting metaphysical visions of a world constituted exclusively of truths or facts, and of a world consisting of an island of truth surrounded by an ocean of undetermined logical possibilities do not allow any scope for compromise. Either idle questions have answers or they do not. This metaphysical notion of having an answer has the curious property, however, that its use in formulating one's philosophical position presupposes an understanding of its intended use in the description of the opposed position. We have already described one direction of this dependence: the world of possibilities does not contain or preserve the answers to idle questions in the sense of the metaphors used to describe the world of truth. However, in order to understand those metaphors, it is equally necessary to understand the alternative that they are meant to rule out: that the world contains the answers to all our idle questions implies the existence of a container full to the brim with facts, with no empty space inside; that truths are preserved makes sense only in defiance of the threat that they might otherwise be obliterated or lost. There is no way to break into this circle. All we can say is that one party seems to affirm a position, while the other seems to deny it; but as to what it is that is being affirmed or denied the philosopher is none the wiser.

The only conclusion to draw under these circumstances is that both positions are false. It is meaningless, and therefore false, to assert that idle questions have answers, or that our world is the world of truth; and it is equally meaningless and false to assert that idle questions to not have answers, that our world is only the world of possibilities. Both parties must, in the end, acknowledge that no form of words would ever be adequate to express either position, let alone prove it. Just because each defines itself directly and exclusively in terms of the other, there is nothing for the truth of either theory to consist in other than one's immediate metaphysical intuition of the falsity of the theory which it claims to reject. From whichever side one begins, therefore, the very existence of an alternative position constitutes a conclusive refutation of that starting point.

8. Irrespective of whether one feels inclined to say, or assert vehemently, either that idle questions have answers or that they do not have answers, the very possibility that someone else can with equal right say the opposite shows that both positions are false. The basis for this claim is an assumption concerning what it is that ultimately makes a metaphysical assertion true. By contrast with ordinary, factual assertions, we have no conception of what could make one of two opposed metaphysical assertions true other than the existence of something in virtue of which it would be possible to produce an argument that logically ruled out one in favour of the other. The world may indeed be so constituted as to make it impossible ever to determine which of two incompatible scientific theories is true. That is a possibility which both the realist and anti-realist understand equally well, even though they claim to give different accounts of the significance of asserting the disjunction of two such theories. What is, by contrast, incomprehensible is the idea of a world in which certain metaphysical propositions are true, but where it is impossible in principle for conscious subjects to decide by means of logical argument between those propositions and their negations. Yet the possibility of producing a logical argument is just what is ruled out in the present case. Since there is nothing that could ever make either one or other of the two opposed theories of truth true, both must be false; for to assert either is to imply the existence of a state of affairs that could not be.

9. This verificationism with respect to the truths of metaphysics may be seen as the one useful legacy of positivism, with its emphasis on relating the content of our assertions to what we do with them. Of course, we do something rather special with metaphysical assertions; indeed our methods of verifying them bear little resemblance to the methods of science, features to which the positivists notoriously showed little sensitivity. The close historical association between metaphysics and theology, however, should warn us that our principle of metaphysical verification may well appear to some simply question-begging. Thus an objector might maintain that there is one necessary exception to the general rule that the truth of a metaphysical assertion consists in the possibility of constructing an argument which would rule out all its competitors. There is one and only one unprovable metaphysical fact: the fact that God exists. Even though our conception of this metaphysical fact is very imperfect, that does not prevent one from believing that the proposition 'God exists,' states a truth.

236

Now, if God does exist, then, since he is all-knowing, any statement which is idle as far as we are concerned is still known by him to be true or to be false. That, it seems, is all it would take to ensure that any idle question has an answer. In that case, it might be argued realism is true: our world is the world of truth. If, on the contrary, God does not exist then both metaphysical theories are false. Anyone who believes in God is therefore committed to believing in realism. At the very least, since no-one can be certain that God does not exist, we cannot assert dogmatically that realism is false.

The claim that if God exists then our world is the world of truth may seem self-evident. Certainly, that is the way God has traditionally been represented. However, the claim may still be challenged. Let us suppose that one were to take to its logical conclusion the conjunction of the following three ideas: first, that the whole world is continually dependent upon God's creative power, secondly, that the world exists exclusively for our benefit, and thirdly, that this best of all possible worlds is the most economical, in the sense that God would not exert his power in order to maintain in existence anything which it was not necessary to his purpose to do so. Given these three premisses, one might argue that God had no sufficient reason to create a world full of unknowable and therefore unnecessary detail, as we take the world of truth to be. For the more economical alternative is a world whose forms and qualities God decides upon only in response to our investigations: a backdrop, like that of a cosmic film set under a continual process of reconstruction, containing just enough detail at any particular time to match our capacity for knowledge. Though we may believe otherwise, our idle questions are directed only towards the formless void that lies behind the backdrop; even God does not know the answer, since they have every possible answer.

There may be sound theological reasons why such a conception is abhorrent; but we are not concerned with the God of any particular religion. A more pressing objection might be that God could not destroy the past; once an event has taken place, that is a fact which must remain in God's memory, even if the whole universe were to be destroyed. In reply, one may concede that it is beyond our understanding how the past could be simply done away with. Yet that may just be a prejudice based on our very limited view of reality.

It cannot be maintained, therefore, that if God exists then our world is the world of truth. The most one can say is that if God exists then he knows whether the world he created is the world of truth or the world of possibilities. One therefore needs not one unprovable metaphysical fact but two: the existence of God and the metaphysical nature of the world he chose to create. This seriously weakens the objection under consideration, for it would be only a short step to dismiss the question of the existence of God as redundant. One might just as well maintain that the one unprovable metaphysical fact by virtue of whose obtaining one or other of the opposed metaphysical positions is true, is simply that the world is the way the metaphysic describes it. In response to the criticism that we have no conception of any such unprovable metaphysical fact, the objector can only resort to the facile explanation, 'whatever God, if he existed, would know to be a metaphysical fact'.

10. In spite of these criticisms, however, the objector can still hold on. All that would seem to be required in order to keep open the possibility that one of the metaphysical positions might be true is the possibility that God exists. Let us then suppose that God does exist, and that he chose not to create the economical world described above. In that case, statements which are idle as far as we are concerned are known by God to be true or to be false. Now it is crucial to the expression of the realist's vision of a world of truth that idle questions can have answers in some other manner than by turning out not to have been idle. We are concerned only with questions to which we believe we can never know the answer; if God exists, then if any question is to be regarded as idle, it must definitely be ruled out that God will ever inform anyone of the correct answer. If that is not ruled out, then that would be tantamount to saying that any ungrounded speculation we make, however trivial, is a question directed to God: it is always possible that God will tell me, and indeed convince me, that the die did indeed fall on three. A world in which this was the case would not, strictly speaking, be the world of truth, for with God's aid human knowledge could penetrate into the deepest recesses of reality, leaving no room for a gap between a question's having an answer and the possibility of our coming to know that answer.

Consider then an idle question of the form: 'Is it the case that P?' God knows whether P. But what is that to us? The question whether God knows that P is just another idle question. If God knows that P, then it is indeed the case that P; if God knows that not-P, then it is not the case that P. However, anyone who denies that the question whether P has an answer can just as easily deny that the question whether God knows that P rather than not-P has an answer. (It is irrelevant that as far as God is concerned the question does have an answer; we can only speak for ourselves, we cannot speak for God.) In that case, the existence of a God who knows the answers to our idle questions is compatible equally with the world of truth and the world of possibilities.

There remains only one way in which the existence of God could decide the truth or falsity of the opposed metaphysical positions. If God did choose to create the economical world, then our world could not be the world of truth. This is not quite a reductio ad absurdum of the original objection, for its aim would have been accomplished, albeit in a manner contrary to its original intention. Whether anyone would still wish to maintain the objection is another matter. For anyone who refuses to grant the coherence of the appeal to the possible existence of God, however, or to entertain the notion of unprovable metaphysical fact, the earlier argument still stands: the realist vision of a world of truth and the anti-realist vision of a world of possibilities will always have, as far as metaphysics is concerned, equal claim to validity; therefore both must be rejected as false.

11. We come finally to the question of interpretation. It is a negative attribute of the objective world to be neither a world of truth nor a world of possibilities. What kind of positive vision of the objective world does this result reveal to us? And how does that lead to a diagnosis of the source of the metaphysical illusion involved in the futile dispute between the realist and the anti-realist? If it is false to say that unknowable facts are there in the world, and equally false to say that unknowable facts are not there in the world, then logic dictates there can be no such place in the world, empty or filled, as 'there'. How are we to picture this? If there is an objective world then of course there is something there: what is it, then, that is not there?

In chapter 6, we argued that the denial of the identity of subjective and objective aspects by the refined cartesian dualist, and the opposed assertion of identity amounted to no more than a combat between two metaphors – that of my physical body as a window through which others could in principle perceive my mental states, versus that of a screen onto which the objective aspects of my mental states were projected – whose contents could not ultimately be distinguished from one another. The contradiction between their declared opposition and total mutual dependency entailed the refutation of the two positions. We argued that the illusory metaphysical vision responsible for the dispute was the notion of my subjective *this* as an entity or constituent of reality, concerning which the question of its identity or non-identity with objective constituents of reality inevitably arises. If there is a fruitful analogy to be drawn here with the dispute over unknowable facts, it will be in the way that both positions result from a distorted perception of certain features of our two-world metaphysic.

Thus one might argue that failure to grasp the nature of the contradiction between the subjective and objective standpoints results in a notion of truth torn in two opposite directions. Our discovery of the insufficiency of the objective standpoint to account for the whole of reality leads us to mistakenly identify the notion of truth as the medium through which subjectivity enters the picture. Truth cannot simply belong to the world; it must belong to us. It must somehow be shaped to fit the subject, if the subject is ever to be said to reside in the truth, rather than apart from the truth, that is to say, in unreality and illusion. As these remarks stand, however, they are far too general and imprecise. We need to get inside the vision of an objective world embodied in our two-world metaphysic, in order to see how it could be neither a world of truth nor a world of possibilities; but at the same time, why it inevitably appears as something which must be one or other of those two alternatives.

The thought that I am essentially nothing more, when viewed from the objective standpoint, than one self-conscious being amongst others, suggests the picture of a part of me which is able somehow to get outside my own skin, of a mental faculty of self-transcendence. It is this transcendent self that surveys the world from no particular point of view, and locates the subject known as Klempner within a common space shared by many such subjects. That is what Nagel calls the 'objective self' (*The View From Nowhere* pp. 62ff; cf. our discussion in chapter 6). For us, the idea works well enough as a heuristic device: the very fact that the subjective and objective worlds stand in a relation of metaphysical contradiction means that one cannot describe what it is to contemplate the reality of the two worlds other than in terms of the metaphor of moving from one standpoint to the other and back again. Taken literally, however, the metaphor becomes sheer mythology. Just because my subjective standpoint is the ultimate, the place where my metaphysical investigation of reality begins and where it remains forever rooted, the only objective world I can ever talk about, in answer to the metaphysical doubts I myself have raised, is that objective world whose reality I come to recognize when I acknowledge the authority of other persons to correct my judgements. The objective world can only ever be our objective world.

The meeting point between self and other is that which presents itself as the object of our mutual demonstrative knowledge: call it *that*. That is for us the point of actuality from which our common world spreads out. Yet one seems to possess another, more general notion of actuality which has nothing to do with *that*. In this latter sense, what is actual is not tied down to any particular point of reference. It is simply what fills the framework within which all particular points of reference are located, a framework grasped from no particular standpoint. However, there is a tension here. For if one thinks of the actual purely in terms of filling a framework, then there is no room for an additional *that*. Whatever the content with which the framework is filled, and even if it remains partially unfilled, there is nothing the *that* can add to what is already there. Every point in the framework is equally 'that'. The *that* cannot therefore be actual. It seems as if the objective world as such, the world as it is grasped from no particular point of view, has no more room for the demonstrative *that* of our objective world than it had for the non-demonstrative *this* of my subjective world.

Now of course one could avoid having to make a choice here by positing a third world, so that our metaphysic embraced three worlds: my subjective world, our objective world, and the objective world as such. There is no objection in principle to such a move (in the last chapter, we shall consider the possibility of a third, ultimate standpoint which stands in an analogous relation to the objective standpoint as the objective stands to the subjective). However, in the present context it would be quite unwarranted. For the only argument we have for an objective world is for our objective world and not an 'objective world as such'. That world whose actuality would consist purely in the filling of a framework has, therefore, no legitimate claim to reality.

12. What then is it that being actual adds to being merely possible? That may seem a very strange question. Someone who did not know the difference between actuality and possibility would have no grasp of reality at all. The events described in a novel would be just as real as those reported in the news. What then is the difference? In virtue of what does the image on my television set refer to something actual, while the words in the novel I am reading refer to something merely possible? It seems impossible to give a non-tautological answer to this question, one which does not carry an implicit reference to how it is in general that I know that certain things are actual and others not. Yet the question I put to myself was not about knowledge. The difference between what was actual and what was merely possible would be no less real, or so it seems, even if no conscious beings had ever existed.

Picture a Leibnizian deity, deciding which of all possible worlds to make actual. Each individual world glows dimly in God's mind, a constellation of lights of every conceivable colour and shape. Then, as God makes his choice, one light shines out, drowning the others in its brilliance. Why must the others be drowned out? Clearly it would not suffice to make a possible world actual that it shone a little more brightly than any of the others. Yet merely to increase the brightness, by any imaginable degree, can never consummate the act of creation.

Rendering the other possible worlds invisible merely blinds us to the inadequacy of this image. The brightest and dimmest of lights are, after all, only different degrees of brightness; there is no absolute difference. As an account of the actuality of the actual, the picture is fatally flawed.

It is clear that no process of thinking will arrive at actuality if it does not begin with it: what is actual is the given, that which is there for us. Now all one can do is give examples: the book, the television set, the keyboard. What is 'the' book? It is not just a book with such-and-such properties, it is that book. And surely nothing one could ever think of can be actual if it does not belong with *that*. For someone who, by contrast, denies the ultimate reality of *that*, who claims that every point in the framework of the objective world is equally 'that', actuality can only ever be an object of thought, an idea in the mind of God. Now, belatedly, knowledge enters the picture. Only it is not actual knowledge, the knowledge that I and the other gather about our objective world, but the mere concept of knowledge, the idea of the dependence of actuality on what can be known by subjects in a situation such as ours. The conclusion of this dialectic is a logical antinomy. What is true, what is actual, says one party, must already be there; the framework of the objective world must at all times be filled with sheer, solid fact, otherwise it cannot be at all. The other party, perceiving the emptiness of that claim, insists that only knowledge can supply the filling; there is nothing actual or true that cannot be known by an actual subject. Yet this claim turns out to be no less empty: for the possibility of knowledge in general that would supply the filling has no more actuality than the sheer fact for which it was meant to be the substitute.

242

17 Relativity of our objective world

1. OUR discovery that the objective world is neither the realist's world of determinate truth nor the anti-realist's world of undetermined possibilities has uncovered a new definition of the objective world: that whose being actual consists in its belonging with or spreading out from *that,* the immediate environment of demonstrative reference, the place where self and other meet. By virtue of the primacy of *that*, actuality can only have a local and never a global sense: what is actual is there, as well as here, because it is here, not because (as the realist and anti-realist wrongly assume) it is everywhere, that is to say, nowhere in particular. The actual is always here going towards there, the place of the other, or there coming towards here. Thus, the objective world is never simply the objective world but is always our objective world. Whatever I say or do results, at greater or lesser remove, in changes to the actual state of things which give expression to my judgements, effects that cumulatively build up a picture of me which is more than a mere picture, but rather my very reality in the eyes of others. That is my conception of the objective world in which I live and move, the only world whose reality is in question for me, from the standpoint of my subjective world.

Placing this result alongside our refutation of anti-materialism in chapter 15, and also the conclusion of chapter 14 establishing the reality of now, we may say that the objective world is, first and foremost, the material here-and-now, the moment of my physical action, and of my transaction with the other. If one compares this notion of an objective world with the nonegocentrist's view from nowhere, the picture with which our inquiry began, then one may gain a sense of how far we have travelled towards our goal of

243

reconciling the subjective and objective standpoints. In a similar way, the subjective world began as the egocentrist's 'world of my possible experience' and transformed into a structure of material objects. Under pressure of philosophic criticism, each standpoint has begun increasingly to display the attributes of the other.

Viewed in the context of the history of metaphysics, the pre-eminent reality of our material here-and-now will no doubt appear an ironic outcome, a strange content indeed for a metaphysical vision. For two-and-a-half thousand years, philosophers have struggled to direct our gaze to the stars; now, it turns out, reality was all along back here in our cave: the fire that warms us, the walls that surround us, the immediate concerns of the moment. What makes the difference is the journey taken to get here, the dialectic. Our early forbears never doubted that what was actual was that which was present, a world revealed in the immediacy of perception and action. Yet it was historically necessary that doubts should arise, that we should seek to transcend the here-and-now; just so that we could after all the twists and turns of the dialectic find ourselves again back again where we started. In order to reject metaphysical illusions, it is first necessary to suffer from them.

However, there is more to the story: to return to the cave is not to abandon metaphysics, but to make a new beginning. There are other attributes of our objective world to be described. Primary amongst the questions that confront us is whether there is just one objective world, or more than one. Just how far does our objective world spread out? Could there be worlds that remained forever beyond our grasp? That in turn raises the question of the relativity of knowledge. It is a familiar idea from anthropology that peoples who belong to societies or cultures separated from ours inhabit, in some sense, different worlds; worlds that we are prevented from entering by our cultural conditioning, just as members of those other cultures are prevented from entering ours. This clash lies at a deeper level than simply a conflict between different sets of values, for it concerns the very notion of rationality itself. If talk of different worlds is more than just a metaphor, if we renounce – as some philosophers have been persuaded to do – the possibility of timeless, cross-cultural standards for the rationality of belief in favour of standards relative to a given culture, then our claim to know how things stand in a world that is there for us independent of differences in culture must it seems be surrendered. Yet if knowledge is only knowledge of the world of our culture, and not of a world existing independently of our contingent, culturally informed understanding, then it becomes open to question whether we have the right to call it knowledge at all.

2. The objective world is, in the first place, the subject matter of our mundane discourse. Everything under the sun, or beyond, every subject matter for judgements whose truth or falsity can be a matter of agreement between myself and other persons – even if only in principle, or only after an indefinitely protracted investigation – belongs ultimately to our objective world. Now in relation to this definition, there appear two different ways in which other objective worlds might arise. The first would be if there existed judgements which were true with respect to one objective world, but false with respect to another. We could imagine, for example, a process of argument between two groups of individuals which over a period of time led to an increasing divergence of views; a disagreement which as it developed took in more and more beliefs, until two incompatible but internally coherent systems of beliefs had formed, between which there was no possibility of reconciliation. In this picture, a proponent of one system of beliefs would be fully aware of what a proponent of the other system believed, but would disagree with it absolutely, in a manner that ruled out any further argument. While each group remained convinced that the other group were wrong, an impartial observer could only conclude that each group had equal claim to their own truth: each inhabited a different objective world.

However, a second, more radical way in which other objective worlds might appear would be if there existed other systems of mundane discourse, other languages incompatible with our own, so that the possibility of argument was ruled out from the start. Judgements expressed in one language would be incapable of being translated into judgements expressed in the other. One could not even speak of disagreement, for there would be no identifiable subject matter for the disagreement to be about. Resorting to metaphor, one might say that, whereas in the first case the two objective worlds, though incompatible in their detailed structure, were at least made out of the same kind of basic material, in the second case there would be no substance in common that could be identified between one world and the other. Or, alternatively, it would be as if, in the first case, the two worlds were so far apart that one could never travel from one to the other, whereas in the second case they were not even located in the same space.

On reflection, it becomes apparent that these descriptions as they stand embody several questionable assumptions. First, the definition of sameness of objective world on which they are based refers to an indefinite future time. Yet who is to say that a divergence of belief systems will not at some time perhaps far in the future turn round and become a convergence, so that even the most fundamental disagreements will eventually be resolved? Or, if the difference is the more radical one of incompatible languages, who is to say that languages that we now find impossible to translate will not, at some time in the future, yield to translation? It would seem that the hypothesis of different worlds is one that, in an actual case, could never be conclusively verified: time could always prove us wrong. Reflecting further, one might even begin to doubt whether there is any significant content to the notion that an unverifiable absolute difference between worlds, referring as it does to an indefinite future time, might, for all we could ever know, and independently of any explanation or ground, just happen to obtain.

The second questionable assumption lies in the very idea that one can logically distinguish between a difference of objective worlds based on a divergence of beliefs, and the supposedly more radical difference based on incompatible languages. If two persons discover that their belief systems clash, how can each be sure that she understands what the other means? Surely, they must agree on something, if they are to establish that they are talking about the same thing. Yet if they can find something to agree on, then that provides a foothold for enlarging the area of agreement; once that process is underway, there is in principle nothing to prevent it from leading to a complete resolution of their dispute. Or, on the other hand, if they are unable to make any progress in resolving their disagreement, then the most that each can say is that she only seems to understand what the other is saying. There is certainly a prima facie difference between seeming to understand and seeming not to understand. However, that difference is not sufficient to underpin the putative logical distinction between divergent belief systems and incompatible languages.

We may, however, waive these two objections, as matters of relative detail. For practical purposes, the reference to an indefinite future can just be taken to mean a time long enough to convince us that the divergence of belief systems or incompatibility of languages can never be overcome. Similarly, the distinction between seeming to understand a language and seeming not to understand it is sufficiently vivid in itself to justify a practical distinction between a divergence of belief systems and an incompatibility of languages; a distinction based on the different stances involved in trying unsuccessfully to persuade and trying unsuccessfully to understand.

There is, however, a third objection which carries far more weight. The idea that the divergence or incompatibility can be understood in terms of a difference between worlds would seem to depend upon the notion of a vantage point outside the two belief systems or languages, from which each may be viewed as equally valid or equally meaningful, the idea of what an impartial observer would judge to be the case. One imagines this hypothetical subject to be located mentally equidistant from the two worlds; able, as were, by looking right or looking left to take in each of the two belief systems or languages in turn. But what does the impartial observer itself believe? What language does the impartial observer speak? One only has to raise the question to realize the absurdity of what we have been attempting to describe. To stand outside a given belief system can only mean to have different beliefs, beliefs according to which the beliefs of those who subscribe to that belief system are not valid, or at least are a matter of doubt. To grasp a language from outside the vantage point of those who seem to understand it can only mean to regard such individuals as having their view of reality restricted by the conceptual limitations which it embodies, while one continues to enjoy the more comprehensive view provided by one's own language. In either case, there is only one objective world, the world of the impartial observer. The two divergent belief systems or incompatible languages which the impartial observer stands outside each give their subscribers only limited, imperfect access to that one objective world.

3. If there is any meaning to the idea of a plurality of objective worlds, it cannot be one that refers, either explicitly or implicitly, to the notion of an impartial observer. What then is the alternative? Let us imagine that proponents of each belief system gradually develop the ability to argue within the framework of the other belief system as if they believed it; or alternatively that speakers of each language gradually learn to speak the other language as if they fully understood it. That is, after all, how the more adventurous anthropologists pursue their investigations into other cultures or societies, by living with the people whose lives they wish to record and understand, until they are able to some extent to see things the way their subjects see them. Now it could conceivably happen that one entered so deeply into the other belief system or language that one's belief or understanding ceased to be merely 'as if'. One might find oneself mentally switching back and forth with increasing ease between one belief system and the other, or between one language and the other, until one's commitment to one's original beliefs or language no longer appeared any deeper than one's commitment to the beliefs or language one had entered into. That is a state of affairs which it is undoubtedly difficult to picture to ourselves; but that may only indicate our lack of the relevant experience.

It is precisely at this point, however, that we part company with the nonegocentrist. For someone who insists on the exclusive reality of the objective standpoint, the idea of switching back and forth between two different objective worlds must appear simply incomprehensible. It is impossible for a genuine nonegocentrist to think about such a state of affairs without importing a notion of what is really going on, what view an impartial observer would take. If one allows that however many of us agreed about the basic structure of our world at any one time, there might conceivably be just as many who with equal right disagreed, then, however wide a view one takes, there will be yet wider views, none of which has any authority to define an objective world. Only an impartial observer, only a being who stood outside the procession of competing viewpoints, would be in a position to judge things as they really are. In that case, a situation in which we seemed to have gained access to two incompatible but equally real objective worlds could only be represented as a life of permanent confusion between appearances and reality.

4. One might remark here on the curious way our description of a plurality of objective worlds appears to mimic the metaphysical duality of subjective and objective worlds. That is no accident: there is a common dialectical form that explains the resemblance between the two cases. Recourse to a plurality of worlds is a solution to a certain form of philosophical problem: the problem of how to grant recognition to conflicting or incompatible realities without falling into self-contradiction. It is a move one would make only as a last resort. The idea of a two or of a dual reality which, as we expressed it in chapter 9, cannot even be thought together as one goes against the very idea of number. For the very act of counting presupposes a single reality, a single frame of reference within which the counting game alone makes sense. Yet that is just what appears to be denied in the case of the duality of subjective and objective worlds, and equally in the case of the plurality of objective worlds. We must, it seems, admit that some very simple numbers cannot be counted.

Care must be taken not to read too much into this formal resemblance. Although we shall argue that only the two-world theory is able to tolerate a plurality of objective worlds, it would be a gross travesty of the argument to suggest, for example, that any philosophy permissive enough to recognize two worlds has thereby opened the floodgates to recognition of any number of distinct worlds. Nor would there be any point in trying to compare the deep sense of paradox invoked when we encounter the contradiction between the subjective and objective worlds, with whatever difficulties we imagine we might face in coming to terms with a plurality of objective worlds. The contradiction between a subjective world that revolves around me, and an objective world where I am just one individual amongst the multitude, gives no guidance when one tries to conceive of what it would be like to move back and forth between two clashing belief systems, or between two incompatible languages.

5. According to the two-world theory, the only objective world that can be in question when one seeks to prove the reality of the objective world is an objective world in relation to an equally real subjective world. Talk of objective worlds that have nothing to do with my subjective world is, as far as I, the person asking the question am concerned, just empty noise. The objective world can only ever be our objective world. Yet now it seems we must recognize that there might be more than one such world; with 'our' in each case carrying a different sense (though the references would still coincide, were the two objective worlds to be shared by the very same group of individuals). Any objective world that can be real for me – that is to say, real simpliciter – must be one concerning which I might conceivably find myself in a position to make judgements; judgements that other subjects in that world had the authority to correct.

We can afford to be generous in speculating upon the changes that one might conceivably undergo, in the process of becoming acquainted with other objective worlds. Back in chapter 6, we argued against Nagel that it is indeed possible that I should come to know what it is like to be a bat – by acquiring the ability periodically to change into one. (The objection that I should only know what it was like to be a bat-human and not a common bat has no more force than the thought, discussed in chapter 14, that I cannot know what it was like to have been sitting at this desk an hour ago, on the grounds that I did not know then what words I would now be writing.) One might say that there is no upper limit to the elasticity of the I, to what it might change into or assimilate. That is not because the absolute I of my subjective world possesses an identity over time that could survive the most extreme changes in my external circumstances, but precisely for the opposite reason that the absolute I has no identity over time (cf. chapter 10). Insofar as conditions do exist for the identity of an I, they are objective conditions for the identity of my relative I. However, these refer not to what I can now conceive of happening to me, but only to what, as an agent and language user, I might become in the eyes of some other subject who had the authority to correct my judgements: say, another bat-human, or another anthropologist entering with me into the objective world of a radically different culture. In acquiring a new system of concepts, a new way of experiencing or picturing the world, my future self would indeed find itself making judgements I might now simply refuse to admit I could ever make, or indeed speaking a language of which I can now form no conception. For my present self has no authority to speak for my future self. By definition, the alternative world that awaits me in the future is still beyond my cognitive or conceptual grasp: for if I did grasp it, then it would not be future but present.

6. Yet there does seem at first an uncomfortable circularity in the idea that my experience of another objective world might be vouchsafed by some other person who shared the experience with me. If I go mad, and another person goes mad at the same time, that does not make us both sane. There are two observations one can make here. The first is that if there really were a circularity in the idea that the objectivity of my judgements depended on nothing other than my recognition of another person's authority to correct them, then, far from merely rejecting the possibility of a second objective world, one ought to reject the very notion of an objective world as we have defined it and become an egocentrist. Nor does it make any essential difference how many other persons, as a matter of contingent fact, happen now to be in a position to judge the reliability of my powers of judgement. If there was only one such person, then I might, given a sufficiently dramatic change in my circumstances, entertain doubts about my sanity. However, the content of those doubts would be precisely that I did not grant my companion authority to correct my judgements but regarded the correctness of his judgements purely as a matter for my own judgement; in which case, according to our refutation of egocentrism, I must be prepared to acknowledge the authority of persons other than my companion to correct my judgements. It must be possible for someone to be in a position to judge the reliability of my powers of judgement; but there is no reason why that someone should not be a person who shares my experience of an alternative world.

The second point to make in regard to the alleged circularity is that there are in fact real restrictions on what could logically give another person in the same predicament as myself the authority to correct my judgements, and, consequently on what kind of thing could be an alternative world. When we discussed Quinton's thought experiment of two spatially unrelated worlds in chapter 9, we argued that no-one who shared my situation, who like me had to wait to be whisked away from one world to the other could have the authority to correct my judgements, now made in world 1, about events in world 2. What is missing in this latter case is any notion of what would logically distinguish our shared experience of another spatially unrelated world from a mere collective hallucination. For the problem is that all the judgements that we could now, in principle, make about world 2 ultimately depend on memory judgements. Just because we do not believe that world 2 stands in any spatial relation to where we are now, we have denied ourselves the conception of the actual reality in virtue of which those memory judgements might be correct or incorrect: instead, whatever the majority says goes. By contrast, when I and my bat-human companion change back into human form, or when I return with my fellow anthropologist to our own living quarters, we still find ourselves in the same physical frame of reference – however differently our surroundings now appear to us – that we inhabited only a short while before. It is this common space that forms the minimal point of contact between our two alternative objective worlds. One might say that the two worlds necessarily spread out from or belong with the very same *that*. The reason this does not make the two objective worlds into one world is that the *that* has no authority to dictate what judgements should be made about it, or even what concepts should be used in its description. We cannot say what the *that* is without entering into one or other of the two alternative worlds.

The requirement that any objective world other than the one I now inhabit be capable of becoming our objective world, where the reference of 'our' depends upon whoever has the authority to correct my judgements about that objective world, rules out once and for all any notion that a belief system that I regarded myself as barred from ever entering into, or a language that I could never understand might, for all I could ever know, relate to another objective world, no less real than my own. This requirement, as a direct consequence of the theory of subjective and objective worlds, is clearly unavailable to the nonegocentrist. However, with the loss of that subjective criterion, the floodgates do indeed threaten to open. For all the nonegocentrist could ever determine, there might exist an infinite number of worlds, all equally objective. What objection could possibly be raised against such a hypothesis? Only the one we considered earlier: for an impartial observer located outside the relative worlds of divergent belief systems or incompatible languages, there can only be one truly objective world, the world of the observer's own beliefs and language. In the absence of my recognition of that special authority of other individual subjects with whom I communicate to correct my judgements, all that remains for the nonegocentrist is either an absolute authority whose recognition does not come from anywhere, embodied in the notion of what an impartial observer would judge to be the case, or no authority at all. Either there is just one objective world, or else any number you like.

7. Having established the logical possibility that a limited number of other objective worlds might exist, we move on the question of knowledge: what right do we have, as inhabitants of the dual reality of subjective and objective worlds, to claim knowledge that things are thus-and-so, and not otherwise? Traditional discussions of knowledge begin with Descartes' sceptical question, How do I know that I am not dreaming?, or, in the more up-to-date science-fiction version, How do I know that I am not in a scientist's laboratory, having 'experiences' fed into my sleeping body by a cable attached to my brain? Within the two-world theory, however, neither of these hypotheses makes any sense. Descartes is asking how I can know anything other than my own subjective states, how I can know that there is a world outside my own mind. We saw in chapter 3 that as soon as one allows such a question to be raised, the dialectic cannot be halted at that point, but carries one forward inexorably to the egocentrist's ruthless denial of the reality of the objective world.

In the more up-to-date version, the existence of an objective world is apparently not put into question. All I am invited to doubt is whether I am now in cognitive contact with that objective world in the way I take myself to be: whether my eyes really see, whether my ears really hear, whether my fingers really feel. We learned in chapter 5 that I can exist as a thinking subject, that is to say as an individual who makes judgements and entertains hypotheses, only so long as I remain an agent and language user; only on that condition are others in a position to judge the reliability of my powers of judgement.

In either case, then, I cannot entertain the sceptical doubt concerning the objective world without at the same time undermining my belief that I am a subject who knows what things are like for me, or indeed that I exist. Egocentrism, in trying to maintain the exclusive reality of my subjective standpoint, loses everything; while a being who cannot exist as a thinking subject as far as the objective standpoint is concerned, cannot be said to have any thoughts at all, and a fortiori any thoughts about itself or its own subjective states.

Still, one might encounter a really determined sceptic who on principle doubted everything, including her own existence. How could one deal with such a person? More to the point, are we really so sure that we could never fall victim to such all-consuming doubt? Our answer to both questions is rather unsubtle: there is no way of dealing philosophically with a really determined sceptic, nor can we ever ensure that we shall not fall victim to the sceptic's doubts. At this root level, logical argument is simply irrelevant. I do not, as a matter of fact, doubt my existence, or that I have knowledge of an objective world. That is not because I am not a deep enough thinker, but simply because I do not know how to doubt these things. There is nothing in the thought of an empty realm without either a subjective or objective world that my mind can catch hold of. I can only say, along with Parmenides, that a reality which is just nothing, a world constituted exclusively of what is not, is unthinkable; or, at least, unthinkable for me. If I did know how, then I might, just for the same of experiment, entertain the sceptic's doubts; perhaps the determined sceptic is right in claiming that all one has to do is really mean one's doubt, just for a single moment, and one will never find one's way out of it. For if total doubt can ever be seriously entertained, then I must doubt everything always; I cannot allow myself the luxury of keeping my mind open lest something appear that there was reason not to doubt. Yet if I must doubt everything always, then I must deny it also.

Someone might claim, in spite of this, that it is really quite easy to entertain sceptical doubt. All one need do is imagine, for example, having the experience of waking up to find oneself on the table in the scientist's laboratory. Can we really say that we know, without a shadow of a doubt, that we shall never have such an experience? The answer to that question is that an imagined doubt is not yet a doubt, not yet a doubt really meant. Now there are many things we normally say we know without any possibility of doubt, of which we are very sure, but which we should cease to put our trust in under certain circumstances. It might be that the consequences of being wrong in a particular case would be disastrous. Yet that cannot be all there is to it. My very life depends on there not being a yawning chasm behind my front door as I step out; still, I do not pause to check. Behind this confidence lies an implicit prudential calculation. Even with the stakes raised so high, it is simply not worth checking all the things one would have to check if imagined doubts such as this were to be granted any credibility. Life would become impossible.

Let there arise, on the other hand, some particular reason for focusing on this particular doubt amongst the multitude of imaginable doubts, then one would indeed find oneself taking steps to ensure that the imagined possibility was not realized. The discovery that one's house had been built on old mine workings that had begun to subside would be one such reason. Or it might be no more than a momentary irrational fear brought on by watching a horror film on television the night before. Could anything, then, make me focus in this sense on the imagined doubt that I may be lying on a table in the scientist's laboratory? Suppose that I have a part-time job with the cleaning staff at the local university, working in the science labs. That evening, on the six o'clock news, there is a report of a successful experiment at my university of feeding experiences into the brains of human subjects while they are asleep. The next day, I answer the door to find a smartly dressed man who tells me that I have won £1,000,000 on the football pools. How should I react? I might try pinching myself, but that would not prove anything; nor would a visit to the laboratory where the reported experiments took place. There is no action I could take to prove that I was not really asleep, being fed experiences. In that case, however, there is no function that meaning my doubt as opposed to merely imagining it could perform. (Suppose that my doubt tells me I must postpone my celebrations: for how long should I postpone them?)

8. Our unsubtle point against the sceptic might be illuminatingly compared with the discussion, in chapter 13, of theoretical and practical solipsism. There is, we conceded, no way to argue against a practical solipsist, who acts with complete indifference to the interests of others or to the rules of moral conduct. We would be wrong, however, to think that this was a failure on our part; that we are obliged to produce an effective argument, but are unable to meet that obligation. The task for the moral philosopher is only to refute the theoretical solipsist's claim that moral conduct lacks any logical basis.

By contrast, there could never be a practical sceptic; there is nothing a person could do that would be consistent with the denial that he had any knowledge about an objective world. One can, perhaps, picture someone whose mind was so mesmerized by imagined doubts that he simply refused to do anything at all. However, even doing nothing would not suffice for the total sceptic: to stand still in the path of an oncoming bus is after all a positive action. Yet supposing ourselves faced with someone who remained immobile, refusing to speak, on whose countenance was drawn a profound, unnameable dread, that would still mean nothing to us, for we could conjecture any explanation we liked.

I know at least that I am not such a person; I still find myself wanting to do things: that is all one can add in the way of a philosophical argument against theoretical scepticism. There is no question here of searching for a logical basis for my knowledge of an objective world, parallel to our logical basis for moral conduct; a proof that I should be irrational to give in to paralysing doubt. The search for such a basis would indeed be doomed to failure from the start. – If that is all one can say, however, then the determined sceptic, the resolute proponent of what is not, stands as a symbol for an obligation that reason can never meet.

9. Is there then any form of scepticism, apart the kind we have been discussing, combating which can supply the philosopher with useful employment? Just because total scepticism is the absolute negation of every knowledge claim, it does not touch our concept of knowledge in any way. What we are looking for, by contrast, is a form of scepticism that would make the question of the revision of what we take to be knowledge a real issue. A more fruitful line to pursue is the challenge arising from our acknowledgement of the potential existence of other objective worlds. The thought that I might at some time develop the facility to think and act within a completely divergent system of beliefs from the one I have always known, or learn to describe the world in ways I could never have comprehended in terms of my native tongue, urges the question whether what my own well-trusted system of beliefs or my unreflective use of my familiar tongue intend – to put me in touch with a world whose forms and qualities my beliefs and language more or less accurately reflect – matches what they are actually able to achieve. For if there can be a plurality of objective worlds, then it appears that things are the other way around. My beliefs and language do not reflect the nature of the objective world as it really is; rather, what I call 'our world' is just the reflection of the language and beliefs I happen to have acquired. If the world itself has no authority to dictate the choice of belief system or language, then there is nothing, short of an impartial observer, that can offer any standard or guidance: the decision is ultimately up to me.

Discussions of the relativity of knowledge have in the past been bedevilled by such banal questions as, How many different ways could there be to describe a cat on a mat? One pictures the world as made up of things, the familiar objects of sense perception, standing in various relations to other things. One can no more easily transform, by means of mere words, our given world into a world of different objects standing in different relations than one could with an abracadabra transform a quartz watch into one that ran on clockwork. Lest any reader think that our argument involves an implicit appeal to some form of metaphysical alchemy, there are two sober points to be made.

First, there is no reason why the basic perceptual vocabularies of different objective worlds should not coincide, at least to some extent. (We have already anticipated something of this in the requirement that different objective worlds retain a point of contact.) All it takes to make two worlds rather than one is that their systems of classification or explanatory concepts should be incompatible with one another. It has been said that nothing is more effective in proving the absolute supremacy of an explanatory system than a hydrogen bomb. However, that ignores the fact that there might exist cultures for whom such dramatic demonstrations of technological power appeared unimpressive and trivial, a proof of our total lack of understanding, in the light of our failure to grasp the really significant explanatory connections between things.

The second point is that there is no reason in principle why we should not acquire new forms of perception. This point is more difficult to drive home, since there is no way one can provide an example, or even an adequate analogy, that might show us what having such unknown forms of perception would be like. (A bat has, after all, only different organs of perception.) One can, however, suggest things that these new forms of perception might do. Consider just one example. All our senses relate back to a body physically located at a specific place in our familiar three-dimensional spatial world. However, we might conceivably discover that we possessed extended bodies that reached to the very limits of the universe, so that each of us was in reality located everywhere, while yet leaving room for one another, and for a world of similarly extended objects. The piece-meal way in which we now construct our knowledge of the objective world, by identifying individual things and connecting them together (so deplored by philosophers such as Bradley) might then come into conflict with an altogether different way of perceiving and knowing, not tied down in that way to our present physical limitations.

10. In exploring these issues, the most serious obstacle is the ingrained prejudice that one cannot coherently represent to oneself a possibility of understanding that one does not yet understand. It is not being advocated that we abandon all restraint and intoxicate ourselves with every sort of speculation and fancy. However, if one learns anything from the study of metaphysics, it is that we are constantly impelled to reach beyond the assumed limits of our understanding. There is no greater intellectual tyranny than the doctrine that where one cannot think or speak clearly, one must not think or speak at all. With this in mind, let us try to take an unbiased look at the argument that relativity undermines the claims or the intention of knowledge.

In order to consider the argument in its strongest form, we may think of how it would be assessed at a time when the existence of other objective worlds was as commonplace and uncontroversial as the existence of other planets is now. How would the philosopher defend our claims to knowledge? If each belief system or language creates its own objective world, if internal consistency and not correspondence with one single, absolutely objective world is the only criterion of truth, then surely all our supposed knowledge is only our invention: is that argument valid? It would be, if we were free to construct new objective worlds simply by inventing new belief systems or languages. However, nothing we have said implies any such thing. It remains an essential feature of belief that it possesses the attribute of something that arises from the effect upon us of things that happen in the world. We are not free to choose how the world will impress itself on us. In that case, our recognition of an actual plurality of objective worlds could only take the form of our being pulled, independently of our will, towards each world in turn. There has to be the mental equivalent of gravitational attraction which each world is able to exercise on our thoughts. If the recognition did not take this form, if it appeared that one could stand back from the various conflicting ways of representing a world and view them purely aesthetically, as one views works of art, then they would no longer have the status of beliefs.

It is, admittedly, hard to imagine what it would be like to live with a plurality of objective worlds. One might well wonder how one it would be possible, under such stress, retain one's sense of self-identity: how could I regard my various objective incarnations as mere facets of the life of one and the same agent? – The very fact that such a problem should arise effectively rebuts the sceptic: the theoretical and practical difficulty in resolving it is the measure of how far belief is from something that could be merely invented.

18 The world, I and now

1. WE approach our destination leaving many questions still unanswered. Some press their claims upon us, others, no doubt, we have not even thought to ask. Had one known more – or better – this book would probably not have been written. However, comfort may be taken in the thought that metaphysics is not like any other field of human inquiry. Everyone is a beginner. It is hard enough to make a start. And if one can find reason to keep going for a while without running out of problems, that is cause to rejoice. It would be pleasant indeed, at this late stage, to be able to report that all that remained to do is tidy up a few loose ends, or express the confident assurance that nothing important has been omitted from our account of existence. In the light of the history of the subject, it is far more likely that, despite our very best efforts, we have allowed some essential aspect of the problem of defining reality – or some vital clue to its solution – to pass by unnoticed. As for loose ends, the idea that such an open-ended inquiry as this could ever be tidied up is simply foolish.

Yet apart from all the questions we have silently passed over, or mentioned briefly and then forgotten, there is one that remains constantly before our vision; taunting us, leading us on, daring us to say more than we know can be said, or at least said intelligibly: Why is there anything? Surely there is no greater indication of the power of language than that in those few words one can put the whole of existence into question. Only it seems this power is one that no finite being can ever exploit. Nor are there many persons capable of defying all existence, and extending their power of negation to the point at which one could assert instead the fatal proposition, 'It is not.' How the Gods must laugh! and the sceptic too!

What then is the point of our efforts? Why should anyone struggle to harness logic to the contradictory metaphysic of subjective and objective standpoints if one did not believe, along with the Gods, that there are no philosophical questions, even the ultimate questions of existence, that cannot be answered? It is surely the most outrageous of conceits to think that existence is nothing but a puzzle to be solved, a problem of logic. Yet if we banish this conceit, what should we then say? That there is a puzzle, but that it is not to be solved? Or, with the early Wittgenstein, that a puzzle that cannot be solved is no real problem at all? These are not meant as rhetorical questions. We have described three mutually exclusive alternatives which, for anyone but the total sceptic, exhaust all the possibilities. Yet to choose any one of them appears equally absurd and outrageous.

2. Let us then not choose. What we do not have we do not have; and whether it is in some sense there to be had, or there beyond our having, or only that which would expose the illusion of a beyond or of something to be had, is a question that does not lead anywhere. By contrast, we have seen that the question, 'What is it of which we ask the question why there is anything?' does lead somewhere. It leads to the two-world metaphysic of subjective and objective standpoints. There is the objective world. There is my subjective world. And there is also now.

Each of these three statements states a simple metaphysical fact. By that is meant a fact whose proof consists in the logical impossibility of one's thinking it to be a mere illusion. If the objective world is an illusion, then all that exists is the world of my subjective standpoint, the world of my possible experience. But then there would be nothing by virtue of which my judgements about my world could either be reliable or unreliable: I could think or say whatever I liked and never be wrong; which is the same as saying I could not think or say anything at all. If, on the other hand, I try to think of my subjective world as an illusion, then the sheer fact of the illusion is something I cannot sincerely regard as illusory; it must be real. Yet the undeniable reality of that illusion is all it takes to endorse my incommunicable sense of my own unique existence, to prove the reality of my subjective world. Nor can the fact that the time is now be illusory unless my agency, for which the fact that the time is now is the ultimate issue, is itself unreal. Yet if my agency is unreal then, as we saw in chapters 10 and 11, there can be no bridge between the subjective and objective worlds; the two-world metaphysic is reduced to an intolerable double vision, splitting my own existence into two irreconcilable halves.

Yet these simple metaphysical facts, of the world, I and now, each lead on to further questions whose answers would appear far from simple. That there is an objective world does not explain why, of all the possible ways things might have been, our objective world is the way it is. That there is my subjective world does not explain why, of all the persons that exist or have existed, my world is the subjective world of the individual standing here, the author of these words. That there is the unique time we call now does not explain why this time, of all the times that make up the history of the world, is happening now. Why is the world the way it is? Why am I here? Why is the time now?

3. Without going so far as trying to explain why there is anything at all, there is much that we can say about these questions. One issue we first explored back in chapter 2 was the thought that the world is the way it is because God, in creating the world, decided that it should be that way. We found two difficulties with this familiar idea. The first was that from God's objective or 'super-objective' standpoint, from which the contents of every finite consciousness, including my own, lie open to view, my subjective standpoint as such remains invisible. Even if God did create the objective world, that still leaves open the question of how my subjective world came to exist. For if the God of the objective world cannot even see my subjective world, as a reality whose existence remains unaccounted for by the existence of the objective Klempner, then the act of creation could at most be regarded as the occasion for my subjective world's coming to be, and not something that the objective deity could in any way have intended or be held accountable for. All one can say in response to this logical difficulty is that there must, in some sense, also exist a god of my subjective world. However, that is merely to give a name to the problem, not to solve it.

The second problem arose when we considered what it could mean for a deity to have chosen to create this actual objective world out of all the worlds he might have chosen to bring into existence. If God did choose to create this world, then he must have originally occupied the ultimate standpoint from which all possible worlds appear equally real. Yet from that standpoint, there can be no feature that marks our world out as being actual and not merely possible; the world that God did actually bring into existence. It seems that, just as there is nothing an objective deity could add to the person with my objective attributes to make him into the individual with my subjective world, so there is nothing an ultimate deity could add to any of the merely possible worlds to make that world into our actual world.

To these two difficulties, we can now add a point that emerges from the discussion of time. The fact or issue that the time is now, bound as it is to the reality of my subjective standpoint as agent, is no more visible to the standpoint of an objective deity than is my subjective standpoint itself. Just as the objective deity is unable to see which person is I, so he is unable to see which time is now: for him, all times are equally 'now', just as all persons are equally 'I'. – It might indeed be said that all these difficulties concern the construction of a metaphysic as such, and are not special problems for religious belief. That is true. What they do count against, however, is the idea that, for the believer, one's metaphysic and one's religion can be kept in logically separate compartments. If we must be metaphysicians, then we must be consistent metaphysicians.

4. If we do not appeal to an inexplicable act of creation, we are left with three facts that seem to demand, yet at the same time prohibit explanation: the actuality of the actual world, the I-ness of I, and the nowness of now. One angle to investigate is the extent to which one may perceive a parallel structure within these three inexplicable facts. For example, they all share the common feature of defining a sense of possibility. Out of all the possible worlds that might have been actual, only one is the world we call the actual world. Out of all the self-conscious subjects to which 'I' could possibly refer, only one is my actual self. Out of all possible times, past, present and future, only one is the time of events which are actually happening now. Perhaps one of these three facts can be used as the model for understanding the other two: a way of interpreting the other facts or a form for describing them that would render them less inexplicable, or at least lessen the sense of vertigo induced by our recognition of their inexplicability.

Before exploring that suggestion – which will occupy the bulk of this chapter – let us first consider them individually. We shall begin with time. The sense of sheer amazement that the time is now, that the entire history of the world should have led up to this moment and no other, is to some extent reduced to its proper perspective when one considers that every other time, whether past or future, even the most insignificant, has had or will have its brief moment of glory: every time gets its turn to be now. Yet although this fact ought to be obvious, in our actual lives few of us are willing or able to make the mental effort required to take full cognizance of it. The effort is one associated traditionally with the attitude of the philosopher: the attempt to conceive of the world sub specie aeternitatis.

The task that faces us, by contrast, is not that of transcending time or temporality as such. For we rejected, in chapter 14, the notion that the before-and-after series of events, whether conceived of from God's eternal standpoint or only from the temporally neutral standpoint of tenseless truth-conditions, is all there is to time; the view that denies that the nowness of now is itself any kind of fact. The question remains to what extent the attempt to think of now as no more than one time amongst others can succeed without the aid of such a prop. It would surely take a true philosopher, a person who probably has never existed, to recognize while under torture that this present moment of agony, though an absolute fact whose reality cannot be argued away, is still only one now amongst other nows.

5. When we come to my sense of amazement that I should be the individual that I am, that my subjective world should be the world of this objective person and no other, it is difficult even to state what it is that I am amazed by. One wants to say that it is the fact that my subjective world is the world of this individual, the person standing in these shoes, rather than some other person. However, it is far from clear what it means to say that my subjective world might have been the world of some other person. Might I, for example, have been Napoleon? Leibniz comments that to imagine myself becoming Napoleon is to imagine myself ceasing to exist, and Napoleon existing in my place. In other words, if one takes away all my thoughts, feelings and perceptions, and replaces them with Napoleon's, then there is simply nothing left in me to think such a thought as, 'Now I know what it is like to be Napoleon!'

Nor does there seem to be any other way in which I can conceive that my subjective world might have been that of Napoleon. At the moment of my birth, my thoughts, feelings and perceptions, confused as they were, probably were not that much different from those of any other new-born infant, including Napoleon's. Yet it seems highly dubious to assert that the something Klempner was born with, the thing that makes that individual I, might have been the very something that Napoleon was born with, and not just the same kind of something. If, per impossibile, my subjective standpoint could be identified with a non-physical entity or soul, then one might imagine that that very entity, and not just one like it, might have been born into the body of the infant Napoleon. However, we have already given conclusive reasons, in chapters 6 and 10, why such an identification between the subjective and objective standpoints cannot be made.

Despite that, there does remain a strong sense of the inexplicable contingency of the existence of my subjective world. Perhaps the feeling comes to no more than the point noted at the end of chapter 9: that the person with all Klempner's attributes would still exist for the objective standpoint even if my subjective standpoint ceased to exist, or indeed had never existed. Yet, as we also noted, when I try to think about the contingency of the fact of my subjective world's being there at this moment rather than not being there, I find that I am not thinking of anything at all.

6. We seem to be on much firmer ground when we consider the fact that our objective world is the way it is, rather than some other way; that the world is our actual world rather than some other possible world which might have been actual. The difficulty arises when we seek to account for the status of what is not actual but merely possible. The question what it means to talk of the way things might have been has received much debate in recent years, and has led to a polarization of views between which it is hard to claim any middle ground. On the one side, there are those like David Lewis (*On the Plurality of Worlds*, Introduction) who maintain that other possible worlds are in every sense as real as our actual world, but just happen not to be the worlds we find ourselves in. If one asks where these other real worlds are, one is told that talk of places where things are only makes sense relative to the system of spatio-temporal relations determined by our actual world. In other words, what makes other possible worlds non-actual for us is merely that they are not located in our space or in our time. On the other side, there are philosophers, inspired by the 'state descriptions' of Carnap (*Meaning and Necessity* p. 9), who would dismiss as meaningless talk of states of affairs being simply possible, in themselves, as opposed to talk of descriptions of states of affairs being compatible with descriptions of other states of affairs. It is all right to say that, setting aside what actually happened, and given that I am not under duress, the statement that Klempner decides not to work today has a significant degree of relative probability; it is not all right to say that there exists, in itself, the possible world where he actually takes the day off and goes for a long walk instead.

One widely-held view is that the dispute involves a problem of analysis rather than pure metaphysics; and that it will be resolved by an account of the logical form of modal statements which maximizes 'meaning-theoretic elegance' and 'ontological economy'. For the moment, we may confine ourselves to making two analytical points, one against each position. If it is said that there is no way to make sense of our talk of how things might be or might have been without assuming real possible worlds, each in its own space and time, then the very same argument ought to lead to the conclusion that there exist real impossible worlds also. For many propositions whose truth or falsity we wish to determine, especially in metaphysics, involve stating seriously what would be the case were certain logically impossible states of affairs to obtain: counternecessaryfactuals are the

263

life blood of dialectic. If one rejects the idea of spatio-temporally realized impossible worlds (as indeed Lewis does), then some other interpretation of the kind of reality we mean to refer to when we consider such propositions must be found. There then seems no reason why the same deflationary interpretation should not be extended to statements or arguments which refer to states of affairs which are logically possible.

Turning to the view that rejects all talk of things being simply possible in themselves, we may pose the following dilemma: either it is all right to go on saying that certain things might have been the case, or it is not. If it is all right, then to add that these things are not 'real' possibilities seems no more than an empty verbal quibble; if it is not all right, then we must assert that everything that is the case could not have been otherwise – a very doubtful metaphysical proposition.

Rebounding from both views, what one would like to do is simply accept talk of what might have been, whether possible or impossible, at face value; neither inventing real worlds outside our space and time for such talk to be about, nor deploring the fact that in their absence our talk is empty. Our talk is surely about something, one would like to say, but in a way it is also empty. – As it stands, however, that is to merely restate the problem.

7. Having considered in a preliminary way the significance of the inexplicable facts of the nowness of now, the I-ness of I and the actuality of the actual world, we must now ask whether any one of these facts may be used as a model for understanding either of the others. Of the three, the nowness of now appears in some ways the most straightforward. (We are not now addressing the problem of the nature of time as such.) If someone asks us, 'Why is the time now, rather than some other time?', we can just turn the question around: every time gets its turn to be now, so why not the present? The question is what would be the parallel observations to make about the I-ness of I and the actuality of the actual world.

To begin with, what could it mean to say that every self-conscious being gets its turn to be I? One can think of two very different things it might mean. The first is no more than a colourful way of putting the truistic point that, qua self-conscious subject, I am just one I amongst other I's. The trouble with this is that it answers the question, Why am I the individual that I am?, only when interpreted in a nonegocentrist manner: there is no such thing as my subjective world, the reality which I must regard as necessarily unique and incommunicable. This is where the analogy with the nowness of now breaks down. For we saw that it was not necessary to deny the unique reality of now, amongst all the times that have been or will be now, in order to maintain the philosopher's attitude towards time: the recognition that every time has had or will have this unique status.

The second, and metaphysically more extravagant interpretation of the statement that every self-conscious subject gets its turn to be I does yield the desired result; but only at the cost of taking the notion of getting one's turn quite literally. If I, the possessor of this unique subjective world, have been or will be every self-conscious subject who has ever existed or will ever exist, then we may turn the question around with the l-ness of I in the same way as we did with the nowness of now: why shouldn't I be the individual that I am, since I have been or will be every other individual? One can see how someone might take comfort in the thought that all the goods and evils of this world will in time have been enjoyed or suffered by every I, however slender our grounds for believing that to be true. As a picture, it also provides a strong incentive for moral action; though one which, in view of the argument in chapter 13 establishing a logical basis for moral conduct, would be strictly superfluous (and indeed in its ultimate appeal to the self-interest of the migrating I would seem to undermine the latter argument). The trouble is, as we have already learned from the Napoleon example, it is just not possible to make any sense of the thought that I have been or will be other individuals besides the one I am now.

8. We should not be surprised to discover the same two very different interpretations when we turn to the actuality of the actual world, the inexplicable fact that the world is the way it is. Just as every time gets its turn to be now, so every possible world in some sense gets its turn to be an actual world. The question is whether or not one should understand this as a temporal process. If not, then we find ourselves back with David Lewis' view that other possible worlds are in every sense as real as our actual world, only not located in our space or time. For the individuals living in another possible world, their world is every bit as actual for them as ours is for us. This theory does have one spectacular result. At one stroke, the question why this world, of all possible worlds, should have been actual becomes simply redundant. The problem of evil, the heartbreaking question addressed by theologians over the centuries why, if God is all-benevolent, this world with all its vice and misery should have been chosen to exist out of all the worlds that might have been, disappears. If there is a God, then he is either the Creator of all possible worlds or none. (That might be thought to raise a different and possibly far more agonizing problem: there is nothing so unspeakably evil that is not actually realized in

some possible world.) However, this robust view of possible worlds would not be justified merely on the grounds that it dispensed with the question why the world is the way it is, or abolished the traditional problem of evil. Its logical basis can only be that it provides the only coherent way to justify our belief that there are ways things might have been. In view of the doubts expressed earlier, that is not a proposal we are yet in a position either to accept or reject.

There remains the theory that, in time, all possible worlds will actually come to exist. One can at least say that there is not the same obstacle to believing this as there was in the case of the question why I am the individual that I am. Whereas one simply does not know what it would mean to say that I have been or will be every other individual, that my subjective world will be in each of them just as it is now in the person writing these words, it does seem to make sense to say that in time all possible worlds will exist. Surely, one might think, if time really goes on for ever, then every possibility must eventually be realized; it is just a matter of chance, a roll of the dice, that determines in which order they occur. (That is to assume that the succession of worlds would not, As Nietzsche argued, form an 'eternally recurring' fixed causal loop, from which some possible combinations of the basic elements of reality were forever excluded.) Nor would my belief that such was the case rest on such slender grounds as the corresponding belief I have been or will be every other person, supposing that one did find a way of making sense of this thought. One may leave it to the reader to judge whether the image of an endless sequence of random variations of worlds is preferable to the image of just one world, the world that exists now.

9. Our attempt to comprehend the I-ness of I and the actuality of the actual world in terms of the model of the nowness of now has had mixed results. Let us now consider what would happen if we took each of the other two inexplicable facts as our model: first, the I-ness of I. My recognition that I cannot conceive of what it would mean for my subjective world to have been the subjective world of some other individual, for example, Napoleon, does in a way lessen my sense of the inexplicability of the fact that I am the individual that I am; it does so by rejecting the question why I am the individual that I am rather than some other individual. That is a very powerful idea: perhaps it could be made to work in the case of the question why the time is now, or why the world is the actual world. Let us start with time.

We have already observed that the philosopher's attitude towards time, which recognizes that now, despite its unique reality for the agent I must necessarily take myself to be, is only one now amongst other nows, is a stance that requires great mental effort. But do we really know what we mean when we say this? We considered the example of a person under torture trying to create a mental distance from the presentness of this present moment of agony; but it is not clear what that proves. It might be argued that when one asks the question, 'Why is the time now?', what one imagines, as one tries to conceive of the present moment as being just one now amongst other nows, is not simply that every time is equal in getting its turn to be now, but rather the far less philosophical idea that now might have been a different time than it in fact is. For example, now might have been the time of the Battle of Austerlitz.

If that is what lies implicitly in our thoughts, then we have indeed fallen into no less an error than one who imagines that he might have been some other individual than he in fact is. Just as in imagining myself to be Napoleon I secretly transfer some of my own thoughts into the mind of Napoleon, so in imagining that now might have been the time of the Battle of Austerlitz, rather than the time it in fact is, we keep one portion of time back, secretly appealing to a second time outside the historical order of events, the time experienced by a deity who could have chosen to set that train of events in motion earlier or later. In that case, we have embarked on an infinite regress. For one must now call up a third time, the time of a superior deity, in which the series of events that form the content of the consciousness of the first deity may be imagined to have reached a different moment in time than they in fact reached, and so on. Thus, if the fantasy of a time outside of time is what is implicit in the question, 'Why is the time now?' then the correct response is to follow the model of the I-ness of I and reject the question outright.

10. The complications are mounting up, but let us press on. How might the I-ness of I serve as the model for grasping the actuality of the actual world? It can hardly be by rejecting the question why the world is the actual world rather than some other possible world. For the parallel argument would have to be that we are wrong in thinking that the world might have been different from the way it in fact is; an assertion which we remarked above is a very doubtful metaphysical proposition. However, one can see another use for the model. The problem with the I-ness of I was that the existence of my subjective world is a fact that cannot be generalized simply by reducing myself and the other to two of the same, for that would mean reverting to the objective standpoint. I cannot, logically, talk of another person's subjective world; I can only repeat the argument that one cannot treat as a mere illusion one's incommunicable sense of one's own unique

267

existence, an argument which the other person must then understand in her own way. As a consequence of this, no-one else can grasp the fact that I am Klempner in the way that I grasp it; the fact is indeed a fact only for me.

Now we referred earlier to the discussion in chapter 2 concerning the question whether God occupies an ultimate standpoint from which all possible worlds appear equally real, or only the objective standpoint (along with all the gods of all the other possible objective worlds), from which our world appears the actual world and all other possible worlds are no more than possible. The question that comes to mind here is how far we can develop the analogy between the two cases: between the relation of the subjective standpoint to the objective, and the relation of the objective standpoint to the ultimate. Just as there exists a clash between egocentrism, which maintains the reality of the subjective standpoint to the exclusion of the objective, and nonegocentrism, which maintains the reality of the objective standpoint to the exclusion of the subjective, so one might expect to find a clash between those who maintain the reality of the objective standpoint to the exclusion of the ultimate, and those who maintain the reality of the ultimate standpoint to the exclusion of the objective. Echoing what we said about the subjective standpoint, one might say that the fact that our objective world is the actual world is a fact only for us; from the ultimate standpoint, the unique actuality of our actual world is only a logical mirage, for all possible worlds appear equally real, equally actual.

Thus, the robust view of possible worlds discussed earlier, according to which each possible world actually exists in its own space and time, in effect maintains the reality of the ultimate standpoint to the exclusion of the objective. Moreover, if the analogy between the subjective and objective on the one hand, and the objective and ultimate on the other does hold, then one might expect the objection against the robust account to possess a form similar to the objection we raised against the nonegocentrist's belief in the exclusive reality of the objective standpoint. We can even imagine a nonegocentrist arguing, against the theorist of the ultimate standpoint, that it is impossible to think away, to treat as nothing, the sheer actuality of our actual objective world. However, the nonegocentrist is on treacherous ground here. For, as we saw in chapter 16, the nonegocentrist's global account of actuality, in terms of the filling of a framework in which all points of reference are equally 'that', misses out the very thing that could alone justify an absolute distinction between what is actual and what is merely possible. The actuality of the nonegocentrist's actual world can, in the end, be pictured only as a light shining in the consciousness of a

Leibnizian deity, a light whose overpoweringly greater brilliance than the lights of all other possible worlds still remains ultimately a matter of mere degree.

By stark contrast, from the point of view of our two-world metaphysic, what counts against the exclusive reality of the ultimate standpoint is the reality of *that*, the environment of public demonstrative reference where self and other meet. The theorist of the ultimate standpoint has no more right to deny that reality, than the nonegocentrist had to deny the reality of the non-demonstrative *this* of my subjective standpoint. However, that is by no means the end of the argument. Someone who maintained the reality of the subjective and objective standpoints to the exclusion of the ultimate might be accused with equal justification by the theorist of the ultimate standpoint of failing to account for our ability to make true or false judgements about what might have been the case, echoing our objection against egocentrism, that it failed to account for the possibility of my making true or false judgements about what is actually the case. (There is even an analogue to Kantian egocentrism in the ersatz, linguistic account of possible worlds offered by the philosopher who rejects the reality of the ultimate standpoint.) It might well seem that, for the theorist of the ultimate standpoint, only an ultimate deity who saw all possible worlds as equally real would have any genuine authority to correct our modal judgements. Even if that were the case, the theorist of the ultimate standpoint could still argue that the alternative remains far less palatable: anyone who believes that the ultimate standpoint is unreal must also believe that there is simply nothing for modal judgements to be about. In that case, the only consistent course is to renounce modal judgements altogether: to maintain a steadfast silence about what might have been the case.

Extending the analogy one last step, one might admit the partial truth embodied in both positions. The ultimate standpoint cannot be granted reality to the exclusion of the subjective and objective standpoints; but nor can the subjective and objective standpoints be granted reality to the exclusion of the ultimate. In other words, all three standpoints are real. The correct account would then be one that recognized an unavoidable contradiction between the objective and ultimate standpoints, parallel to the contradiction between the subjective and objective standpoints. The idea canvassed earlier that modal talk is both 'about' something and also 'empty', would then in a sense have been vindicated. (There remains the worrying problem of explaining the place of impossible worlds in the context of the ultimate standpoint: so the join is by no means seamless.) Objectively, talk of possible worlds is empty: the only worlds that can exist are actual objective worlds. In making modal judgements, however, we are not confined to what is objectively real, to what exists; for what we are talking about, what we have our sights set on, is something altogether different. If we refuse to say what that something is, that is not because we refuse to face the question of its ontological status, but rather because any attempt to understand the possible in terms of the concepts of existence or actuality entails a failure to acknowledge the contradiction between the objective and ultimate standpoints. If, on the other hand, someone asks, 'Where is the possible?' then we can give a more positive reply. Wherever one looks, one cannot but see beyond the actual; for our objective world gains its meaning and articulation only in the light of the ultimate standpoint of ways our world might possibly have been.

11. There are just two more cases to consider. We once more pass over what has gone before and start again from the beginning, this time taking the actuality of the actual world as our model for understanding, first, the nowness of now, and secondly, the I-ness of I. For some, this would be the most obvious starting point. For the question why the world is the way it is appears far closer to our familiar notion of explanation than the question why the time is now, or why I am the individual that I am. It is, one may agree, superficially closer; but it remains ultimately unintelligible. To seek an explanation of a fact involves seeking prior factual conditions from which that fact can be deduced. The objective world as a whole has no factual conditions in this sense. If one continues to insist that there must be an explanation for the existence of our world, then one can only have in mind the idea of God's choice of this world from out of all the worlds that might have been, as the one factual condition which is itself unconditioned.

Thus, according to Leibniz, the existence of God is the one fact not requiring any explanation, for God is necessarily such as to contain the sufficient reason for his existence within himself. As difficult as this idea is to conceive, we may take Leibniz's point that it is no less difficult to conceive of an infinite regress of conditions, which never amounts to a sufficient reason why there should be anything at all, let alone the world we know. However, our objection to the idea of divine creation back in chapter 2, and repeated above, is not based on the difficulty of conceiving of a deity as such, but rather questions the notion that he could have been in a position to make a choice of our world out of all the worlds he might have created. From the ultimate standpoint, there is nothing God can add to a possible world to make it

270

actual; while from the objective standpoint, the choice has already been taken care of, and so is out of God's hands.

Let us suppose, however, that this objection could be met; say, by recognizing the contradiction between the objective and ultimate standpoints. (Someone might argue that just as one has to divide up the labour of creating the whole individual who is myself between a subjective and an objective deity, so one must divide up the work of creating an objective world, and the work of choosing a world to create, between an objective and an ultimate deity.) Can we use the actuality of the actual world as the model to make sense of the idea of there being a sufficient reason why the time is now? There is a fallacy to which we are sometimes prone, in our less philosophical moments, when we are tempted to regard our momentary sense of amazement that the time is now as an intimation that it possesses a special significance for our lives; that some important event is about to happen, or some vital decision about to be made. Of course, that is patently not the case; the amazement may come upon us at the most insignificant moment. Yet this idea that there must be a reason why the time is now, when it does arise, is very difficult to get rid of. Where then does one imagine such a reason might be found? We have already dismissed the idea that the time might have been earlier or later than it in fact is. The hypothesis that now might remain in the same place while the history of the whole universe was shifted backwards or forwards in time is unintelligible. The model of factual explanation, whether we think of an infinite regress of conditions or of a series of conditions leading back to a God as the one unconditioned condition, therefore has no conceivable application to the fact that the time is now.

12. Just as we sometimes fall into the primitive fallacy of thinking there must be something significant about the present moment that it should be this time, amongst all the times that have been or will be, so one may on occasion be tempted to infer fallaciously that God must have had some special reason for making me me, rather than someone else. Since in this case I cannot even conceive of how I might be or might have been a different individual, for example, Napoleon, there does not appear to be room for even the question of the sufficient reason why I am the individual that I am. So far, then, the nowness of now and the I-ness of I are not parallel. For we can at least say that now has in fact been or will be other times than it is now.

However, the failure of correspondence between the two cases can be remedied by the following thought experiment. It is only a contingent fact that there are not an infinite number of individuals who share all of my attributes; individuals who, from the objective standpoint, are similar to me in every respect. I can imagine, for example, that this room is one of an infinite three-dimensional array of identical rooms, each with identical contents. There is nothing else in the whole universe. As I step through a door into another room exactly like this one, I catch sight of one of my infinitely many doubles stepping through the door opposite me into the next room along. As I cry out, 'Why am I here?', I hear 'my' voice echoing back from the other rooms with the very same question. Yet it is a fact: I am the person standing in this doorway and not any of my doubles. What then is the explanation of this fact? What would be a sufficient reason in this case which accounted for my being here rather than there?

Clearly, there is nothing for any kind of factual condition to get a grip on, even if we imagine that condition to be God's exercise of his creative power. For if it is said that there is a non-physical soul which God put in me, which is different from the souls which God put into any of my doubles, then the question has not yet been answered. If the souls are merely numerically different, then the very same question can be asked again; if, on the other hand, my soul has a unique attribute which none of the souls of my doubles possess, then that goes back on the hypothesis that we are identical in every objective respect. This is merely one more version of the argument that, from the standpoint of an objective deity, what makes a certain individual me, the possessor of my subjective standpoint, remains invisible. Here then is a fact which seems to demand a sufficient reason; yet, as with the nowness of now, I cannot even imagine where this reason might be found. The conclusion must therefore be the same: in thinking there might be a reason why I am I, I have merely become the victim of a metaphysical illusion.

13. It is time to call a halt to these strained speculations. We have come a long way since we first encountered the baffling problem of the subjective and objective standpoints. Yet, as should by now have become apparent, the distance we have actually travelled is comparatively short. The end of the marathon is not so very far from the beginning; for we have not been running in a straight line, nor, fortunately, in a circle, but in an inward-turning spiral. Our goal, a vision of the nature of reality, a vision which is able to reconcile its own perpetually discordant elements, stands out with greater clarity now that we have seen it from every side. However, we have not reached that goal. The centre of the spiral still appears infinitely distant. Whether it is so in fact one would not venture to say. In the past, when a sense of the unlimited powers of human reason led

philosophers to construct ever more ambitious philosophical systems, a last chapter such as this would have been the place to reflect on the crowning achievements of our theory, a coping stone to the great edifice. For us, entangled as we are in the problems of building a secure foundation, there is less to boast about. It may seem to the reader, weary from toil, that having set out to write the alphabet of existence, we have spent all our time worrying whether A should come before B, or B before A. It would be fatuous to express one's assurance, or even the hope that all our work has not been in vain; that is something only time can tell. If there is a single thought one should like the reader to have gained from these pages, it is that to remain true to one's vision and never let up is all anyone can hope to do in philosophy. If we can do that, then the numerous obstacles we have encountered along the way, and the innumerably more that lie ahead fully merit the time and energy needed to surmount them.

Two last comments. We have talked about reconciliation, and also about security. These themes of human existence go far beyond metaphysics, nor do they come originally from there. One of the consolations of philosophy, it is said, is the promise it holds out of an arena where we can flee from conflict and insecurity. In the calm of our metaphysical vision, where all conflict is resolved and all our most cherished beliefs find an unassailable foundation, lies a bulwark against the tumult and uncertainty of the world of practical affairs. What we have discovered leads to a less optimistic and more ambivalent conclusion.

We set out with the optimistic hope of reconciling the subjective and objective standpoints. As a result of our investigations, each standpoint has acquired some of the colouring of the other: the subjective standpoint is no longer an endless parade of experiences but a world of material objects; the objective standpoint, far from being the view from nowhere, has become our world, the view from here, the place where I meet the other in collective endeavour and in our common language. The co-ordinate notions of agency and matter provide the bridge that brings the subjective and objective standpoints even closer together, warding off the threat of a metaphysical double vision. Yet these measures only serve to bring into greater clarity the perpetual conflict between the two worlds, the stubborn resistance of the I to give itself up exclusively to one standpoint or other. There can be no reconciliation here, not even in the minimal sense of agreeing to differ. Nor can we ever reconcile ourselves to the role of perpetually ineffective peacemakers.

Is there then no escape from conflict, even in the calm of philosophic contemplation? Perhaps we should re-examine our fear of conflict. The reverse side of that fear, it seems, is the desire for victory and domination. All must submit to the same ruler, all must convert to the same faith. Yet what if reality, the truth itself, contains discordant elements that will never submit to a single rule? That is a thought which in the eyes of the philosophical tradition appears the ultimate heresy. In reacting in that way, however, the tradition reveals itself not as a lover of peace but as a lover of war. For only by war can a single element rise up above all opposition and banish the discord; only by war can it aspire to comprehend the totality of all there is.

What, then, of security? It is only practical commonsense that leads us to seek secure foundations for our metaphysic. Engaging in far flung speculation in the absence of a sound logical basis may amuse for a while; but once the novelty wears off, one can only rue the waste of one's time and passion. Yet in a metaphysic which acknowledges the ultimate reality of our agency, the reality of our freedom to act for good or ill, there can be no denying in thought the perpetual insecurity of our existence in the world. Whatever consolation our metaphysical vision may provide, it is not the consolation of knowing that our insecurity is an illusion and all our fears unreal. On the contrary, it is surely the mark of the true strength of a philosophy that it does not retreat into a world of pure thought where all is secure, but encourages us to face up to the real world, with all its perils.

Two of our deepest fears do indeed prove illusory. As we learned in chapter 10, the fear of death, when that is understood not as the fear of the pain of dying, nor as the biological instinct for survival, but as the terror at the thought that some day one's subjective world will cease to continue, is revealed, in the light of the non-continuity of my subjective world, to be empty, a fear for the loss of something that one never had. Nor, as we discovered in the last chapter, is there any ground for fearing that we shall never have knowledge of the real world, just because we might encounter others who know things in a way that contradicts our way of knowing them, or who grasp a reality that does not exist for us. Knowledge that recognizes that there may be actual objective worlds other than the one we know gives up its claim to absolute security; but is not on that account undermined. My own existence, and the existence of the objective world, though each in different ways metaphysically ultimate, are not the absolutes I once took them to be. In that case, I must live in a world without absolutes. It is a lesson that takes time to learn. The impulse to flee from reality is not just the predilection of philosophers; it is in all of us.

Bibliography

List A contains books and articles referred to in the text, except for those classical works for which no particular edition is specified, which will be found in List B. No single principle determines membership of List C.

List A

Bradley, F.H. (1897), *Appearance and Reality*, 2nd edn, Allen and Unwin, London.

Beck, L.W. (1975), *The Actor and the Spectator*, Yale, London.

Carnap, R. (1947), *Meaning and Necessity*, University of Chicago Press.

Davidson, D. (1963), 'Actions, Reasons and Causes', *J.Phil*, vol. 60, pp. 685–700.

Dennett, D.C. (1978), *Brainstorms*, Harvester, Sussex.

Dummett, M. (1973), *Frege Philosophy of Language*, Duckworth, London.

Dummett, M. (1978), 'Truth', in *Truth and Other Enigmas*, Duckworth, London, pp. 1–24.

Evans, G. (1982), *Varieties of Reference*, Clarendon Press, Oxford.

Evans, G. (1985), 'Things Without the Mind', in *Collected Papers*, Clarendon Press, Oxford, pp. 249–90.

Frege, G. (1967), 'The Thought', in *Philosophical Logic*, Strawson, P.F. (ed.), Oxford University Press, pp. 17–38.

Heidegger, M. (1978), *Being and Time*, Macquarrie, J. and Robinson, E. (trs), Blackwell, Oxford.

275

Husserl, E. (1973), *Cartesian Meditations*, Cairns, D. (tr.), Nijhoff, The Hague.

Lewis, D.K. (1986), *On the Plurality of Worlds*, Blackwell, Oxford.

Kripke, S. (1980), *Naming and Necessity*, Blackwell, Oxford.

McDowell, J.H. (1978), 'On "The Reality of the Past"', in *Action and Interpretation*, Hookway, C. and Pettit, P. (eds), Cambridge University Press , pp. 127–44.

Mellor, D.H. (1981), *Real Time*, Cambridge University Press.

Nagel, T. (1974), 'What is it Like to be a Bat?', *Philosophical Review*, vol. 83, pp. 435–50.

Nagel, T. (1986), *The View from Nowhere*, Oxford University Press.

Parfit, D. (1984), *Reasons and Persons*, Clarendon Press, Oxford.

Ryle, G. (1949), *The Concept of Mind*, Hutchinson, London.

Quinton, A. (1962), 'Spaces and Times', *Philosophy*, vol. 37, pp. 130-46.

Schopenhauer, A. (1969), *The World as Will and Representation*, Payne, E.J.F. (tr.), Dover, New York.

Strawson, P.F. (1959), *Individuals: An Essay in Descriptive Metaphysics*, Methuen, London.

Strawson, P.F. (1974), 'Freedom and Resentment', in *Freedom and Resentment and Other Essays*, Methuen, London, pp. 1–25.

Wiggins, D. (1973), 'Towards a Reasonable Libertarianism', in *Essays on Freedom of Action*, Honderich, T. (ed.), Routledge, London, pp. 33–61.

Wiggins, D. (1980), *Sameness and Substance*, Blackwell, Oxford.

Wittgenstein, L. (1953), *Philosophical Investigations*, Anscombe, G.E.M. (tr.), Blackwell, Oxford.

Wittgenstein, L. (1961), *Tractatus Logico-Philosophicus*, Pears, D.F. and McGuinness, B.F. (trs), Routledge, London.

Wittgenstein, L. (1967), *Zettel*, Anscombe, G.E.M. (tr.), Blackwell, Oxford.

List B

Aristotle, *Metaphysics*.

Descartes, R. (1641), *Meditations on First Philosophy*.

Hegel, G.W.F. (1807), *Phenomenology of Spirit*.

Hume, D. (1739), *A Treatise on Human Nature*.

Kant, I. (1781/7), *Critique of Pure Reason*, 1st and 2nd edns.

Locke, J. (1694), *Essay Concerning Human Understanding*.

Plato, *Phaedo*

Plato, *Theaetetus*.

Spinoza, B. (1677), *Ethics*.

List C

Armour, L. (1969), *The Concept of Truth*, Van Gorcum, Assen.

Armour, L. (1972), *Logic and Reality*, Van Gorcum, Assen.

Buber, M. (1958), *I and Thou*, Smith, R.S. (tr.), T. & T. Clark, Edinburgh.

Buber, M. (1961), 'The Question to the Single One', in *Between Man and Man*, Smith, R.S. (tr.), Fontana Library.

Browning, D. (1964), *Act and Agent*, University of Miami Press.

Cumming, R.D. (1979), *Starting Point: An Introduction to the Dialectic of Existence*, University of Chicago Press.

Emmett, D.M. (1961), *The Nature of Metaphysical Thinking*, MacMillan, London.

Hamlyn, D.W. (1984), *Metaphysics*, Cambridge University Press.

Hatano, S. (1963), *Time and Eternity*, Suzuki, I. (tr.), Printing Bureau, Japanese Government (National Commission for UNESCO).

Levinas, I. (1969), *Totality and Infinity*, Lignis, A. (tr.), Nijhoff, The Hague.

MacKinnon, D.M. (1974), *The Problem of Metaphysics*, Cambridge University Press.

MacMurray, J. (1957), *The Self as Agent* (1953 Gifford Lectures), Faber, London.

MacMurray, J. (1961), *Persons in Relation* (1954 Gifford Lectures), Faber, London.

Mallik, B.K. (1940), *The Real and the Negative*, Allen and Unwin, London.

Mallik, B.K. (1956), *Non-Absolutes*, Vincent Stuart, London.

Munz, P. (1964), *Relationship and Solitude*, Eyre and Spottiswoode, London.

Ortega y Gasset, J. (1967), *The Origin of Philosophy*, Talbot, T. (tr.), Norton, New York.

Ortega y Gasset, J. (1969), *Some Lessons in Metaphysics*, Adams, M. (tr.), Norton, New York.

Ramsay, I. (ed.) (1961), *Prospect for Metaphysics*, Allen and Unwin, London.

Stirner, M. (1973), *The Ego and His Own*, Byington, S.T. (tr.), Dover, New York.

Taylor, A.E. (1924), *Elements of Metaphysics*, 7th revised edition, Methuen, London.

Whiteley, C.H. (1950), *An Introduction to Metaphysics*, Methuen, London.